THE 50 BEST
family
hikes
IN IRELAND

**Mairéad Furlong
& Fergal McLoughlin**

GILL BOOKS

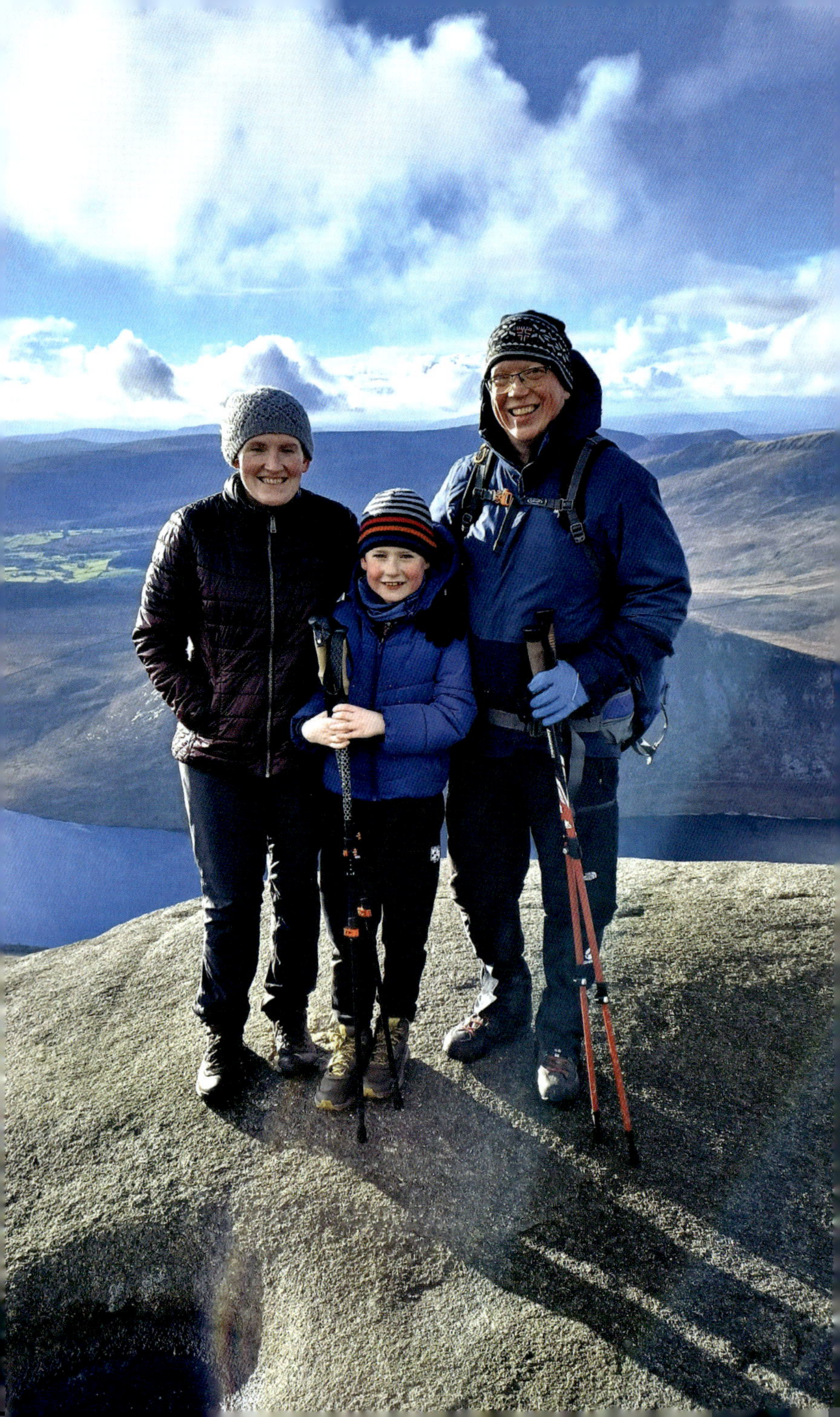

Mairéad Furlong and Fergal McLoughlin are psychologists with a passion for hiking. With over twenty years' experience of working closely with families and children they have merged this knowledge with their love for hiking and show how a love of the outdoors can create bonds in families steeped in a love for nature. Together with their young son they have climbed more than 200 of Ireland's mountains, including all the country's county high points. All photographs are the work of Fergal and Mairéad.

Hiking is a risk activity. The authors and publishers accept no responsibility for any injury, loss or inconvenience sustained by anyone using this guidebook. Every effort has been made to ensure the accuracy of the hikes in this book.

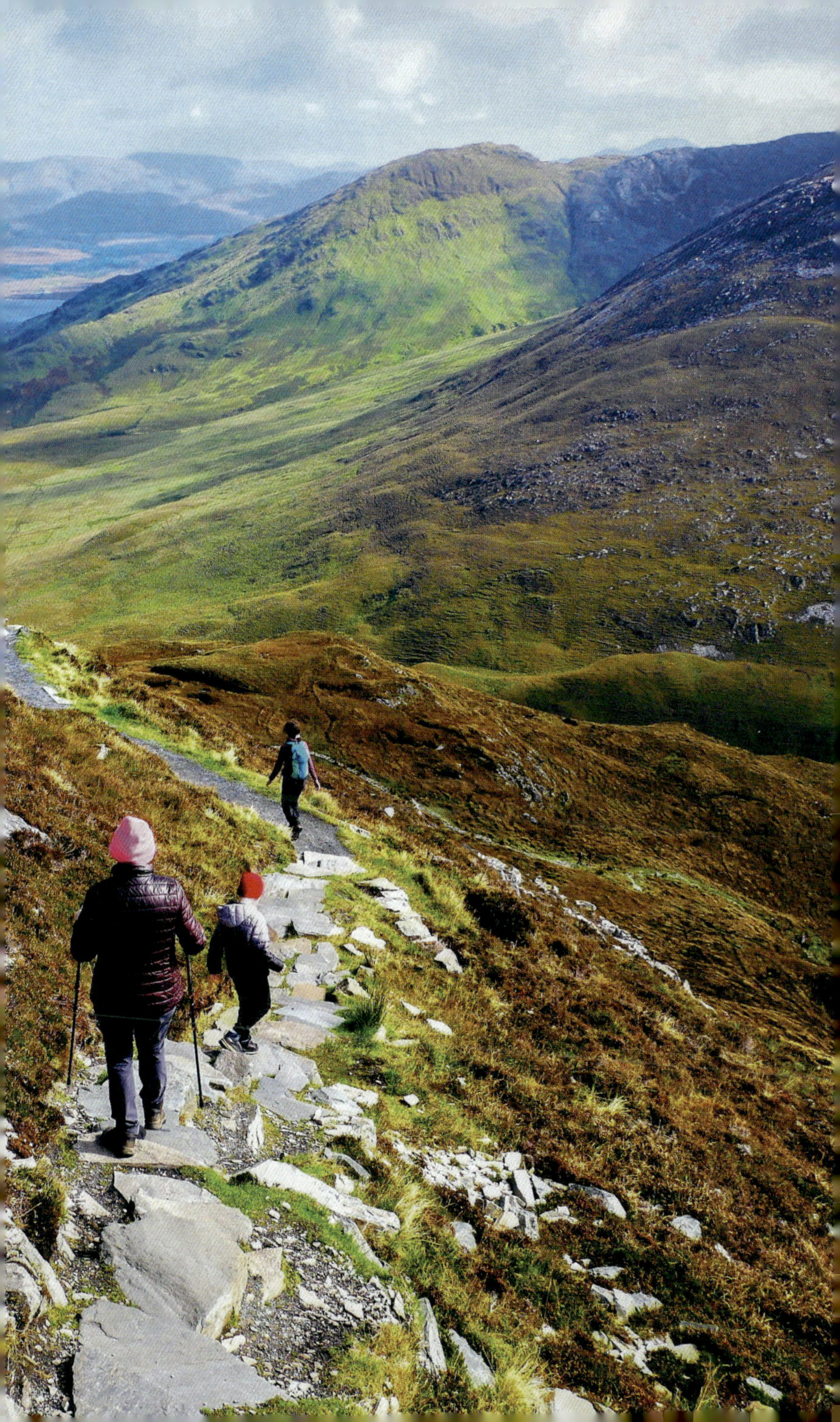

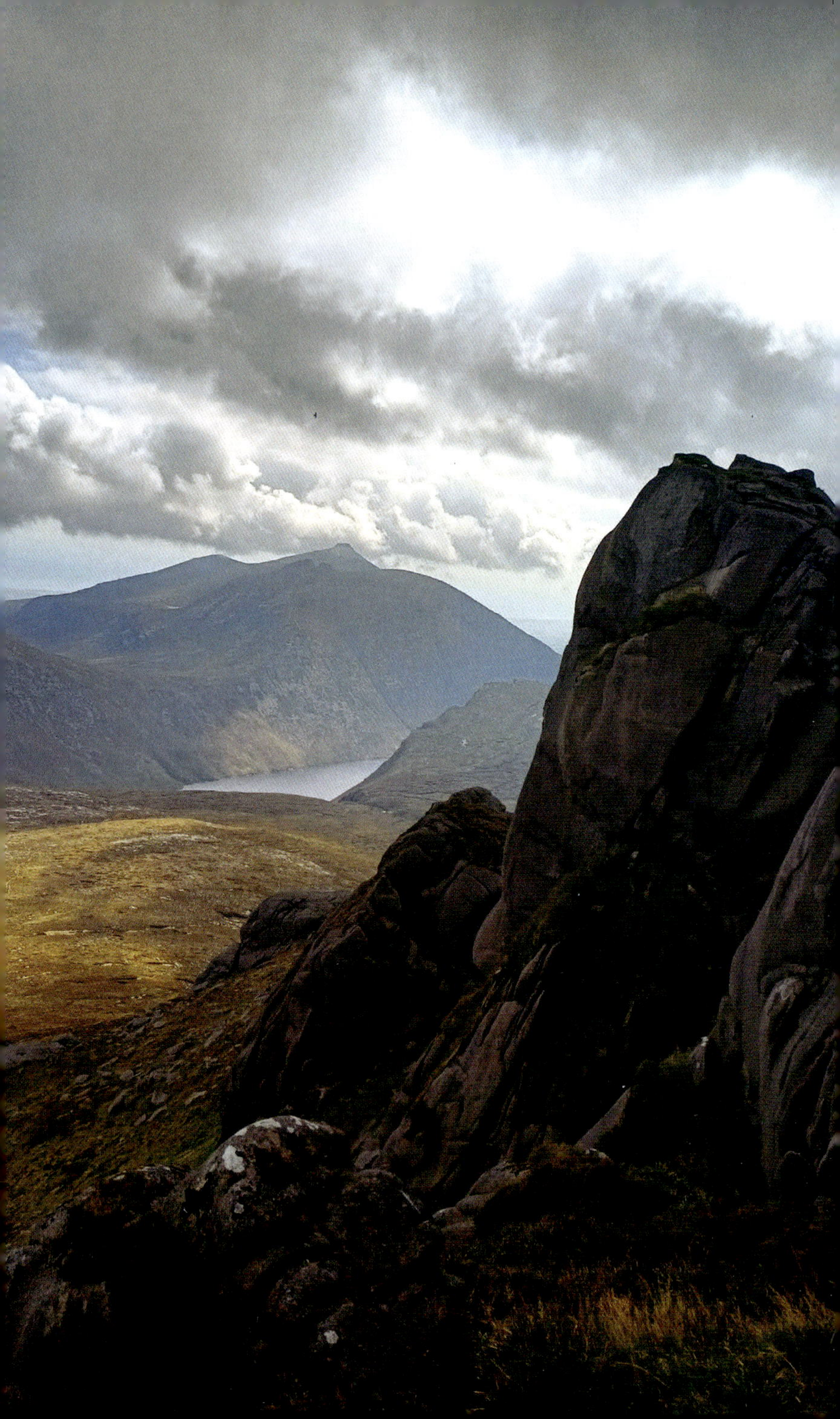

Contents

The Midlands

The North

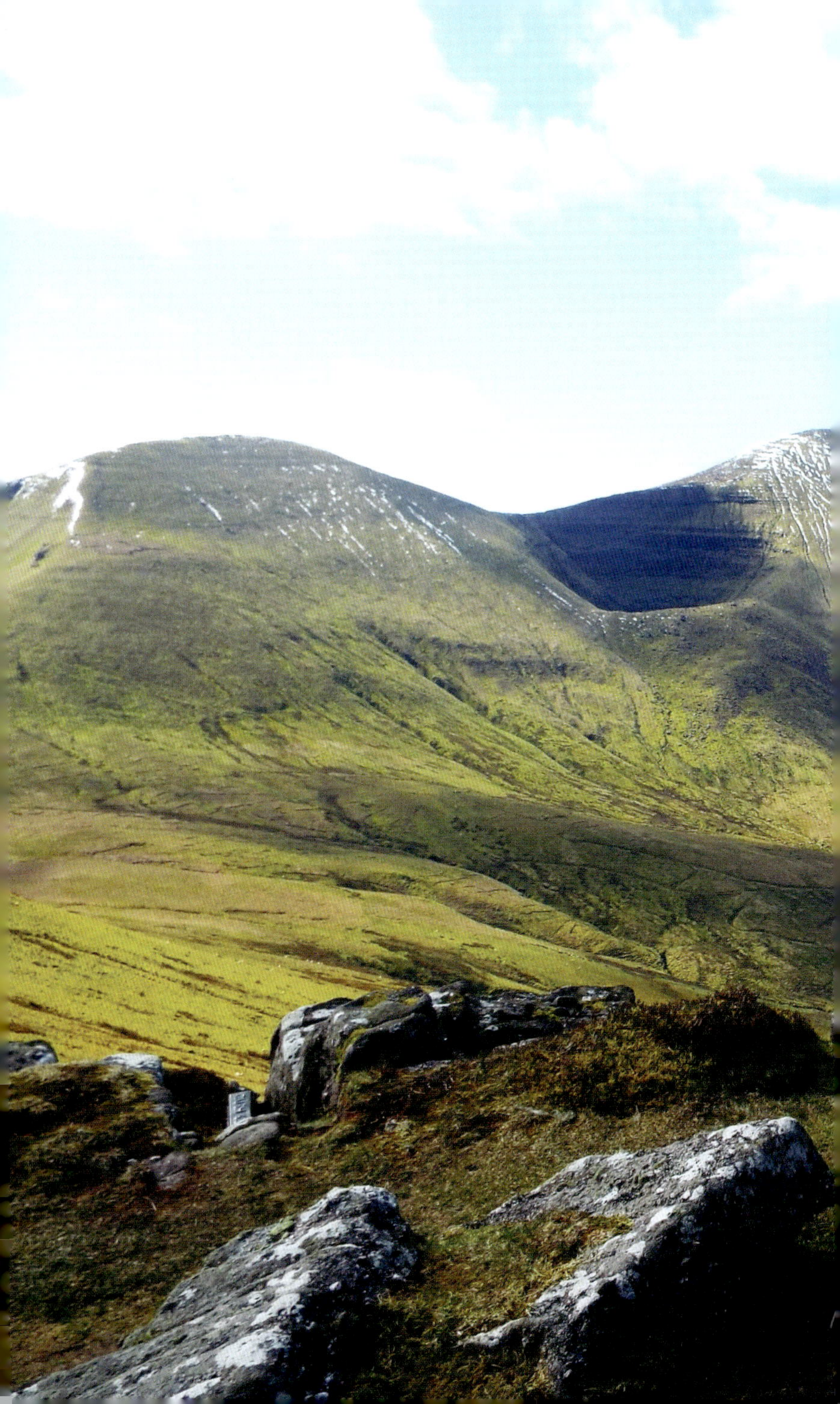

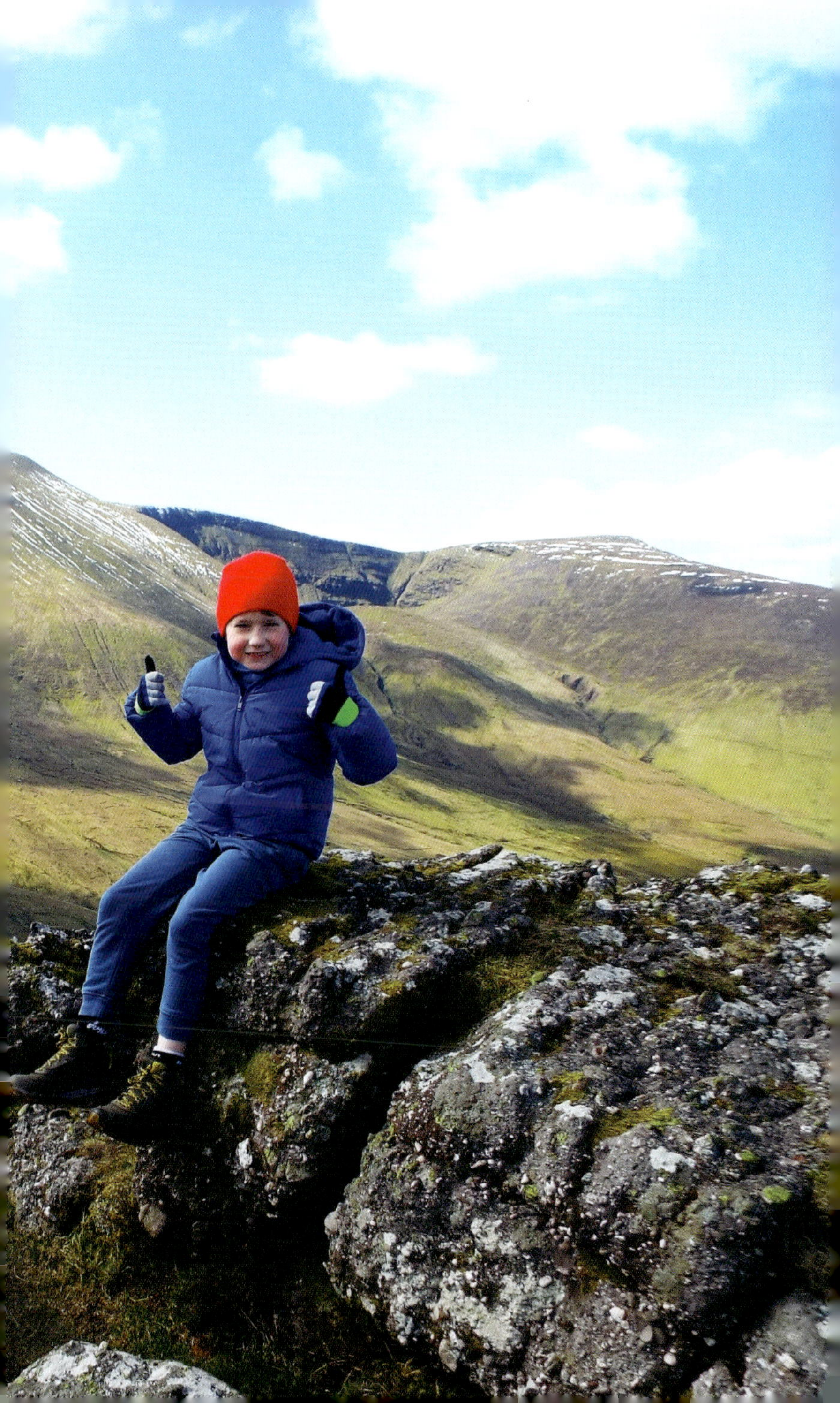

42

43 44 45

41
40

46

1 2 4 50

49 48 47
30
3 5 32 31

29

6
7
9 8

33
34

28

35 27
25
10 36 37 22 23 26 24
11
21

38

39
20

19

12
15
13 16
14 18

17

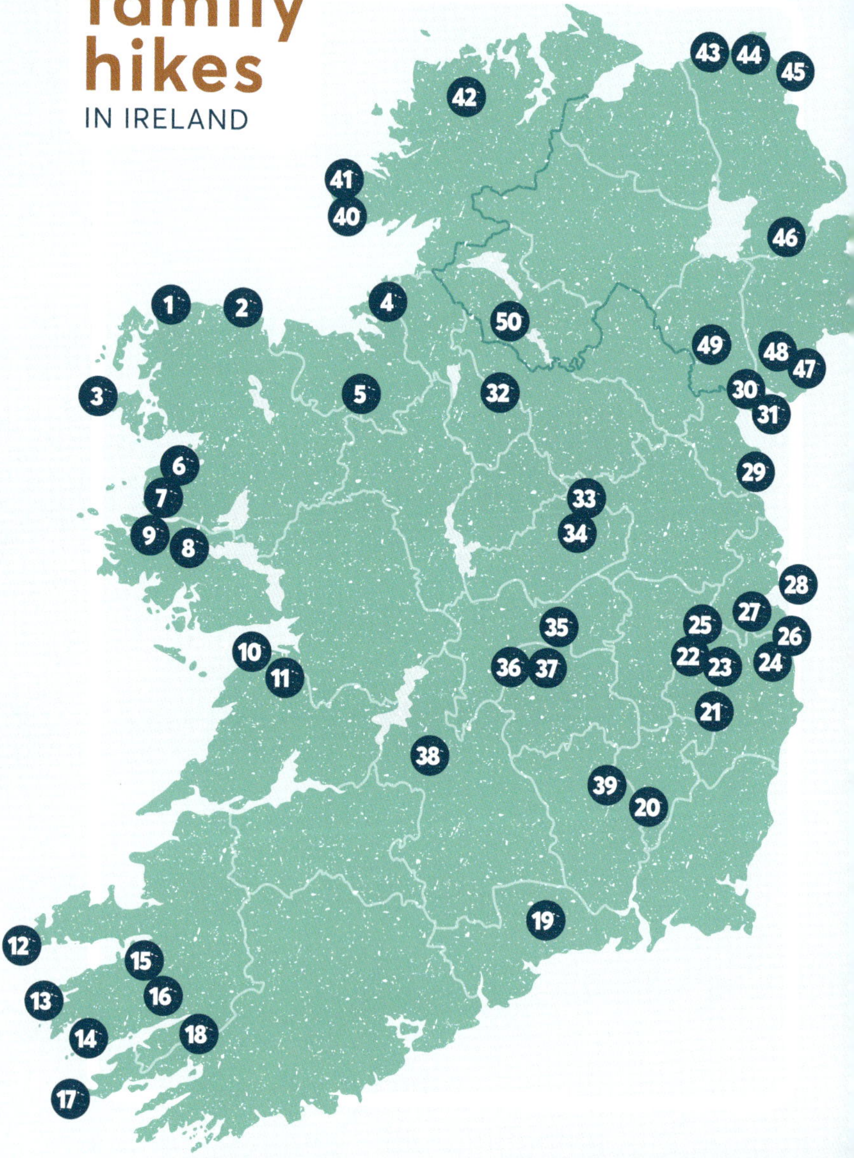

Hike reference table

No	Walk	County	Grade	Length	Time
THE WEST					
1	Benwee cliffs	Mayo	Easy–Experienced	2–11.5km	1–5 h
2	Downpatrick Head	Mayo	Easy	3km	1–2 h
3	Croaghaun cliffs, Achill Island	Mayo	Experienced	7km	4–5 h
4	Benbulbin	Sligo	Experienced	11km	4–5 h
5	Caves of Kesh	Sligo	Easy	2km	1 h
6	Croagh Patrick	Mayo	Medium	8km	3–4 h
7	Mweelrea	Mayo	Experienced	9.5km	4–5 h
8	Mám Éan	Galway	Easy	4km	1–2 h
9	Diamond Hill	Galway	Easy–Medium	3–7km	1–3 h
10	Black Head Loop, Burren	Clare	Experienced	16.5km	5–6 h
11	Mullaghmore, Burren	Clare	Medium	6km	2–3 h
THE SOUTH					
12	Great Blasket Island	Kerry	Easy–Medium	2–9km	2–4 h
13	Bray Head, Valentia	Kerry	Medium	5km	1–2 h
14	Caherdaniel Loop	Kerry	Medium	8km	3–4 h
15	Carrauntoohil	Kerry	Medium–Experienced	9–15.5km	4–7 h

16	Torc Mountain, Killarney	Kerry	Medium	8km	3–4 h
17	Dursey Island	Cork	Easy–Experienced	3.5–11km	1.5–5 h
18	An Cailleach Béara	Cork/Kerry	Experienced	10km	4–5 h
19	Coumshingaun	Waterford	Medium–Experienced	4–9km	2–5 h
20	Mount Leinster and Slievebawn	Carlow/Wexford	Easy–Experienced	2.5–13km	1–5 h

THE EAST

21	Lugnaquilla	Wicklow	Experienced	14km	5–6 h
22	Spinc Mountain, Glendalough	Wicklow	Medium	9km	4 h
23	Mullacor and Derrybawn, Glendalough	Wicklow	Experienced	12km	5 h
24	Great Sugarloaf	Wicklow	Medium	6km	3–4 h
25	Djouce	Wicklow	Easy–Medium	3–9km	1.5–3 h
26	Bray Head	Wicklow	Medium	7km	2–3 h
27	Tibradden via Ticknock	Dublin	Medium–Experienced	10–16km	3–5 h
28	The Bog of Frogs Loop, Howth	Dublin	Medium	11.5km	4 h
29	Clogherhead Walk	Louth	Easy	4km	2–3 h
30	Carnavaddy, Cooley Mountains	Louth	Easy–Experienced	5–17km	2–6 h
31	Slieve Foye, Cooley Mountains	Louth	Experienced	10km	4–5 h

THE MIDLANDS

32	Iron Mountain	Leitrim	Easy–Medium	3–6km	1.5–4 h
33	Mullaghmeen Forest	Westmeath	Easy–Medium	3.5–7.5km	1–3 h

34	Lakeland Trails	Westmeath	Easy	1–3km (per trail)	1–4 h
35	Croghan Hill	Offaly	Easy	2.5km	1 h
36	Glenbarrow, Slieve Blooms	Laois/Offaly	Easy–Experienced	3–14km	1.5–5 h
37	Giant's Grave to Silver River gorge	Laois/Offaly	Easy–Experienced	5–13km	1.5–4 h
38	Silvermines Ridge	Tipperary	Medium	6km	2–3 h
39	Brandon Hill	Kilkenny	Medium	7.5km	2–3 h

THE NORTH

40	Slieve League	Donegal	Easy–Medium	5–9km	2–4 h
41	Glencolmcille to the Sturrall	Donegal	Easy–Medium	4–6km	1.5–3 h
42	Mount Errigal	Donegal	Medium	6km	2–3 h
43	Dunseverick Castle to the Giant's Causeway	Antrim	Medium–Experienced	7–14km	4–6 h
44	Carrick-a-Rede Rope Bridge	Antrim	Easy	3km	1–2 h
45	Fair Head	Antrim	Easy–Medium	5–7km	1.5–3 h
46	Cave Hill, Belfast	Antrim	Medium	7km	3 h
47	Slieve Donard, Mourne Mountains	Down	Experienced	9.5km	4–5 h
48	Slieve Binnian, Mourne Mountains	Down	Experienced	11km	5 h
49	Slieve Gullion	Armagh	Easy–Experienced	3–15km	1–5 h
50	Cuilcagh – Stairway to Heaven and Summit	Cavan/Fermanagh	Experienced	10.5–14km	3.5–5 h

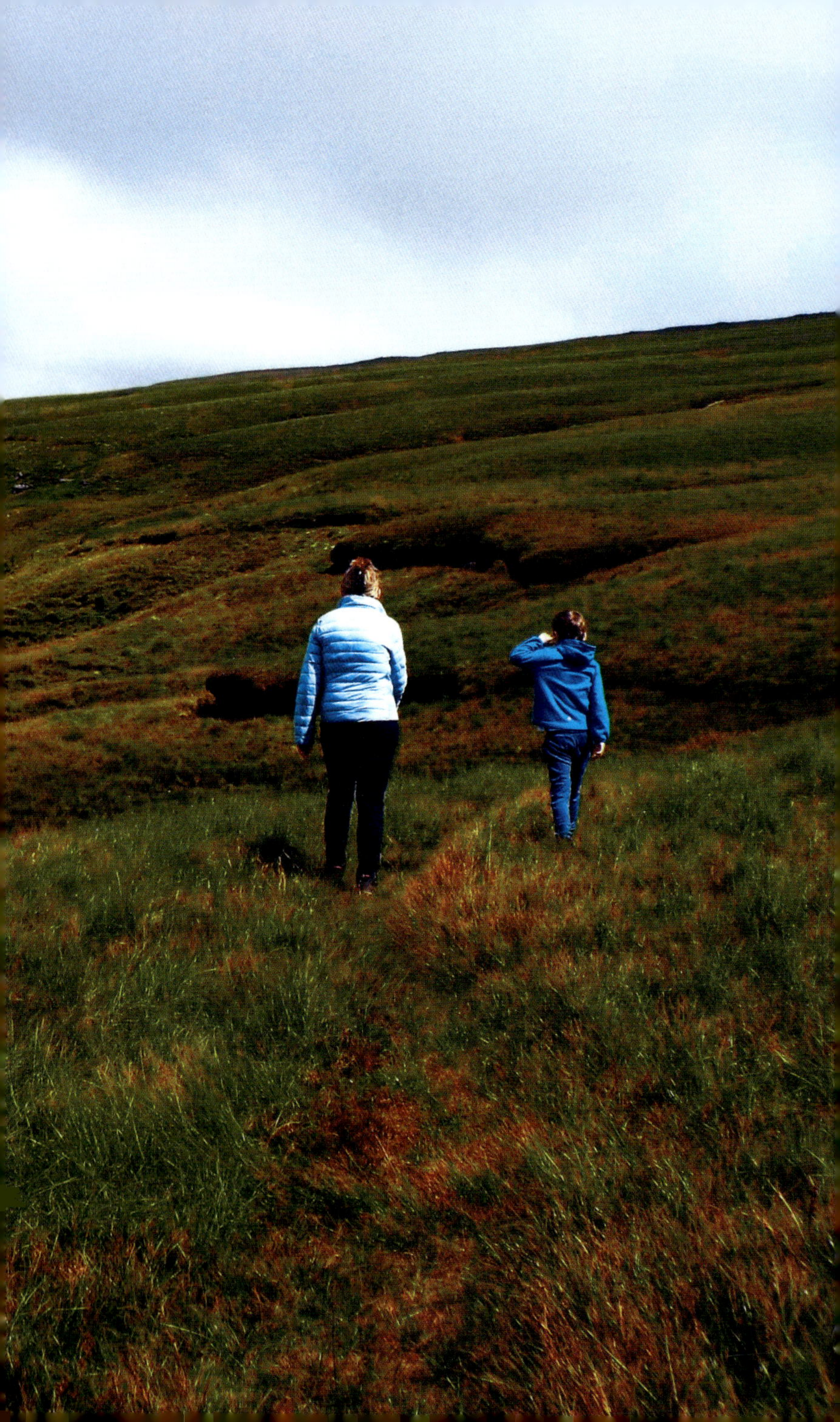

Introduction

Why a hiking guide for families?

We are a family and we love hiking. We started in earnest five years ago when our little boy was three years old. Before that we brought him, as a baby and toddler, on local town, canal and wood walks and saw the fun he had in discovering the outside world. As parents, we wanted our child to experience the beauty, mystery and adventure of Ireland's landscape. We also wanted to experience it ourselves and did not want having children to restrict us! We bought hiking books but there was no advice, guidance or mention of children hiking. We have also noticed a real absence of children in hills and mountains, with the exception of a few hotspots. This was surprising because our boy is often the one out in front and well able to keep up with other hikers. We see how much he loves the hills, how they are an adventure playground for him, and this deepens our bonds as a family.

We want families to realise that children can hike too! All our selected walks have been vetted for child suitability and fun/adventure, and we provide useful tips and advice for parents. With the right level of preparation and enthusiasm, all things are possible.

There are so many benefits to hiking. It helps parents and children become more engaged with nature, not in a dutiful fashion, but in an immersive, awe-inspiring, adventuresome, wild, beautiful and invigorating way. Research shows that hiking and being out in nature have terrific benefits for our physical and mental health, including lowering blood pressure; reducing stress; strengthening the immune system; improving mood; fitness, sleep, cognitive capacity, creativity, problem-solving and altruism; and enhancing family relationships. What's not to like? Without trying, children (and parents) learn about geography, geology, ecology and biodiversity and gain a love for and connection to our beautiful island and planet. We understand in our bones how important it is to maintain and protect our precious ecosystems. Furthermore, regular daytrips to amazing places encourages a holiday spirit throughout the year, an often necessary counterbalance to the stresses of the work–life treadmill.

So let's get started!

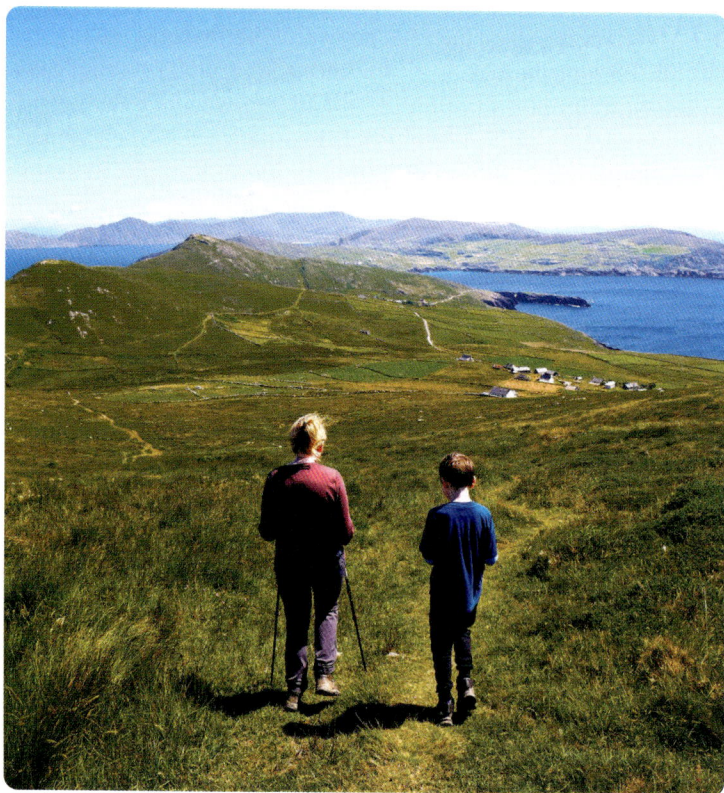

How to get your child (and you!) hiking

The old saying that you have to walk before you can run is also true for hiking – you walk before you hike! Here are some tips:

- Walking can start at any age, but ideally bring your child on interesting walks in woods and by canals, rivers, lakes and the seaside when they are young. If possible, the walks should be inherently interesting and not a boring straight path with little to see. Walking/scootering around town and clambering in parks are also good, but we recommend that children also engage with the natural world as it provides a different, more immersive experience.

- Allow young children time to explore and engage in make-believe when in nature. Be relaxed yourself and have fun, and tell stories and/or play make-believe games if necessary to keep your child going through a boring patch (which is usually a long straight track).

- From three to four years old, your child can start going on slightly longer and more uphill walks. At times, you may need to help them up and down larger steps. Again, the trick is to choose inherently interesting walks so that the rocks, water and scenery carry the load of entertaining your child. Watch your own physical and emotional wellbeing too – try to be in a good mood and not stressed so that you can support your child while also being able to look after yourself.

- When your child is around four to five years old, you can start extending your hiking capacity. For instance, you could undertake a hike that goes an hour one way, then have a sit-down fruit-and-sweets break, and then return/finish your walk. This would be a two-hour walk in total. For the break, we recommend a mandarin and small tub of sweets for each person, with a mat you can sit on in all weathers. Start from a lower baseline of 30–40 minutes each way if needed. With more experience, the time before the 'fruit-and-sweets' break can be extended to 90 minutes or two hours. At this stage, you and your children are able to walk for 3–4 hours in total. Regular water stops and mini rest breaks can be built in along the way, as needed. Over a little more time, walking for 4–5 hours will be well within your capacity, and with more experience, you can extend even longer.

- The more walks you go on, the better hikers you and your children will become. A few uphill hikes on our easier and medium routes are recommended to build up stamina in your calf muscles before you undertake longer, more demanding hikes. We do not recommend starting with Carrauntoohil, the highest mountain in Ireland!

- By steadily increasing your hiking experience, you and your family will be able to climb most mountains in Ireland. Our child was nearly seven when he climbed Carrauntoohil, but he had already had considerable experience in other mountain ranges.

Ireland's landscape and mythology

Ireland is a small country that boasts some of the most stunning and diverse landscapes in the world, including mountains, sea cliffs, sandy coastlines, karst limestone, woods, lakes, rivers and bog. Its compact size is an advantage for getting around. The majority of its mountain peaks encompass a wide panorama of land and sea vistas and at times one can feel the ancient mythologies of Ireland, such as the Fianna and the Tuatha Dé Danann, come alive as one beholds these sights. For instance, walking the Cooley Mountains provides a real sense of the epic Táin Bó Cuailnge (The Cattle Raid of Cooley) where Queen Maeve stole the Brown Bull of Cooley to fight against her husband's prized White Horned Bull. At the pilgrimage mountain of Croagh Patrick in Mayo, St Patrick reportedly banished the pre-Christian serpent goddess, Corra, into Lough Corra at the foot of the mountain. This type of legend is common across Ireland and explains geological features through recounting the triumph of Christianity over the old Irish religions. In another legend, it is said that the winter crone deity – the Cailleach – hid sleeping green things beneath her thick icy cloak and it was not until she had cause for sorrow and wept that she let loose the rivers and dropped many large stones from her apron that became our mountains, hills and valleys. This tale is a beautiful description of how the ice ages and glaciers shaped and scoured the landscape of Ireland. Given the beauty of the island, it is no surprise that Ireland receives its name from Ériu, an old Irish goddess associated with abundance and sovereignty, whose name has been translated to mean 'regular traveller of the heavens'.

Ireland's landscape has a fascinating geological history. Hundreds of millions of years ago, the northern half of Ireland was separated from the southern half by an ocean called Iapetus. The northern part of Ireland was located on the continent of Laurentia, now existing as parts of modern North America. The southern part of Ireland was located on Gondwana, now large parts of Europe, Africa and Australia. Approximately 470 million years ago, these two continents collided, as can be seen in the way that many of the mountain ranges in Ireland run in a south-west to north-east direction. A scar from Dingle on the west Kerry coast to Clogherhead on the east Louth coast shows the line along which the two continents merged.

Later, Ireland moved closer to the Equator and lay under a warm tropical sea, leading to the formation of sedimentary and limestone rocks such as those that can be seen in the Burren. About 60 million years ago, volcanic activity formed the Mourne Mountains, the Giant's Causeway and other ranges in the northern part of the island. Since about 1.7 million years ago, several periods of ice advance and retreat have shaped the face of Ireland, with the most recent ice age ending 10,000 years ago. The impact of this latest glacial erosion can be seen throughout Ireland's topography in its deep mountain corries, sharp arêtes, drumlins, esker ridges and U-shaped valleys.

Access

While Northern Ireland and the Republic of Ireland are two separate political jurisdictions, this makes little practical difference in terms of hiking. The only difference is the different currency used in the shops (sterling in Northern Ireland and the euro in the Republic of Ireland).

The hikes in this guidebook are on a mix of public and private lands but all routes have been checked for access. In theory, it is possible that a previously established route can be withdrawn, but please contact the publishers if access problems arise on any of the walks included in this book.

For each route, we provide travel directions, parking advice and grid coordinates for the walk starting point.

Accommodation

There is a range of accommodation available in most areas, including hotels, B&Bs, holiday homes, hostels and campsites. Check the following websites for information: booking.com, Trivago, Airbnb, campingireland.ie.

For those living in Ireland, depending on location, many hikes can be travelled to and completed within a day and accommodation is not required. Check daylight hours to make sure you have enough time to return from walks. In December, sunrise is at 8.40am and sunset after 4pm, whereas there are over 17 hours of daylight in June.

Climate

Ireland has a mild temperate climate all year round with winds generally coming from the south-west from the Atlantic Ocean across the country. The 'Emerald Isle' gains its verdancy from the amount of rain it receives but the rain usually blows over quickly so there are plenty of fine days (or parts of days) to hike in all seasons. The east of the country is generally drier than the west. It is important to keep in mind that, depending on the route, prolonged rainfall can affect the bogginess of the terrain and the water level of streams and rivers.

Wind chill is the primary risk when hiking in Ireland, even in summer. Temperatures drop 1°C for every 100m elevation and mountain peaks and cols may be windy and cold. Therefore, it is advised to bring appropriate clothing in all seasons, which you can put on and take off as required (see 'What to bring' below).

Weather can change quickly in Ireland. There is a saying that we can have four seasons in one day! This is particularly the case in the mountains, so always check the weather forecast before you leave. Weather apps such as Met Éireann are recommended for the Republic of Ireland and the UK Met Office for Northern Ireland.

Hiking is possible in all seasons in Ireland if the weather is fine. Autumn and winter are particularly delightful with their crisp, clear light, and light frost or snow can transform the landscape.

How to use this book

How hikes are graded

We have given each hike a grading as a guide for you and your child. The gradings have been compiled with children in mind.

★   *Easy:* Short hikes of less than 5km over good paths with clear signage to help. Best suited for three-year-olds and over.

★ ★   *Medium:* Hikes of 6–10km. Generally good paths throughout. Best suited for four-year-olds and over.

★ ★ ★   *Experienced:* Prior hiking experience recommended, and essential if indicated for a particular walk. Hikes are generally over 10km and/or over more difficult terrain. Some navigational skills may be required. Best suited for children over six years of age.

Timings

Timings in this book are based on the length of time it takes to complete the walk, factoring in those all-important breaks. They are calculated with children in mind. They are only a guide and you will soon discover how your pace matches those in the book. All the walks can be shortened to meet your needs. If you need to turn back, do not be hard on yourself; just return another time when things are more in your favour.

Coordinates

Each hike has coordinates for finding the exact parking place at the start of each hike. Just type the coordinates as they appear in the book into Google Maps and they will bring you to where you need to be.

What to bring

Safe hiking is about being organised and equipped but at the same time not carrying more than necessary as this will make climbs harder. Fortunately, there is a great range of lightweight clothes and gear available online or from specialist outdoor/mountaineering stores and websites. We recommend the following as a basic kit.

☑ CLOTHES

Hiking is about dressing appropriately and getting into a 'uniform' so that you are ready to embark on an adventure rather than just going out for a leisurely walk. This is important psychologically in terms of getting into the right frame of mind and also for physical comfort.

We recommend hiking boots with ankle support, and thick socks, for you and your children. The boots should be worn in and well fitting. It is also very important that each person has an insulated, lightweight, waterproof jacket, along with hat and gloves. North Face and Regatta have a good range of suitable jackets. Jog pants or lightweight hiking trousers that dry quickly after rain, and are easy to move in, are recommended. We advise against jeans as they are too tight and heavy and take a long time to dry if you get wet, which is dangerous. It is important that each person wears layers (e.g. long and short T-shirts) that can be put on and taken off as required by weather and exertion.

Even on the warmest days, we recommend bringing hats, coats and gloves as temperatures may be several degrees cooler on a mountain or an unexpected wind may develop. We recommend putting clips onto the hiking bag, where you can hang your coat if you do not need it. In colder weather, with cold winds, we have found that a cowl/snood/neckwarmer helps you stay warm and can be brought up over your mouth and nose if necessary. Your child, and you, will look like super-cool ninjas with your cowls up! Each person should have a full change of clothes in the car for when you return from your hike in case your clothes are wet or dirty. In very boggy terrain, gaiters are a big help.

☑ HIKING POLES

These are for adults: they reduce pressure on your ankle and knee joints and are superb for helping you maintain your balance on the way down a mountain. They are also good at building up arm and back muscles as you walk. Poles range in price but reliable ones can be found on Amazon for about €30.

☑ HIKING BAG/RUCKSACK

It is very important that parents bring a hiking bag. The rucksack should be strong but light and have well-padded shoulder straps and waist-band. Buy a separate waterproof liner for your rucksack, if it doesn't have one, to protect your bag if it rains. Children under 10 years should not be expected to carry a rucksack. The rucksack should contain the following:

☑ WATER

Carry enough water for everyone in the group. On longer walks, this could be 1.5 litres per person. You will drink more climbing up mountains (more exertion) than on the way down and will drink more in the warmer months.

☑ SNACKS

We recommend having a sit-down fruit-and-sweets break after 1.5 to 2 hours of walking. Mandarins are wonderful as they are both food and a drink. A small tub of chocolate sweets (e.g. Celebrations, Heroes) are ideal here too. These tubs are less than three inches in diameter and height. A small tub of grapes and cut-up apples is a welcome treat later on. We also recommend bringing a small tube of Pringles to share later in the hike, especially in summer, to replace body salt lost through sweat. Additional supplies could include Smarties or fruit pastilles as these provide a hit of glucose and come in handy to keep children going towards the end of a hike or along a boring section.

☑ SEATS

Lightweight, foldable, durable and waterproof mats are invaluable when you want a sit-down break but the ground is wet, as it often is in Ireland. They are available on Amazon, where you can buy three for around €6.

☑ SUNSCREEN AND SUNHAT

Sun and wind burn can easily happen on the mountains. Apply sunscreen factor 50 before you start the hike. Bring some with you in case you sweat it off.

☑ PHONE AND HIKING APP

Make sure your phone is fully charged before beginning your hike. Bear in mind that reception can be patchy in low-lying valleys. While you should always bring a physical map with you in case you lose phone signal, we strongly recommend downloading the Hiiker or All Trails app, which will provide you with invaluable information about the walks and even recommend other walks in the area. They also provide an excellent navigational aid that will record your walk and let you know where you are.

☑ MAP AND COMPASS

Each walk has a recommended Ordnance Survey Ireland (OSI) map, along with more detailed maps where available, which you should become familiar with before you start the hike so as to plan your route. Bring your map with you on the hike in case your phone or your hiking app does not work. You should also bring a compass that you know how to use. All hikes in this book have a reference to the best maps available for that area. In general, the OSI 1:50000 Discovery Series covers all hiking areas.

For more detailed maps, the excellent EastWest Mapping 25 Series provides precise coverage at 1:25000 and is available on the Hiiker App. In addition, the Harvey Superwalker XT30 series is excellent and has a scale of 1:30000. For Northern Ireland, the Ordnance Survey Activity Map series provides coverage at 1:25000.

☑ HIKING GUIDEBOOK

Bring this book in your bag to check the route and for advice if needed in an emergency.

☑ CLIPS

Use these to clip your jackets to the back of your rucksack when the weather becomes warm.

☑ FIRST AID KIT

Bring plasters, paracetamol and any other medication required.

☑ BATTERY PACK

A charged battery pack with connecting lead is important to recharge a dying phone.

☑ SPACE BLANKETS

Emergency blankets are inexpensive, easy to source and carry and are essential in an emergency, for instance if someone gets sick or hurts their leg and you need to sit in the cold waiting to recover or waiting for help.

☑ HEAD LAMP

This is useful in an emergency or if the light begins to fade.

☑ TISSUES AND HAND SANITISER

Nature will call on longer hikes.

☑ HAND WARMERS

These are useful on very cold days. They look like teabags and give warmth for ten hours each.

☑ CAMERA

This is optional but it can provide you with better quality pictures and also reduces the demand on your mobile phone, which you may need for navigational purposes.

☑ PICNIC

Depending on the length of the hike, you can bring one with you in your rucksack or leave it in the car and enjoy it when you return from your hike. Food always tastes at least ten times better during or after a hike. We bring a flask of tea, sandwiches, a small chocolate bar and crisps, but do what works best for you.

⚠️ SAFE AND RESPONSIBLE HIKING

Hiking enjoyably and safely is about being organised, planning the route, being well equipped and having sufficient supplies. Please read the guidance above.

Always check the weather forecast before you start the hike as weather can change quickly in Ireland. Reassess your plans if required.

There are fewer daylight hours in autumn, winter and early spring so check you have enough time to complete your hike.

In the event of an emergency, ring 999 or 112, ask for police and then mountain rescue or coastguard rescue. This applies to both the Republic of Ireland and Northern Ireland. Your phone should allow you to make an emergency call even if the signal is poor. Have your grid coordinates to hand, as found on your map or hiking app. Use the space blanket if needed.

All our walks can be shortened to meet your need. If the weather turns against you or you need to turn back for whatever reason, it is better to be safe and return at another time when things are more in your favour.

It is important to leave no trace on the environment and to show consideration for others. Therefore, be aware of not littering, closing gates behind you and not bringing sheep-worrying dogs with you. See www.leavenotraceireland.org.

USEFUL CONTACTS

Emergencies

Ring 999 or 112 for all emergency services, ask for police and then mountain rescue or coastguard rescue. This applies to both the Republic of Ireland and Northern Ireland. Have your grid coordinates ready as found on your map or hiking app.

Weather

Met Éireann app/website for the Republic of Ireland and the UK Met Office for Northern Ireland.

Hiking gear

Suitable hiking gear can be found on Amazon and at a range of mountaineering stores and websites, including North Face, Regatta, Great Outdoors Ireland and so forth.

Information on mountain hikes

The Hiiker or All Trails apps are highly recommended. There are several good guidebooks on hiking in Ireland available online and in good bookstores but these have not been vetted for child suitability. The website www.mountainviews.ie provides details on all of Ireland's mountains.

Maps

To purchase the best hiking maps, please use the following websites: www.osi.ie, www.eastwestmapping.ie and www.harveymaps.co.uk.

Accommodation

For hotels, hostels, holiday homes and camping sites, go to booking.com, Trivago, Airbnb and campingireland.ie.

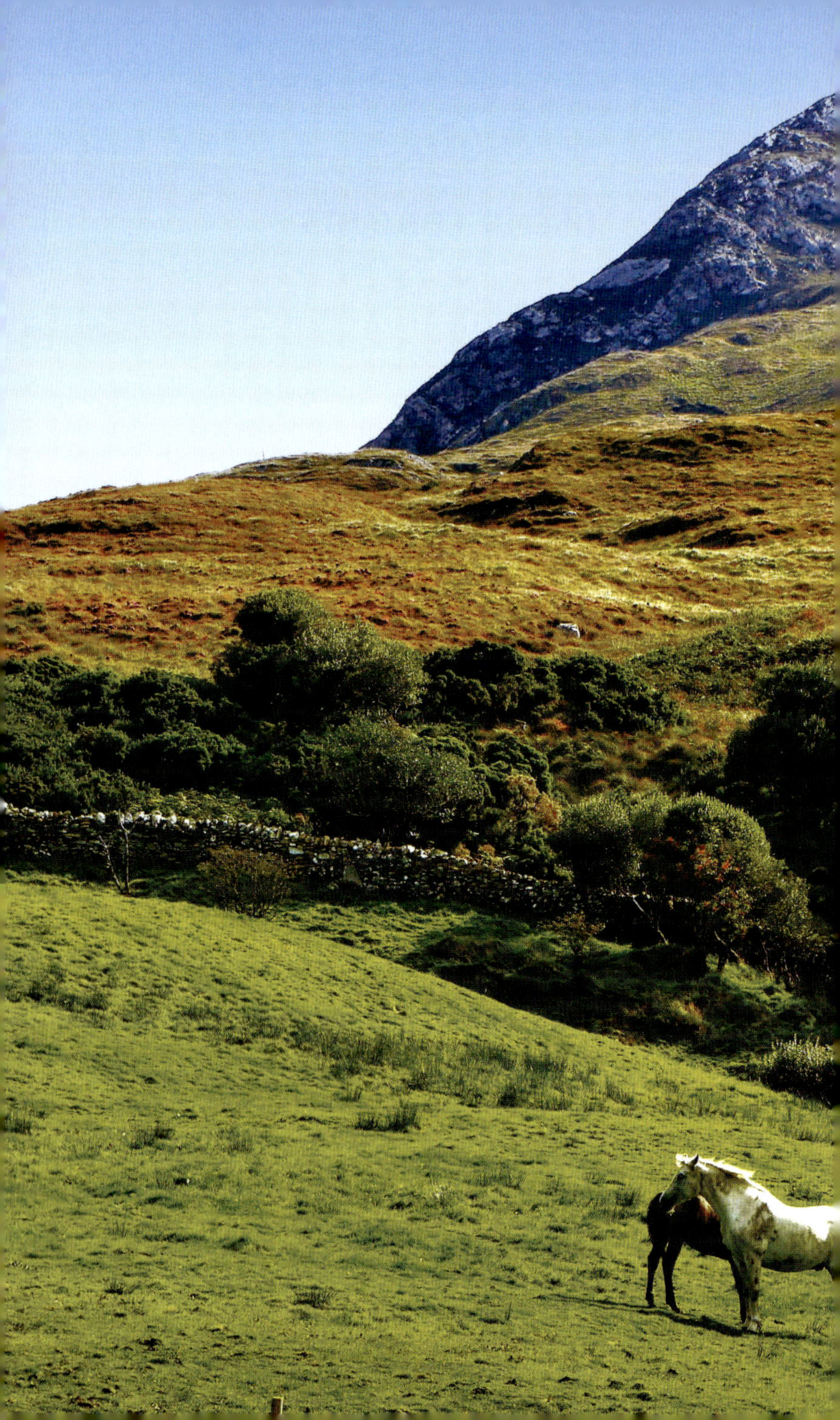

The West

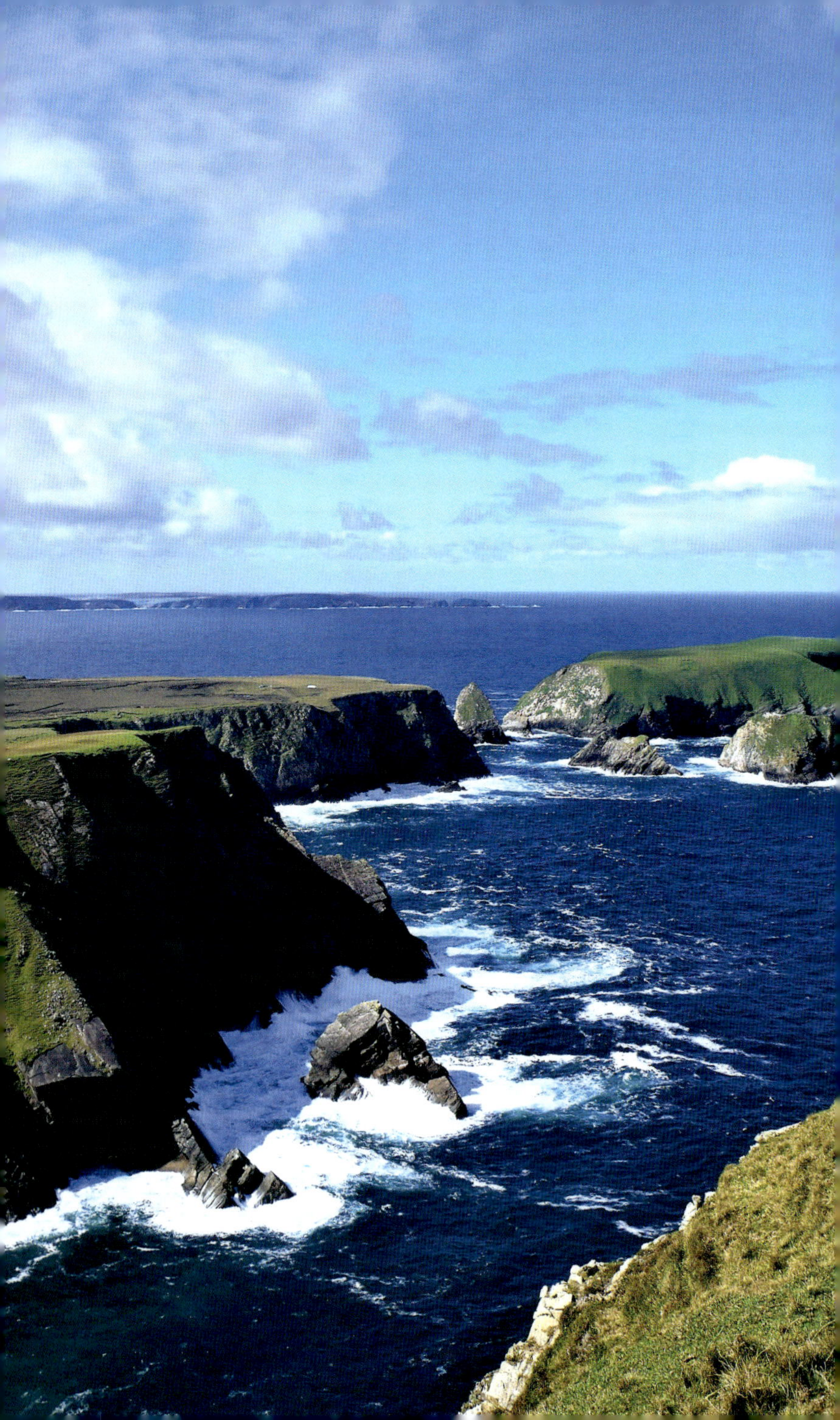

1

Benwee cliffs
Co. Mayo

An amazing cliff-top hike in the land of the Children of Lir

The Benwee cliff walk in remote north-west Co. Mayo boasts some of the most thrilling coastal scenery in Ireland. Features include Kid Island and the Stags of Broadhaven. There are informal grass paths along the headland. You are unlikely to meet many people. Best enjoyed in dry and bright conditions. Hiking boots recommended.

LENGTH:	TIME:	DIFFICULTY:	OSI MAP NO:
2–11.5km	1–5 hours	Easy–Experienced	22

⊙ NEED TO KNOW

From Ballycastle, Co. Mayo, take the R314 west for 27km. Turn right and follow the L1023 for 11km. Then turn left for 3.5km before turning right and following the road to the end, where there is the Wild Atlantic Way Discovery Point for Benwee. The car park is free.

Coordinates: 54.3238 -9.8403

◄ Benwee cliffs with Kid Island, Co. Mayo

The Hike

1 From the car park you may walk on the cliff headland to either your left or right. It is impossible to be disappointed either way and you can walk for as long or as short as you want. For this walk, head right from the car park and follow the way-marker posts you see in front of you. Follow the red arrow uphill and aim for the way-marker post above you.

2 At around 900m, it is more interesting to move away from the way-marked posts. Turn left and follow some informal paths that guide you around the cliff edge. Do not get too close to the cliff edge and exercise a degree of caution, especially in windy conditions.

Transfixed by Benwee cliffs ▲

3 After 2.6km and close to the top of Benwee cliffs, you will meet a fence. Simply follow the fence, keeping it on your left-hand side.

4 At around 4km the fence runs out and you can sit close to the edge for a break while viewing the cliffs and the Stags of Broadhaven. When ready, continue up to the headland in front of you and follow the informal paths around the cliff top. This is a very enjoyable section with stunning views.

5 At just over 6km, you reach another fence. There are lovely views of Portacloy Beach here. This is a good place to now retrace your route to your car.

Myths and legends

The legend of the Children of Lir tells of a story back in druidic times in which four children are malevolently turned into swans by their stepmother Aoife and condemned to wander the Irish countryside for 900 years. Aoife was jealous of the love that her husband, Lir, had for his children and wanted him only for herself. The last 300 of the 900 years were spent on the desolate north Mayo island, Inishglora, which is near the Benwee cliffs. The swans briefly regained human form at the end of the 900 years before they died of old age. They met St Patrick just before they died. The name Inishglora translates as 'Isle of Purity' from the belief that human remains do not decompose on the island. The island is also dedicated to St Brendan the Navigator, who undertook his legendary sea voyage to America in his currach boat in the sixth century AD.

Enjoying a break near the Stags of Broadhaven ▲

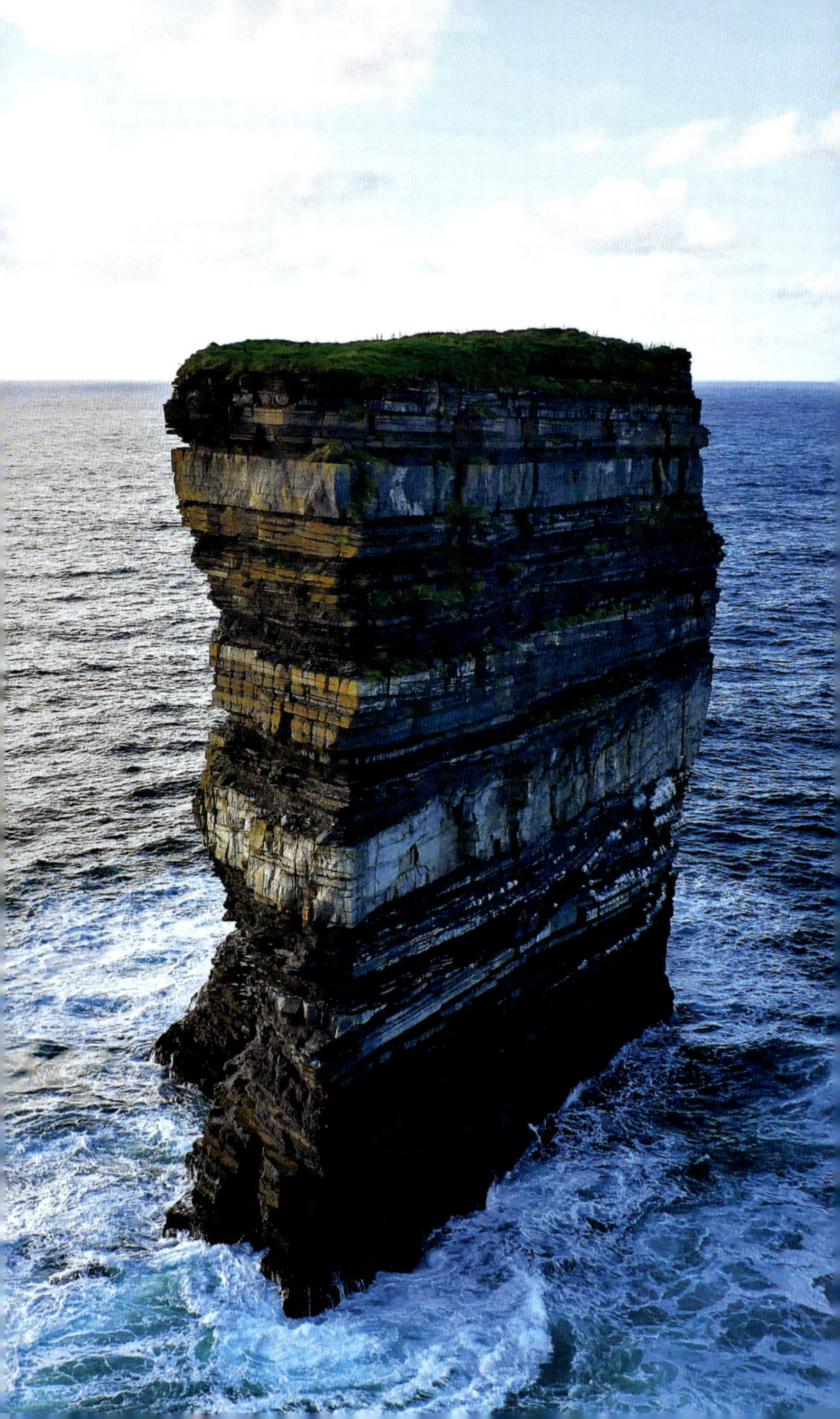

2

Downpatrick Head
Co. Mayo

THE WEST // THE 50 BEST FAMILY HIKES IN IRELAND

A short 'black' hike with fascinating cliff features

An easy yet exhilarating cliff walk along Downpatrick Head with amazing features, including the Dún Briste sea stack, an enormous blowhole and the Stags of Broadhaven. Seabirds nesting here during the summer include puffins, kittiwakes and cormorants. Clear paths throughout. Hiking boots recommended.

LENGTH:	TIME:	DIFFICULTY:	OSI MAP NO:
3km	1–2 hours	Easy	23

⊚ NEED TO KNOW

From Ballycastle, Co. Mayo, take the R314 east for 300 metres. Then turn left and follow the road for just over 4km before turning left again. Follow the narrow road to the end, where a free car park awaits you.

Coordinates: 54.3218 -9.3441

◄ Dún Bríste sea stack, Downpatrick Head

The Hike

1 From the car park, go through a metal gate and walk up the wide path. Go through the next metal gate and you are now on the headland.

2 You will soon see a viewing point for an incredible blowhole. The viewing point also has very interesting information boards that tell you about the geology and folklore of Downpatrick Head. When ready, go towards the cliffs and behold the Dún Briste sea stack off the coast. Take your time to walk around the cliff edge, and when ready make your way back to the car park.

The roiling sea at Downpatrick Head ▲

Myths and legends

Several myths developed to explain the formation of the geological features at Downpatrick Head. One tale brings St Patrick into one of his many confrontations with the demon Crom Dubh (the 'black stooped one'). Crom Dubh was a Celtic fertility and harvest god in pre-Christian Ireland and was also associated with the dark arts. Crom Dubh attempted to throw St Patrick into an eternal fire at Downpatrick Head but St Patrick threw a blessed stone into the fire, at which the ground collapsed, creating the large blowhole that is known today as Poll a Sean Tine (the Hole of the Old Fire). On seeing this, Crom Dubh retreated to Dún Briste. St Patrick struck the ground with his crozier and Dún Briste broke from the mainland to form the sea stack. Crom Dubh was marooned on the stack and suffered the gruesome and ignominious death of being eaten by midges. A 'Pattern Day' celebrating St Patrick's victory is held annually here on the last Sunday of July, but, interestingly, it is called Domhnach Chruim Duibh (Crom Dubh's Sunday). It is also of note that the event is held at harvest time, the time associated with the old demon!

Walking along the cliff edge at Downpatrick ▲

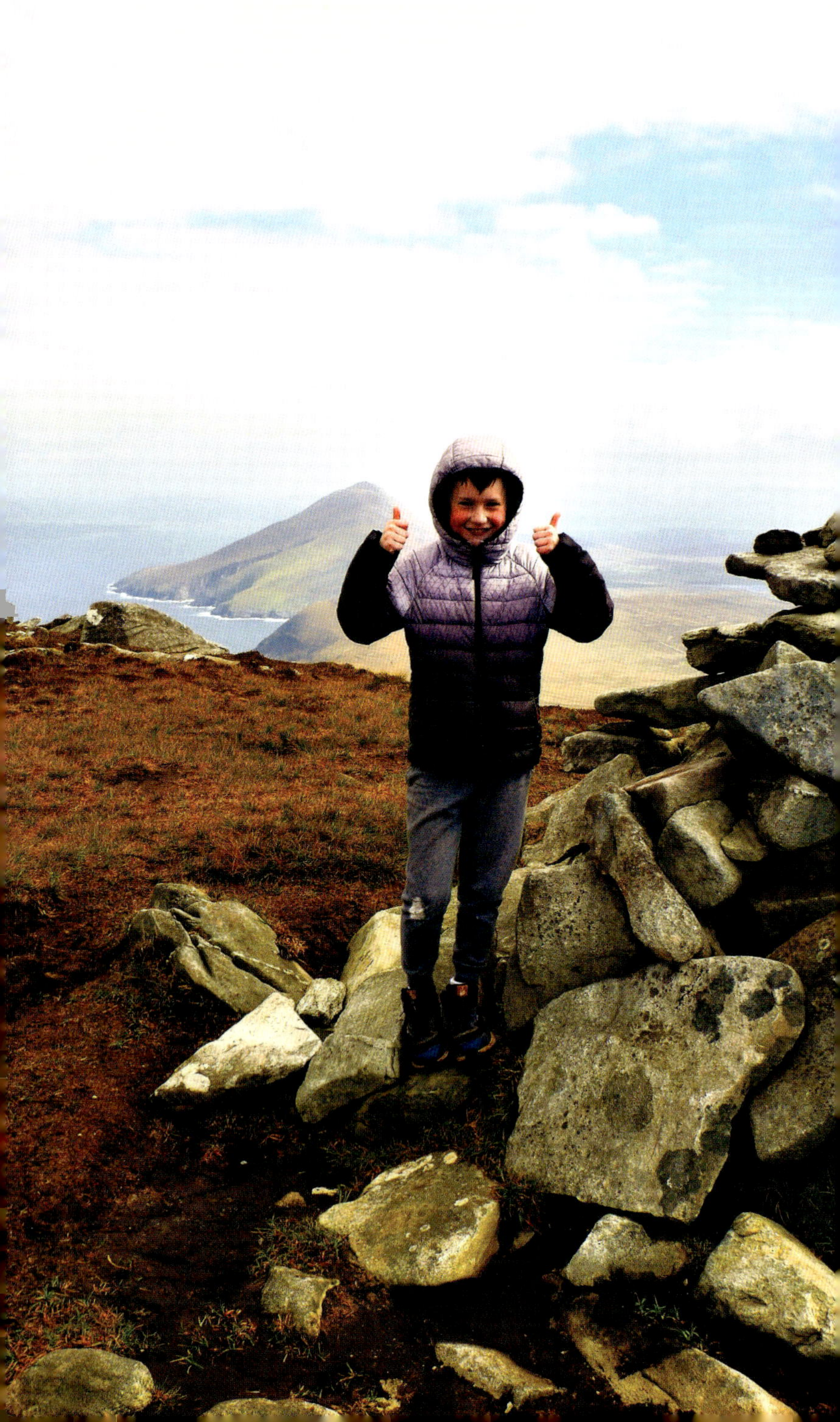

3

Croaghaun cliffs
Achill Island, Co. Mayo

A stunning hike to the highest sea cliffs in Ireland

At 688m, the Croaghaun cliffs on Achill Island, officially the highest sea cliffs in Ireland and the fourth highest in Europe, rise jaggedly above the Atlantic Ocean. The view from the summit is dizzying and stunning. Winds and fast-changing weather make this a hike best enjoyed on a clear, calm day. While there are intermittent informal paths, navigational experience is required for much of the route. Hiking boots essential.

LENGTH:	TIME:	DIFFICULTY:	OSI MAP NO:
7km	4–5 hours	Experienced	22

EASTWEST MAPPING: Achill and Corraun Clare Island

⊙ HOW TO GET THERE

From Westport, Co. Mayo, take the N59 west for 49km past the village of Mallaranny. Then turn left onto the R319 and follow this road for 33km onto Achill Island. Then take a sharp right and follow the road to Lough Accorrymore. The free car park is beside the lake.

Coordinates: 53.9817 -10.1673 (Use the satellite version of Google Maps as the street plan version brings you to the middle of Lough Acorrymore!)

◀ Reaching the summit of Croaghaun

The Hike

1 From the car park, head back up the road you drove in on.

2 After 200m, there is a cattle grid on the road. Leave the tarmac path here for a faint informal grass path to your right. Start climbing up the slope and veer slightly away to your left, i.e. away from the lake. As you look up, you will see the shoulder of the hill above you. Aim for the left-hand side of the shoulder as the slope is less steep here. Once you reach the open ground at the top of the shoulder, start to contour to your right around the mountain. Do not get too tight to the drop-offs on your right. As you climb upwards, pick the easiest line in front of you. There are no defined paths here.

3 At around 1.5km the slope eases and you come to a rocky surface, which you walk across towards Croaghaun, whose summit is now visible straight in front of you. You can climb to the summit directly but we recommend turning right at the base, going around the base where the slope is easier and aiming towards the slight col on the cliff edge. (A col is the low point between two peaks.)

4 After 2.7km, arrive near the cliff edge and get your first sight of the Atlantic Ocean far below. Turn left here and pick up one of the several informal paths that bring you to the top of Croaghaun.

5 At 3.2km, arrive at the summit of Croaghaun. Enjoy stunning views all along the coast. If weather and time allow, continue along the cliff edge to Croaghaun's south-west top. Then retrace your

Ascending Croaghaun and the day is set fair ▲

steps back to point 4 above. This time continue straight ahead and enjoy a very pleasant section of cliff walking with stunning views throughout. After a kilometre, this path begins to bend more inland. The path becomes less defined, but keep to the same line down the mountain.

6   At around 4.7km, start to contour more to your right, but not too tightly. You are contouring around the other cliff edge of Lough Acorrymore that is hidden from your view. As you descend, keep to your left, as the slope is very steep the further right you go. Lough Acorrymore will come into view and soon after you will see the small lake of Lough Choire a' tSamhaidh to the left of Lough Acorrymore. You should aim for well left of Lough Choire a' tSamhaidh as you descend.

7   At 6km, arrive close to Lough Choire a' tSamhaidh and pick up one of the many informal paths that will bring you to the dam bridge at Lough Acorrymore. Cross the bridge and arrive back at your car. Nearby Keem beach is a beautiful spot in which to picnic and relax.

Myths and legends

'The Hawk of Achill' recounts the stories shared between old Fintan MacBochra and a hawk he met while sitting on the cliffs of Achill. Fintan the Wise of the Hundred Lives had lived for over 5,500 years, was said to be a descendant of Noah of the biblical flood and was known as a son of the sea with gifts of wisdom, magic and seeing far-distant times and places. As they talked about past episodes in their lives, it emerged that the hawk had lived just as long as Fintan. In one tale, Fintan related that he had once been changed into a salmon swimming the rivers, lochs and seas of Ireland and that a hawk had plucked out one of his eyes. It turned out the current and the past hawks were one and the same! Fintan was angry but knew it was the nature of the beast and it could be asked for no apology. Fintan recounted how he was then turned into an eagle and then a blue-eyed falcon, and finally the King of the Sun returned him to human form. At the end of the tale, it is revealed that both of them had come to the cliffs of Achill to die. They spoke long into the night, sharing stories about times and heroes long past, until sunrise found them lying side by side, dead.

Achill Island is also home to the sixteenth-century pirate queen Grace O' Malley, who was famous for piracy and being bald! Legend has it that as a young girl she asked her father to take her to sea with him. He refused as he was concerned that her long hair would get tangled in the ropes of the rigging. She cut off her hair and was henceforth known as Gráinne Mhaol, or Bald Grace.

Chilling out on the slopes of Croaghaun ▲

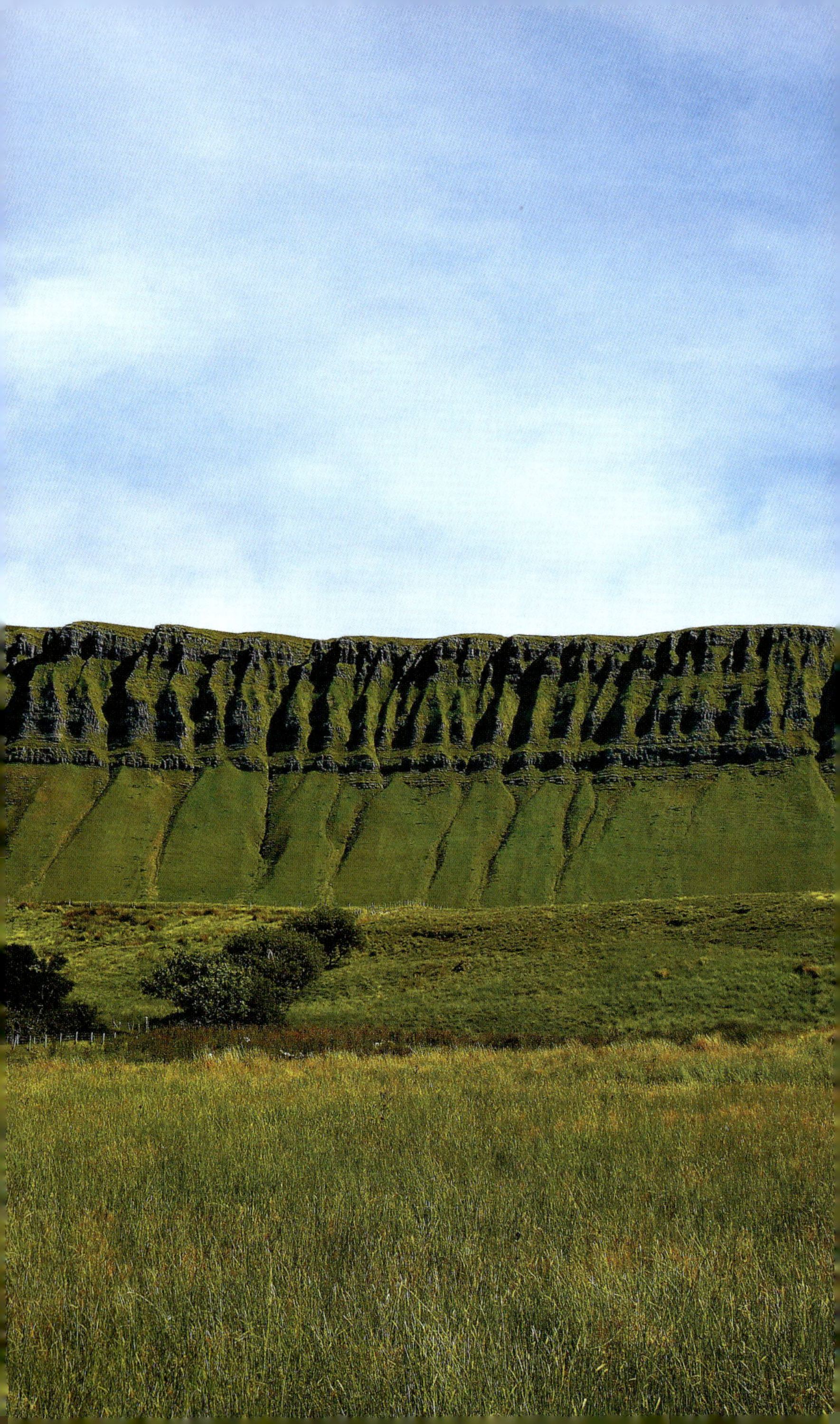

4

Benbulbin
Co. Sligo

A wonderful hike in Yeats country to one of Ireland's most iconic mountains

The iconic table mountain of Benbulbin is the landmark of the Sligo region, towering majestically above Sligo town and W.B. Yeats's grave in nearby Drumcliffe. From the top, there are marvellous views of the Dartry Mountains and the Atlantic Ocean, all the way from Slieve League up in Donegal down to Croagh Patrick in Mayo. Some navigational experience is advised, although the route is generally well defined. Parts of the route can be muddy and boggy if there has been recent rain. Hiking boots essential.

LENGTH:	TIME:	DIFFICULTY:	OSI MAP NO:
11km	4–5 hours	Experienced	16

⊙ NEED TO KNOW

From Sligo town, head north on the N15 for 12km. Turn right onto the L3401, and after just over 2km take the next right onto the L7216. Follow the road for over 2km and arrive at Luke's Bridge, where there is free parking. This can be a busy site in the summer months, so come early.

Coordinates: 54.3735 -8.4664

The Hike

1 From Luke's Bridge, walk straight up the hill with the stream on your right-hand side (do not go left at 150m.) At 750m, cross the bridge and follow the left path. At 950m, keep straight. (Both routes lead to the col, but the straight path is more defined.)

2 At about 2.5km, keep on the path going uphill. The stone track turns more grassy and boggy/muddy and you will cross a few small streams. Find the shortest crossing point at each stream.

3 Walk up the left-hand side of the gully, taking care if it is muddy. The path crosses the stream at point 3. Continue uphill and follow the path that is worn into the grass/bog. You are now gaining the plateau of Benbulbin with sights of Sligo, the Atlantic Ocean and the Dartry Mountains coming into view.

Enjoying the view to Ben Wiskin from Benbulbin ▲

4 At 4.3km, the path moves to your left. Cross a few peat hags, taking your time to find the lowest points to cross. At 4.5km, reach the summit of Benbulbin, which is marked by a trig pillar. Continue on the path in front of you towards the nose of Benbulbin in the direction of the Atlantic Ocean.

5 Reach the end point at 5.5km. Take a well-deserved break and enjoy the views. Retrace your steps back to Luke's Bridge.

Myths and legends

Benbulbin is in the heart of Yeats country. W.B. Yeats is considered one of the greatest poets of the twentieth century and much of his poetry was shaped by ancient Irish folklore and mythology. One of the great romantic and tragic myths associated with this region is the tale of Diarmuid and Gráinne. When Gráinne was a girl, she saw a young, strong man and felt drawn to him, but then he disappeared. Gráinne grew to be a beautiful woman and many suitors proposed to her but she declined them, waiting for the stranger from her girlhood to reappear. As time passed and he didn't appear, Gráinne accepted the proposal of the great Fionn Mac Cumhaill. An engagement party was thrown and it was here that Gráinne at last saw the stranger from her youth again. His name was Diarmuid and he was one of the Fianna soldiers, loyal to Fionn, his chief. Their mutual love could not be denied, however, and Diarmuid and Gráinne ran away to be together. Fionn was furious and gave pursuit. The chase lasted many years, with Diarmuid

▲ Exploring Benbulbin

Crossing the Benbulbin plateau ▲

and Gráinne taking refuge in the mountain ranges of Ireland, including the caves around Benbulbin and Kesh. Unfortunately, it was on the slopes of Benbulbin that tragedy struck. Gráinne was pregnant and as she and Diarmuid were out walking, they came face to face with a magical wild boar. A long-held prophecy had foretold that Diarmuid could be harmed only by a boar. The angry beast bore down on Gráinne, and Diarmuid threw himself in its path. Diarmuid managed to kill the boar but in the process he was mortally wounded. Gráinne took him in her arms but she could not save him. At this moment, Fionn at last caught up with them. Gráinne pleaded with Fionn for help and as he looked on he was moved with pity. He ran to a nearby pool and scooped up a handful of water; Fionn had the incredible gift that those who drank from his hands would live. As Fionn scooped up the water, he turned and saw Gráinne comforting Diarmuid. The rejection and hurt that he had experienced in all of the years of pursuit gathered upon him again and he let the precious water slip through his fingers. Diarmuid breathed his last in the shadow of Benbulbin and died in the arms of his beloved Gráinne.

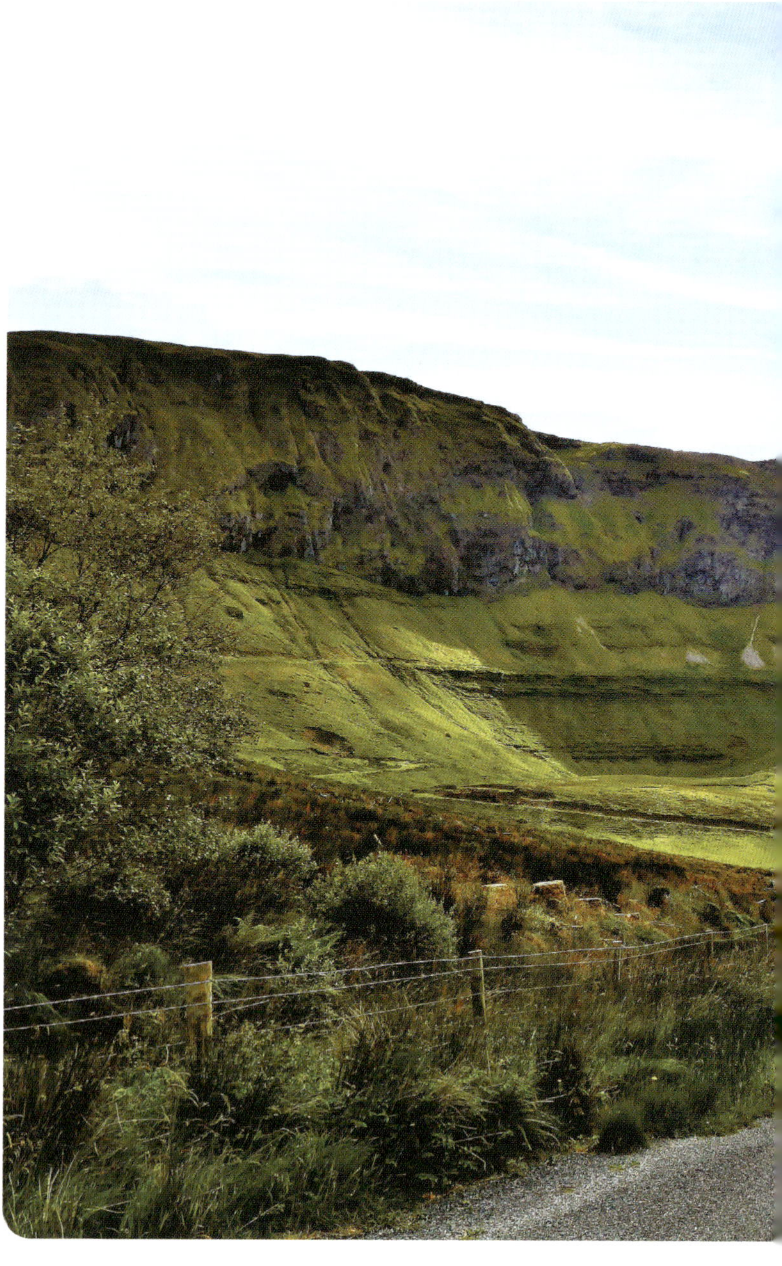

The Dartry Mountains beside Benbulbin ▲

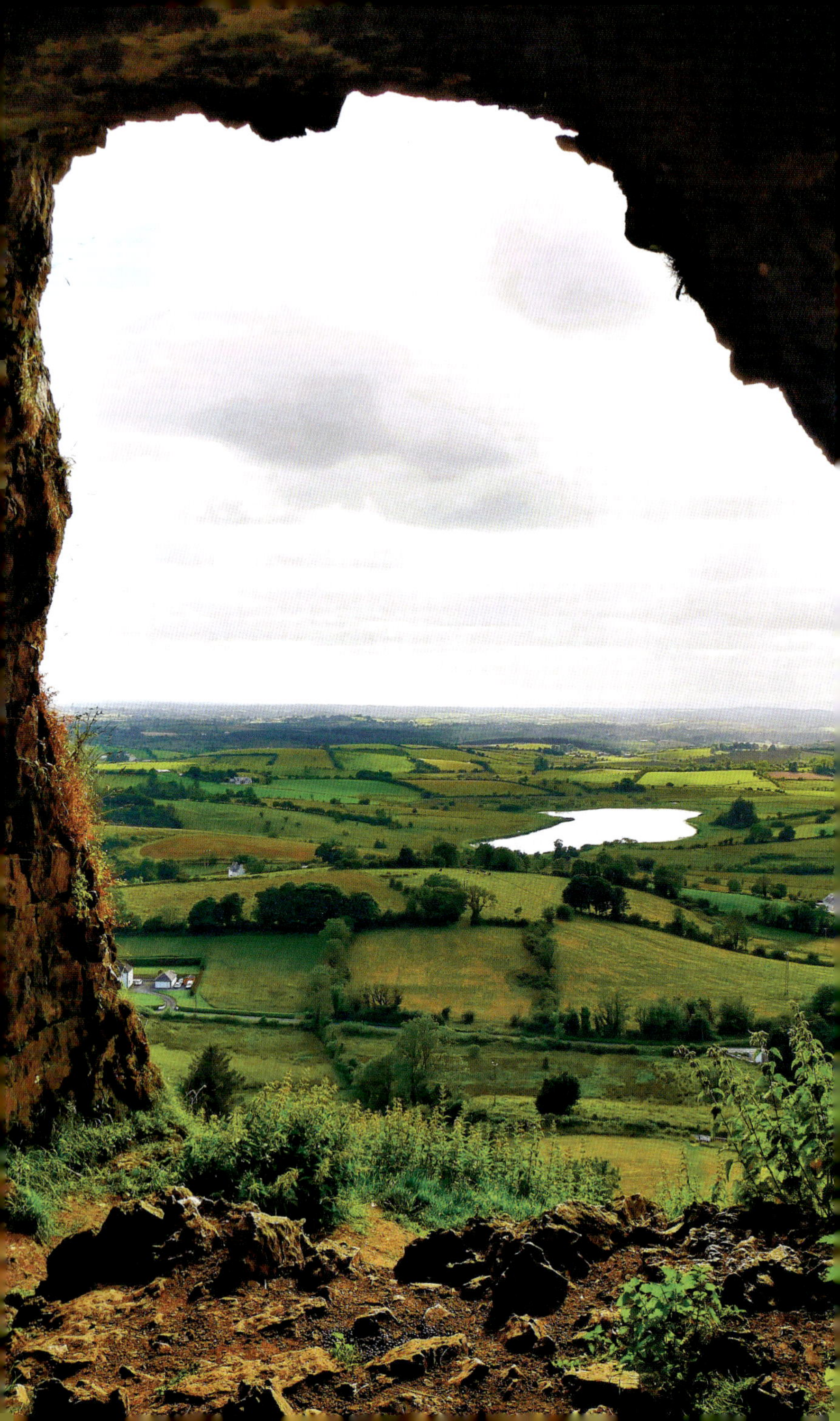

5

Caves of Kesh
Co. Sligo

Enter into the mysterious kingly Caves of Kesh

The seventeen Caves of Kesh are set high in the hillside in Co. Sligo, at the western edge of the Carrowkeel megalithic complex. They are seen as portals to the Otherworld. A short path leads sharply uphill to the caves. The ground outside the caves can be muddy in wet weather. Some of the caves interconnect and it is worth spending time here to absorb the atmosphere. Hiking boots recommended.

LENGTH:	TIME:	DIFFICULTY:	OSI MAP NO:
2km	1 hour	Easy	25

⊙ NEED TO KNOW

From Boyle, Co. Roscommon, take the R294 west for a couple of kilometres before the road turns into the R295. Follow this road for 13km, turn right, then take a left a couple of hundred metres later. After 100m, free parking for the caves is on your right.

Coordinates: 54.0582 -8.4535

Keshcorran
359m

N

Lough Feenagh

500m

The Hike

1 A few metres down from the car park, find a gate that leads across a field in the direction of the caves, which are visible in the hillside. Go through another gate and turn left, keeping on the steep path leading uphill.

2 At 1km, you will reach the caves in the hillside. Several of the caves interconnect. A headlamp is recommended for children who want to explore. When ready, retrace your steps to the car park.

Cave cairns ▲

Myths and legends

The Caves of Kesh are a mysterious set of caves and it is no wonder that many myths are associated with them. Surrounded by large passage tombs nearby, such as Carrowkeel, the caves are strongly linked to one of Ireland's best-known ancient high kings, Cormac mac Airt. In years gone by, the caves were known as the Caves of Cormac mac Airt. It is in these caves that Cormac was raised by a she-wolf after Cormac's mother gave birth in a hedgerow and was too weak to stop the wolf from taking her child. However, Cormac was well raised by the wolves and grew up to become a king of great wisdom and fairness. Indeed, Fionn Mac Cumhaill was one of Cormac's warriors. Another legend says that the Caves of Kesh connect to the underworld of the 'Hell-Mouth Door', which can be found in Oweynagat at the nearby site of Rathcroghan, Co. Roscommon.

Exploring the caves ▲

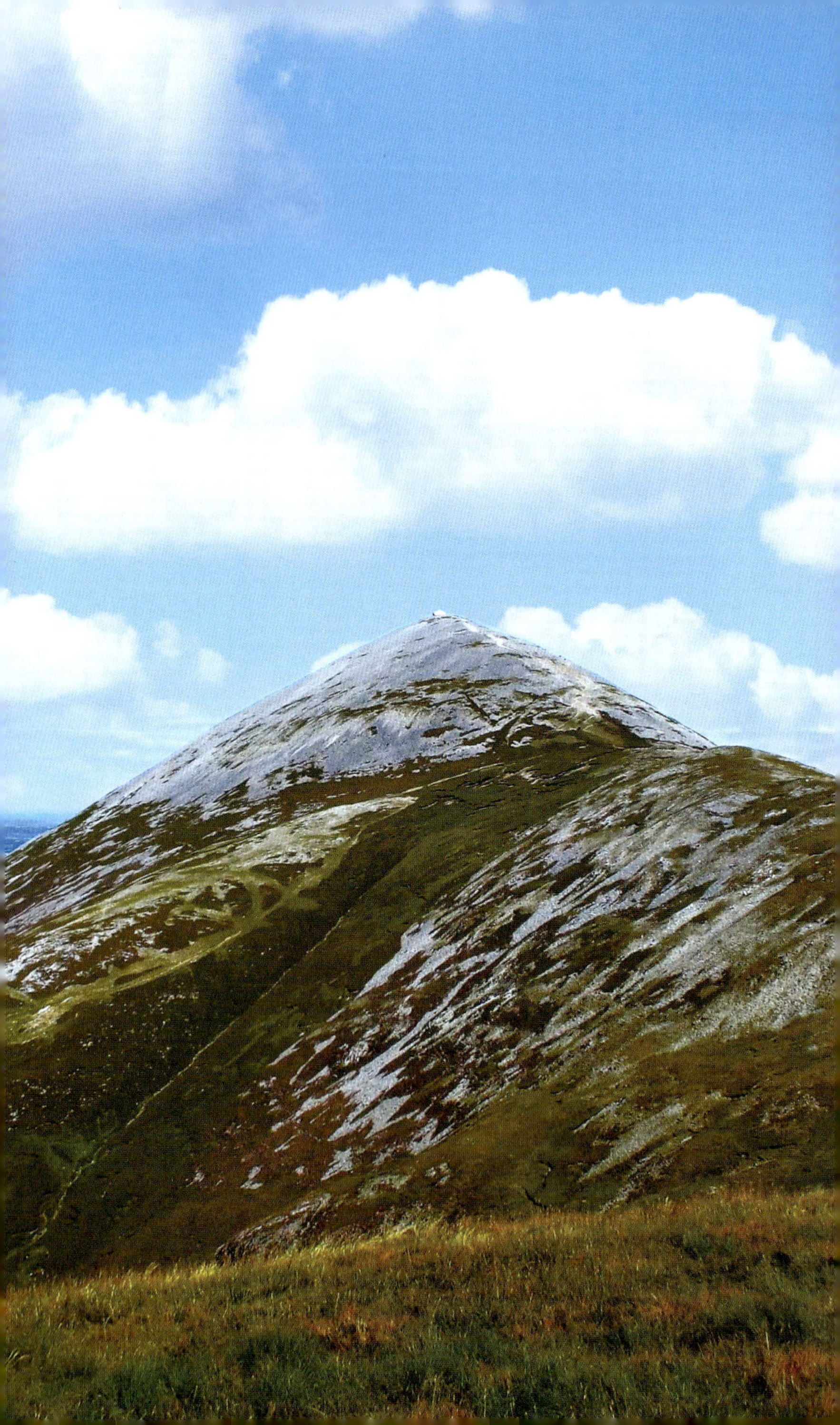

6

Croagh Patrick
Co. Mayo

Take the pilgrims' path to the summit of Ireland's holy mountain

Croagh Patrick is one of the most iconic and most visited mountains in Ireland, especially on Reek Sunday at the end of July. Rising majestically above Clew Bay, Croagh Patrick has been a pilgrimage site for thousands of years. There is a church on the summit, from which there are incredible views of Clew Bay, the Twelve Bens and the Nephin Mountains. There is a clear rock path throughout, and while the going can be tough at times, you will have plenty of company. Best enjoyed in fine weather for the stunning views. Hiking boots recommended.

LENGTH:	TIME:	DIFFICULTY:	OSI MAP NO:
8 km	3–4 hours	Medium	30 and 31

EASTWEST MAPPING: Mweelrea & The Reek

⊙ NEED TO KNOW

From Westport, Co. Mayo, take the R335 west for 8km to the village of Murrisk. Park in the car park on your left. There is a €3 charge for the day. There are toilets and a café on the grounds. Note that on Reek Sunday, the last Sunday in July, thousands arrive to climb the pilgrim mountain so there are different parking arrangements in the village for that day.

Coordinates: 53.7797 -9.6397

◄ Croagh Patrick from Ben Goram

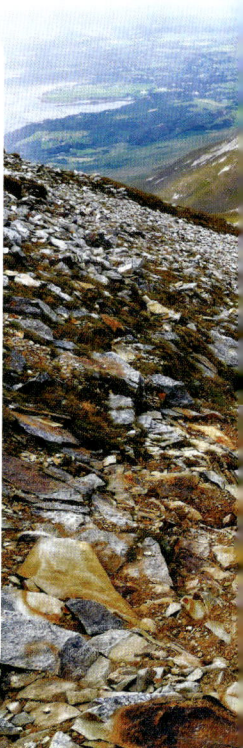

The Hike

1 From the car park, head to your left towards the visitor centre. As you walk up, you will see the uphill route to Croagh Patrick. Follow the signs for Croagh Patrick. After around 800m, pass through a metal gate and keep climbing. Turn around every now and then to enjoy the beautiful emerging vistas of Clew Bay and the Nephins. A lovely mountain stream accompanies you along the way.

2 At about 2.3km, come to the shoulder of the path where the path levels for a while. This is a good place to catch your breath and enjoy the panoramic views, with the Twelve Bens opening up in front of you. When ready, keep along the path where the steep cone of Croagh Patrick now becomes clearer. New steps have been put in recently, which make the climb much safer. This section is very steep so just take your time and take breaks as needed.

Descending through the clouds on Croagh Patrick ▲

3 At 4km, reach the summit. St Patrick's chapel and bed is in front of you. There are incredible views from the summit of Clew Bay, the Nephin Mountains, Twelve Bens, Sheeffry Hills and the mighty peak of Mweelrea, the high point in the province of Connacht. When ready, take your time descending and retrace your steps to the car park.

Myths and legends

While Croagh Patrick is commonly known as a Christian pilgrimage site dedicated to St Patrick, evidence from Stone Age and Bronze Age hill-forts in the area indicate that it was also an assembly point in pre-Christian Ireland. In those days, in late July/early August (the same time as Reek Sunday today), devotion was made to the Celtic harvest gods, Crom Dubh and Lugh (the Irish for the month of August is Lúnasa). The most famous story associated with St Patrick is that he drove the snakes out of Ireland and that is why Ireland doesn't have any snakes today. Interestingly, to the south of Croagh Patrick is a lake called Lough Na Corra, which translates to 'Lake of the Serpent'. Corra was an old serpent goddess in pre-Christian Ireland symbolic of fertility, wisdom and regeneration. Her banishment to the lake represents Christianity's victory over the old religions. On the northern side of the mountain, there is a hollow called Lugnademon ('hollow of the demons'), which was said to be the last place where demons gathered before being banished by St Patrick into the sea.

Croagh Patrick summit ▲

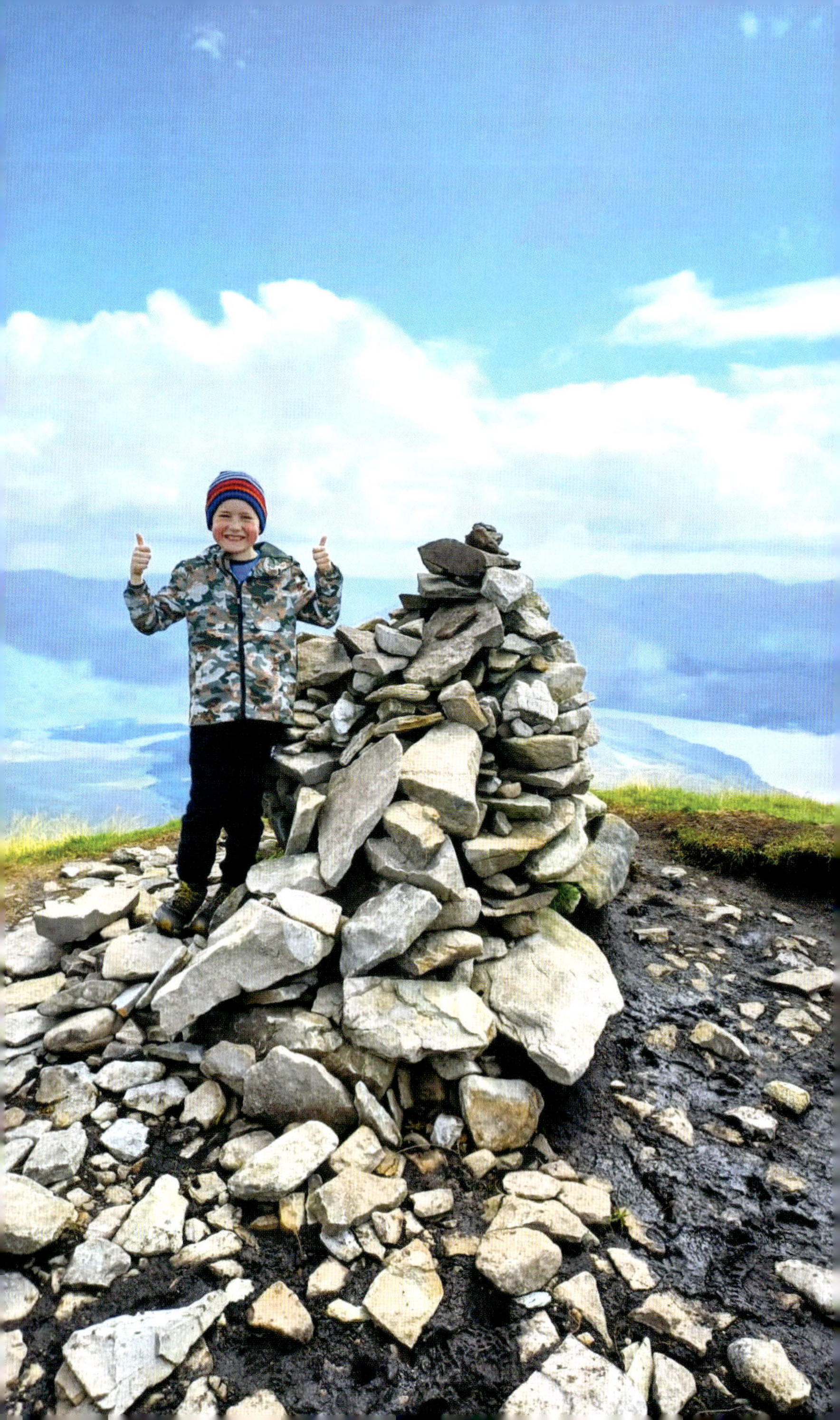

Mweelrea
Co. Mayo

A wild hike to the highest mountain in Connacht

The view from the top of Mweelrea is arguably the finest and most expansive in Ireland. At 814m, it is the highest point in Co. Mayo and in the province of Connacht. There are magnificent views of Ireland's only fjord at Killary Harbour, a glacier valley at Doolough Pass, the Sheeffry Hills and Twelve Bens Mountains. There are many routes to the summit but the route described here is the safest. Navigational skills are required as there are few well-defined paths on the route except for the stone path leading from the col to the summit. Weather conditions can change extremely fast on Mweelrea so this hike should only be attempted when the weather is set fair. Hiking boots essential.

LENGTH:	TIME:	DIFFICULTY:	OSI MAP NO:
9.5km	4–5 hours	Experienced	37

EASTWEST MAPPING: Mweelrea & The Reek

⊙ NEED TO KNOW

From Leenaun in Co. Galway, head north on the N59, and after 3km turn left onto the R335. Follow this road for 19km before turning left onto the R378. Follow this road for just over 13.5km. Park on the side of the road where there is space for three cars. If there is no space, continue down the road to the Silver Strand for free parking. This will add a couple of kilometres to your walk.

Coordinates: 53.6549 -9.8692

◂ Overlooking Killary Harbour from Mweelrea summit

The Hike

1 From your car, walk up the stony lane beside you. A sign says it is a dead end and no dogs are allowed, but you are allowed to walk here. Mweelrea is the highest mountain in front of you, slightly to your right. Pass through a gate on the stony lane, closing it behind you. Head through the reeds on a grass path. A stream will be on your right-hand side, but keep going straight until there is a clear crossing point to your right.

2 Once you cross the stream, you will enter open mountainside and your best line is directly towards Mweelrea summit. Informal grass/bog paths fade in and out, but use them where you find them to help you along. Stunning views of the Silver Strand and Uggool Beach start to open up behind you as you climb.

3 At 2.5km, you reach a large riverbed cut into the valley. Use the river as a guide or handrail towards reaching the col (the low point between the peaks) on your left. Climb initially on the left-hand side of the river, where there is an informal path.

On the edge of the world ▲

4 At 3.1km, you will come to a large set of stones. Turn right here and cross the river to a stony path on the other side. Use this path to bring you to the col above you.

5 At 3.6km, you reach the col and wonderful views of Ben Bury and the Mweelrea range appear. Turn right here towards Mweelrea summit and follow the stone path upwards using the cairn markers on the way.

6 At 4.6km, arrive at the broad summit of Mweelrea. There are incredible views of all the mountain ranges in Connemara, the Atlantic Ocean and Killary Harbour. When ready, retrace your steps to your car.

Myths and legends

Mweelrea translates as Maol Rí – 'the bald king' – or Maol Réidh – 'bald hill with the smooth top'. On a clear day, its hulking mass reveals a bald dome, but just as often it wears a wig of mist and cloud. Local legends reflect the desolation of the area. For instance, the nearby Sheeffry Hills are known as the 'Hills of the Wraith', 'wraith' referring to the legendary Sidhe or fairy people who in pre-Christian times were seen as a remnant of the mighty Tuatha Dé Danann race, who were banished underground when they were defeated in battle by the invading Milesians. The Sidhe are said to reside to this day in the hollow hills or Sidhe mounds. Wraiths are also known as 'banshees' (*bean* – woman and *sidhe* – fairy) and their appearance portends a person's death. Locals say there is an eerie atmosphere in these hills, where mists can descend unexpectedly and a traveller can wander ten miles along a desolate and silent ridge without ever seeing a person, yet at times be troubled by a feeling of another's presence.

The sense of desolation is echoed by what happened during the Great Famine when hundreds of people perished at nearby Doolough Pass in 1849. At Louisburgh in Mayo, the starving people were told to present themselves for inspection at Delphi Hunting Lodge, 20km away, at 7a.m. the next day to check if they were eligible to receive relief. However, bad weather, coupled with sickness, cold and hunger, meant that they never reached the lodge and died at Doolough Pass. In commemoration, a stone cross facing the lake at Doolough bears an inscription from Mahatma Gandhi: 'How can men feel themselves honoured by the humiliation of their fellow beings?'

A view of Mweelrea Range ▲

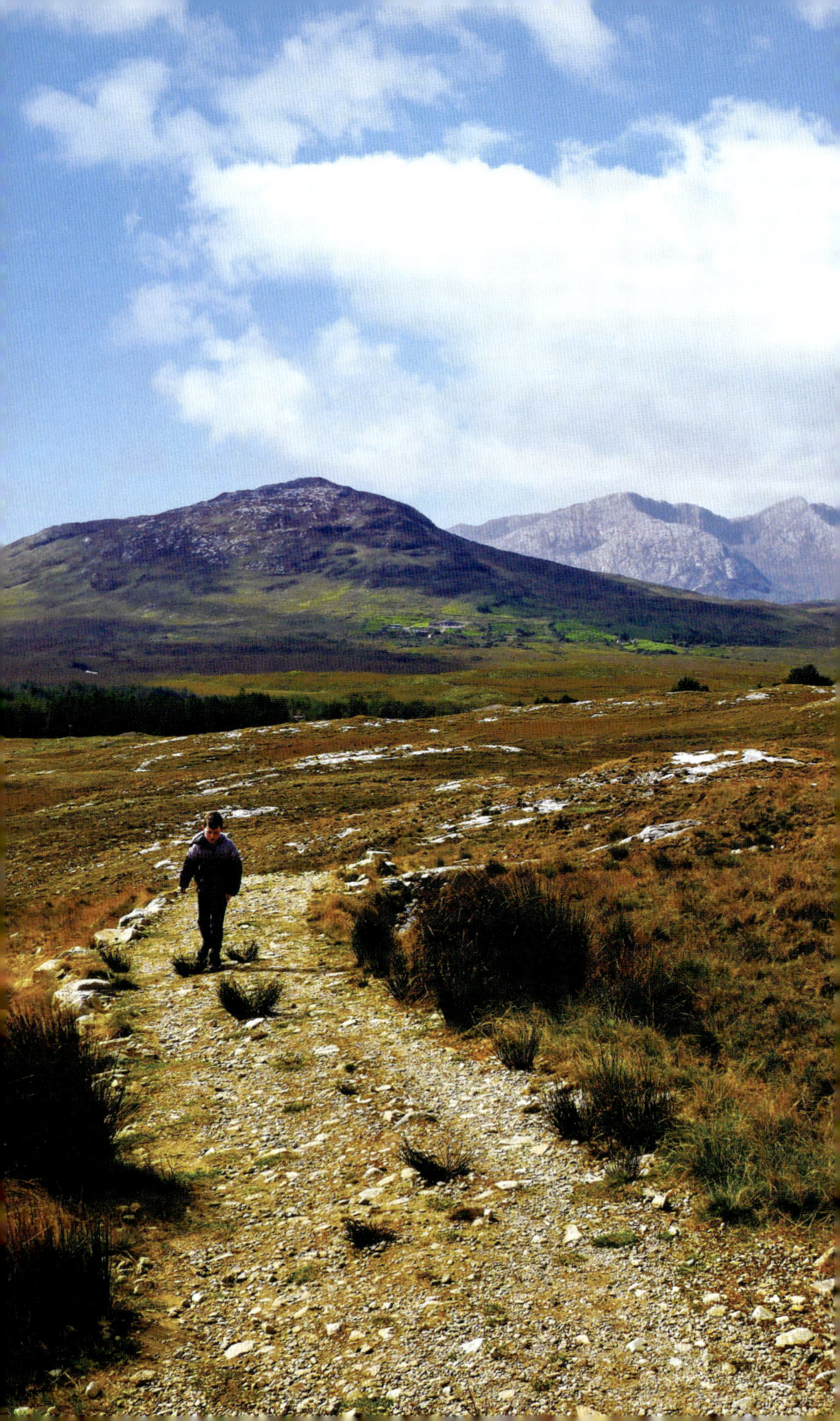

8

Mám Éan
Co. Galway

A beautiful pilgrimage site in the Maumturk Mountains

This is a remote and beautiful hike in the Maumturk Mountains to a pilgrimage site steeped in history and myth. At the pass, there is a statue of St Patrick, a small chapel, a mass altar and Stations of the Cross. There is a well-defined path. Hiking boots recommended.

LENGTH:	TIME:	DIFFICULTY:	OSI MAP NO:
4km	1–2 hours	Easy	37 and 44

EASTWEST MAPPING: Connemara Mountains
SUPERWALKER XT30: Connemara

⊙ NEED TO KNOW

From Letterfrack in Co. Galway, take the N59 north for almost 9km. Then turn right on the R344 for 8km before following a sign for Mám Éan to the left. Follow this narrow road for just over 6km and arrive at a free car park on your left.
Coordinates: 53.4839 -9.6698

◀ A view from Mám Éan towards the majestic Twelve Bens

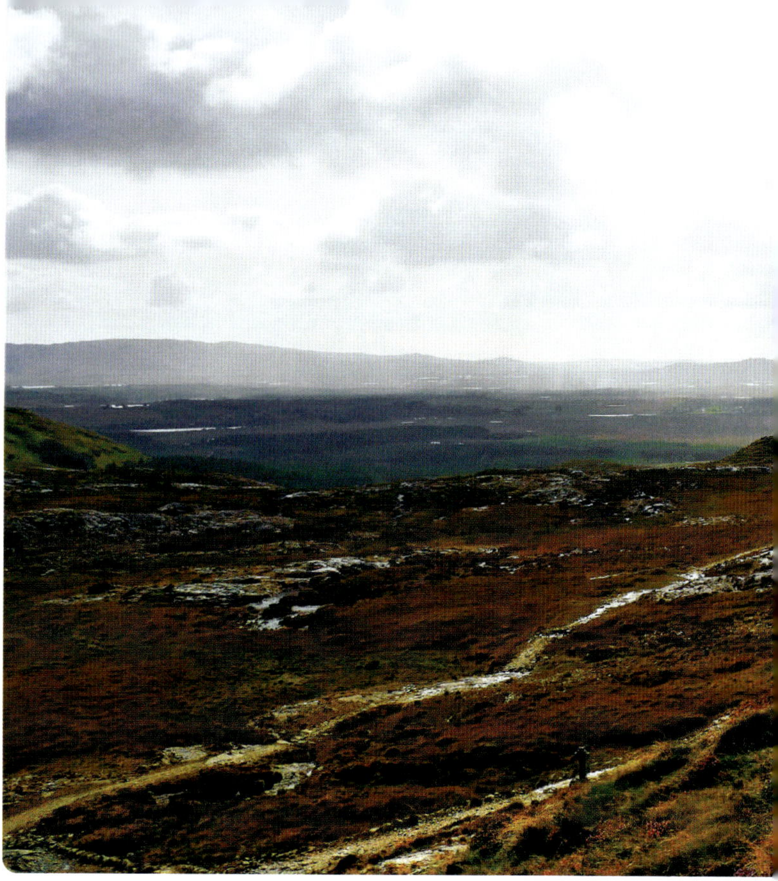

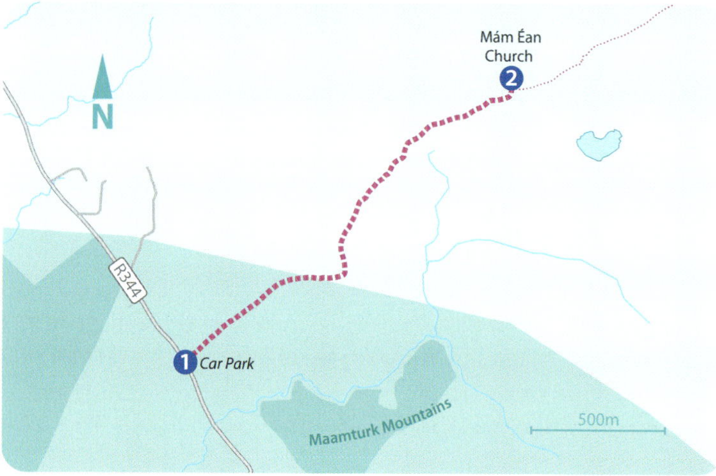
Mám Éan
Church
2
N
R344
1
Car Park
Maamturk Mountains
500m

The Hike

1 From the car park, head up the grassy path in front of you. Pass through a metal gate with Mám Éan written on it and make sure to close it behind you.

2 After 1.8km, arrive at the summit of Mám Éan, where there is a statue of St Patrick, a small church, an altar rock and Stations of the Cross spread across the site. When ready, retrace your steps to your car. If you want to add to the route, there is an informal path that starts up behind the chapel that is worth exploring.

▲ Church and mass rock at Mám Éan

Myths and legends

Mám Éan, which means 'Pass of the Birds', is a beautiful pilgrimage site in the heart of the remote Maumturk Mountains in Connemara. At Mám Éan, St Patrick is said to have fought the pagan harvest god Crom Dubh yet again. Crom Dubh appeared as a speckled bull in these mountains and attacked people who attempted to use the mountain pass. St Patrick drove the bull into the lake near the church that is today called Loch an Tairbh (the Bull's Lake). St Patrick's bed can be found near the church. This site was used as a secret mass rock by Catholics during Penal times in the seventeenth and eighteenth centuries after British rule outlawed practice of the Catholic religion.

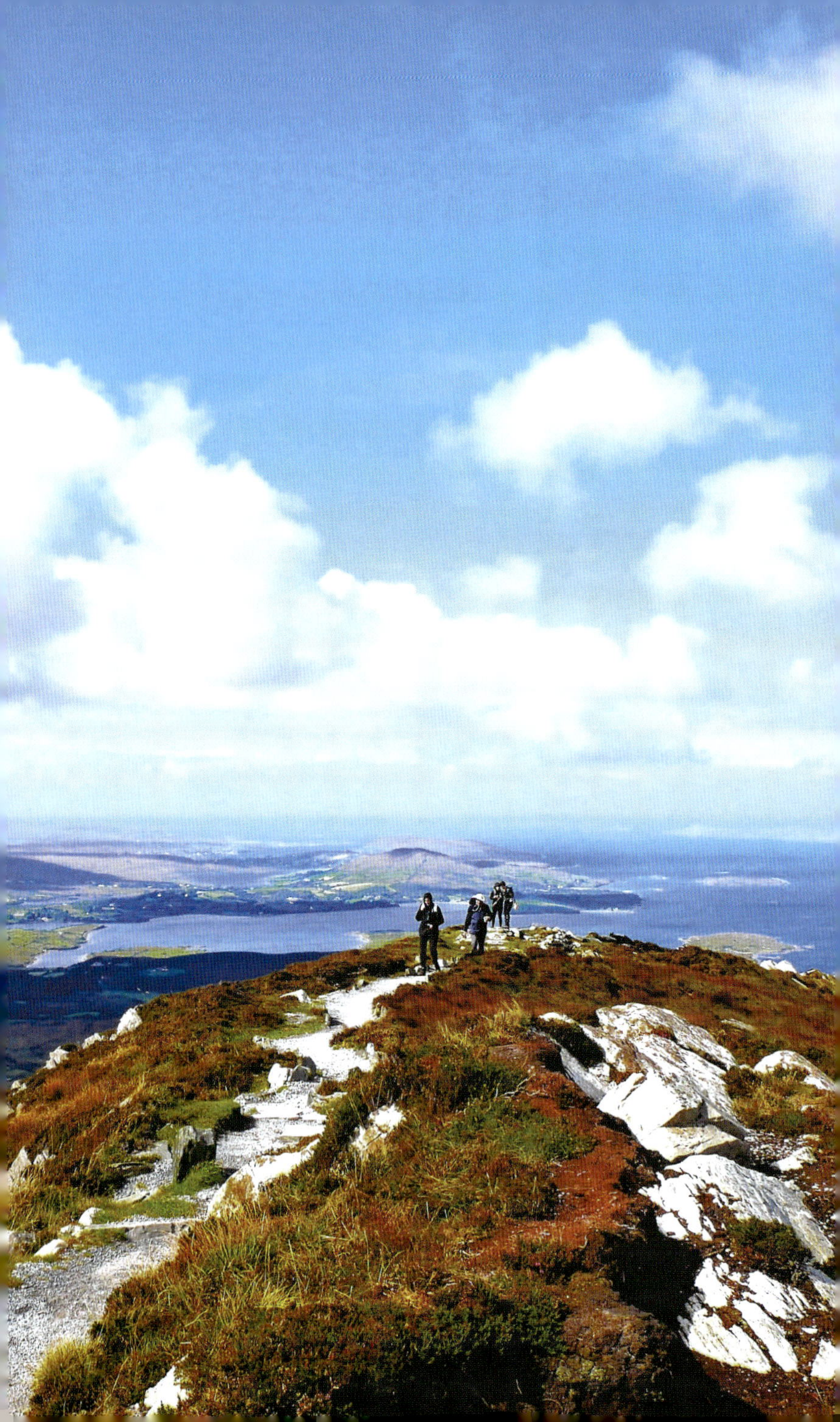

9

Diamond Hill
Co. Galway

An exhilarating hike through Connemara National Park

This is truly a jewel of a hike, with stunning mountain and coastal views and overlooking Kylemore Abbey. Paths are well defined. This hike is best enjoyed in clear, calm weather. Hiking boots recommended.

LENGTH:	TIME:	DIFFICULTY:	OSI MAP NO:
3–7km	45 mins–3 hours	Easy–Medium	37

EASTWEST MAPPING: Connemara Mountains
SUPERWALKER XT30: Connemara

⊙ NEED TO KNOW

From Letterfrack, head south on the N39 and shortly afterwards you will see a sign for Connemara National Park on your left. Turn left and follow the road to the free car park at the end. This can be a busy site, especially in the summer months.

Coordinates: 53.5504 -9.9455

◄ Diamond Hill overlooking the Atlantic Ocean

N59

Letterfrack

Diamond Hill
442m

500m

N

The Hike

1 From the car park, make your way towards a small building and walk around it on the left-hand side. Follow the sign for Diamond Hill and trails. Follow the path downhill. Turn left where there is a sign for Park Centre. Follow the path around the back of the visitor centre. There are toilets on your left and a café and playground on your right. Continue up the path in front of you and follow the sign for Diamond Hill.

2 At 950m, take the path to your left and follow the red and blue arrows. The views start to really open up.

3 At 1.5km, there is a large rock and a junction of paths. For the easy 3km option, take the right path – the Lower Diamond Hill Walk – and follow the blue arrows back to the car park. For the exhilarating Upper Diamond Hill Walk, take the path to the left and follow the red arrow. Four hundred metres later, keep to the left again as there is a sign directing one-way traffic around the upper walk.

Descending Diamond Hill ▲

4   At 3.4km, reach the summit of Diamond Hill. There are stunning views here of the Atlantic coastline and the Twelve Bens Mountains. The beautiful Kylemore Abbey can be seen far below you. When ready, head straight across the summit to the steeply descending path on the other side.

5   At 5.8km, arrive back at the large stone you met at point 3 above. There is an option here to turn left and follow the path back to the visitor centre. Alternatively, turn right and retrace your steps to your car.

Myths and legends

Diamond Hill may be so called due to the glitter of its quartz crystals when the sun shines. In Irish, it is called Binn Ghuaire, meaning 'Guaire's peak'. Guaire most likely refers to Guaire Aidne mac Colmáin (died 663 CE), a King of Connacht renowned for his hospitality and love of poetry. Dunguaire Castle in Kinvara, Co. Galway, was a well-known meeting place for bards and poets. Fionn Mac Cumhaill and Cú Chulainn (another famous Irish warrior hero and demigod) were also said to reside in the Diamond Hill area and often fought with each other. Fionn lived on Diamond Hill and Cú Chulainn lived on the opposite side of the valley on the mountain known as Dúchruach ('Black Stack'), which sits directly behind Kylemore Abbey. One day, during one of their heated arguments, Cú Chulainn threw a massive stone at Fionn. The stone narrowly missed him and landed at an unusual angle on the Kylemore estate, where it lies today. The shape of the stone resembles a traditional iron used for ironing clothes and is known locally as 'The Ironing Stone'. Some use it today as a wishing stone. If you stand with your back against the stone, make a wish and throw a small pebble back over the stone three times, your wish will be granted. *Creid é nó ná creid é!* (Believe it or not!)

On the summit of Diamond Hill ▲

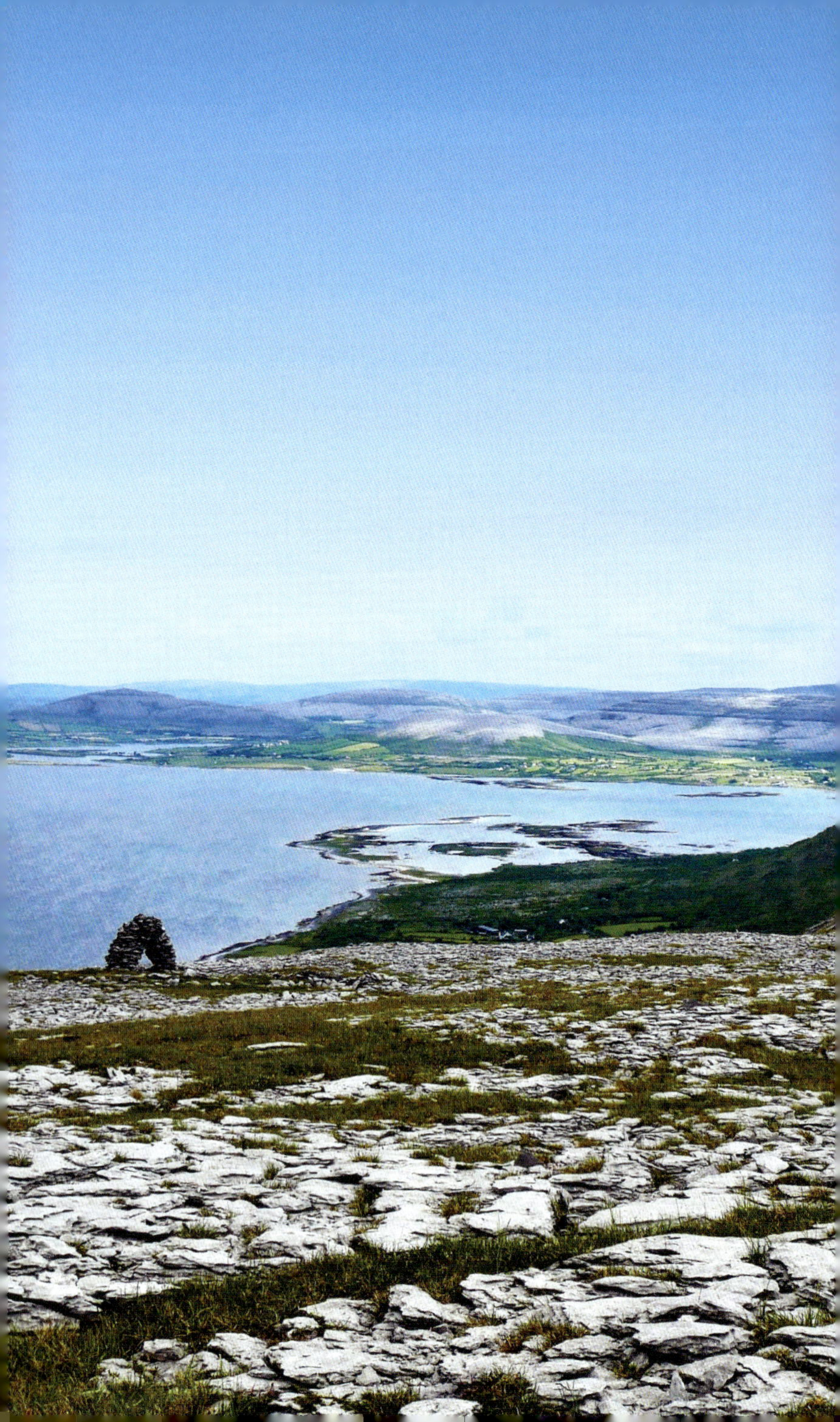

10

Black Head Loop
Burren, Co. Clare

A mesmerising hike through karst limestone

Traversing the karst limestone landscape of the Burren is a mesmerising, adventuresome, unforgettable experience. The coastal and mountain views are breathtaking and include Galway Bay and the Aran Islands. The Burren is particularly special in the summer months, when its unique flora are in full blossom. Navigational skills are required as much of the route has no clear path. Be prepared for wind, whatever the time of year or weather conditions. Hiking boots recommended.

LENGTH:	TIME:	DIFFICULTY:	OSI MAP NO:
16.5km	5–6 hours	Experienced	51

⊙ NEED TO KNOW

From Kinvara, Co. Galway, take the N67 west. Follow this road for 18km into Ballyvaughan village. Turn right onto the R477 and after 13km you will approach Fanore. Turn left here and park outside St Patrick's Church of Ireland church. There is space here for two cars, but if these are taken there is free parking at the nearby Fanore Beach further down the main road.

Coordinates: 53.1246-9.2755

◂ View of Galway Bay from Black Head

The Hike

Black Head

N

Doughbranneen
314m

R477

Gleninagh Mtn
315m

1km

1 After parking carefully outside the church, proceed up the road, which is known locally as the Khyber Road. Follow the red sign at the start for the Caher Valley Loop. Be mindful as there can be traffic on this road. Enjoy the Caher River beside you as it winds its way down the pass.

2 After 4.2km, reach a disjointed crossroads. Ignore the route to the right and turn left a few metres later up a steep stony track. Climb this track, passing some old farm buildings, and continue to the top of the hill where the road levels out. This climbing section is about 1km long.

3 At 5.2km, there is an old ring fort on your right. Turn left here across a stone wall onto the open karst limestone. Aim generally for the green mound you see in front of you off in the distance. As you cross the limestone, there are grikes (crevices), so take care with your footing. You will cross several stone walls en route so look for a low point in the walls. The general direction is north-west or 'one o'clock' from the time you crossed the fence. Keep to the right as the going is easier along this side and the emerging views are incredible.

4 At 8km, you will arrive at the top of Gleninagh Mountain, which has a trig pillar on top of a large mound. This is a good place to rest and enjoy the views. Your route now continues in front of you towards the large cairn you can see on the next mountain

Traversing the karst paving stones, Black Head ▲

called Doughbranneen. Start descending Gleninagh, keeping to your right. You will come across several cliff shelves that need to be descended. The cliffs are lower and more accessible the more you keep to their right. Take your time and you will find a weak spot to climb down. As you descend, aim for the stone wall to your right that leads up along the right-hand side of Doughbranneen.

5 After descending for 1.5km, reach a wide track and bear right. This track leads up the side of Doughbranneen Mountain. As the track climbs, look back and enjoy the stunning coastline views.

6 At any point along the track, you can set off left up towards the top of Doughbranneen. Keep climbing and after 700m see a large pre-historic burial mound called Carn Mhuiriúch Cille (Murrooghkilly Cairn). There are beautiful views here of the Aran Islands. When ready, descend towards the stone fort of Cathair Dhun Irghuis.

Keep to the right and use the cairns as your guide downwards. There are more cliff shelves to be negotiated, so take your time to find the weakest, most accessible points to descend.

7 At 11.7km, arrive at the stone fort of Cathair Dhun Irghuis. This impressive fort is set on the edge of Black Head with panoramic views of the Twelve Bens Mountains in Galway to the Cliffs of Moher in Clare. Descend following the cairns.

8 After 500m, meet a grass path and turn left onto it. You will see a National Looped Walk sign.

9 At 14.8km, cross some steps onto a gravel path and follow it downhill onto the R477. After 1.7km, arrive back at the Caher River and turn left up the L5047 if you parked at the church. If you parked at the beach, continue on the R477 until you reach the Fanore Beach car park on your right. We would recommend finishing the day by enjoying the beautiful Fanore seaside and soaking your tired feet after an amazing Burren adventure.

Myths and legends

Black Head lies at the most northern tip of Co. Clare. The name is a mystery, but the Irish name of Ceann Boirne or Black Head certainly captures the atmosphere of the headland. The stone fort of Cathair Dhun Irghuis was home to the Firbolg chief, Irghus. Irghus was a legendary builder and the stone fort is a testament to his ability. Firbolg means 'men of bags'; the name came from when the Firbolg were enslaved in Greece and were made to carry around heavy bags filled with stone. The Firbolg escaped from Greece and ruled Ireland until the Tuatha Dé Danann arrived and defeated them at the first battle of Moytura. The Firbolg were the fourth group to invade Ireland and it is believed that they descended from the Muintir Nemid, an earlier group who abandoned Ireland and went to different parts of Europe.

A hagstone – one of the many unusual stone formations on Black Head ▲

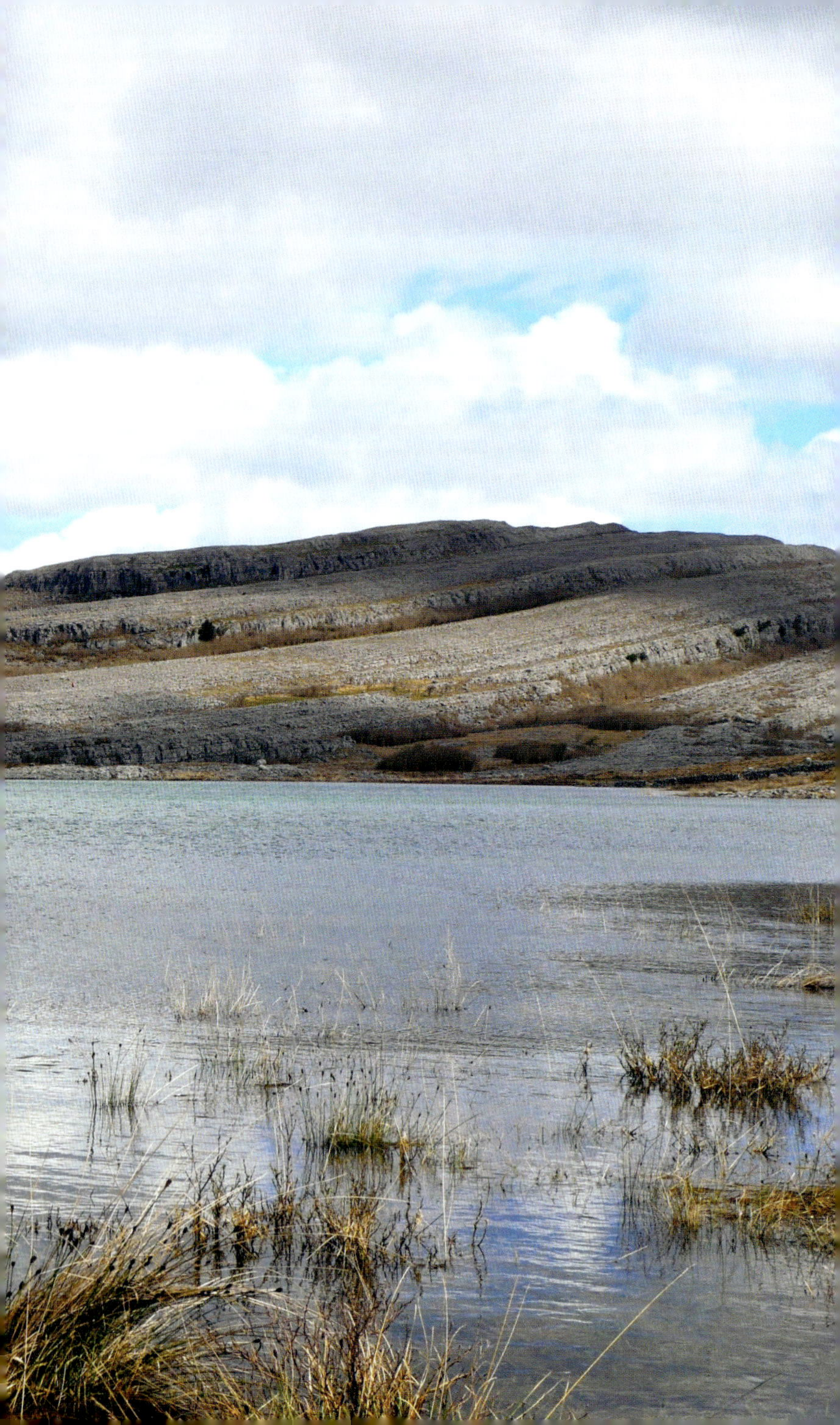

11

Mullaghmore
Burren, Co. Clare

A hike through a fascinating limestone kingdom

Mullaghmore is a karst dome set in the heart of the Burren's karst landscape. Mullaghmore and the surrounding hills look like giant coiled snakes or layercakes, resulting from layers of seabed being twisted skywards 325 million years ago. Paths are across limestone slabs but are well signed throughout. On the far side of Mullaghmore, see Father Ted's house from the comedy show *Father Ted*. Hiking boots recommended.

LENGTH:	TIME:	DIFFICULTY:	OSI MAP NO:
6km	2–3 hours	Medium	51 and 52

⊙ NEED TO KNOW

From Dublin, take the M6 west to Athenry, Co. Galway, and then join the M18 towards Gort. At junction 16, exit onto the R458. Then join the R460 for 16km. Take the next right and follow the road for another 2.5km. Park off the road with consideration for other walkers and motorists in the area.

Coordinates: 52.9958 -9.022

◄ View of Mullaghmore, the jewel in the heart of the Burren

The Hike

1 Cross the wall at a yellow sign and notice the information board showing different walks. For this hike, follow the signs for the blue walk. Lough Gaelan comes into view as you follow the grass path around to your right. After heavy rain this path can sometimes become waterlogged but there is plenty of room to the right-hand side to continue on the path towards Mullaghmore.

2 After 600m, go through a stone wall and keep following the path. Mullaghmore looms before you and the landscape begins to change. After a further 600m, go through another stone wall and continue on the path as it turns left.

3 Cross the limestone slabs for a couple of hundred metres, keeping your eye out for a large rock with a blue sign on it. Keep slightly to the right and you will pick up more blue signs.

4 At 1.5km, you will meet a path winding to your left. This is the path by which you will return later. However, ignore this path for now and instead head up the mountain alongside some hazel trees. Keep following the blue signs uphill. If you turn around, you will start to see some of the beautiful Burren scenery as it stretches out in front of you.

5 At 2km, turn left. Some light scrambling will be required to cross the paving here. Continue across the hill and cross the valley until you reach the next signs.

Returning from a great day on Mullaghmore ▲

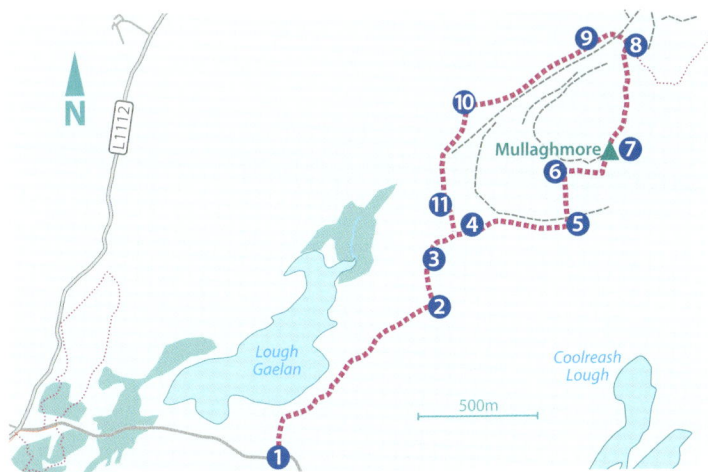

6 After another couple of hundred metres, turn right and start climbing up a steep path. After a short while turn left again, scramble up the rock and go straight across the valley to the next sign. Turn right up the path and shortly afterwards note the blue sign, turn left and ascend to the top of Mullaghmore.

7 At 2.8km, arrive at the top of Mullaghmore and enjoy stunning views across the Burren, including Slieve Roe and Knockane. When ready, continue across the top, following the blue signs. There are great spots here for a well-earned rest and some sustenance.

8 Continue to follow the signs down the mountainside. The path is quite steep and rocky in parts, so take your time descending. At 3km, continue on the blue path and ignore the red and yellow signs pointing you to the right. Keep to the left beside a stone wall on your right. This path leads you around the back of Mullaghmore.

9 After a couple of hundred metres, see in the right distance a large house which was used as Father Ted's house in the iconic comedy show *Father Ted*. Follow this path for one kilometre and enjoy the beautiful views of the Burren lakes.

10 Pass through a gap in the wall and cross the limestone paving again for another 500m.

11 Arrive back at the original path – point 4 on the map – and retrace your footsteps to your car. And why not have a lovely picnic on the rocks?

Myths and legends

As you walk across the limestone pavement, you may think of Colman mac Duagh, a priest and brother to King Guaire, who was King of Connacht in the seventh century and owned nearby Dunguaire Castle. Legend has it that Colman spent forty days fasting during Lent in the Burren with his servant. They only had barley bread, sprigs of cress and water for sustenance. When Easter came, the servant wanted to leave for a decent meal but Colman convinced him to stay and told him a meal was on its way. Back at the castle, a lavish meal was being prepared for King Guaire but suddenly the meal started to levitate and made its way to Colman and the servant in the Burren. The king, along with his guests and dogs, followed the meal but were frozen to the spot while Colman and the servant finished it. When the meal was over, Colman released the guests and dogs from their paralysis. The grikes that you see in the limestone pavements in the Burren are believed to be the tracks of the guests and dogs who followed the levitating food, only to be stuck frozen to the ground!

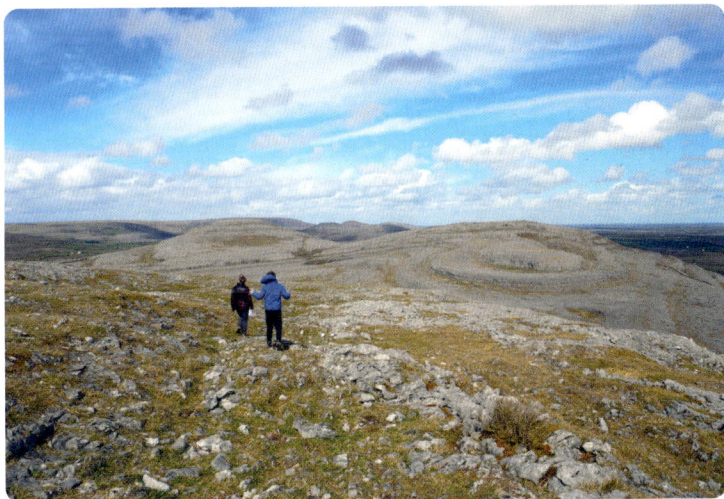

Rambling across Mullaghmore summit ▲

The South

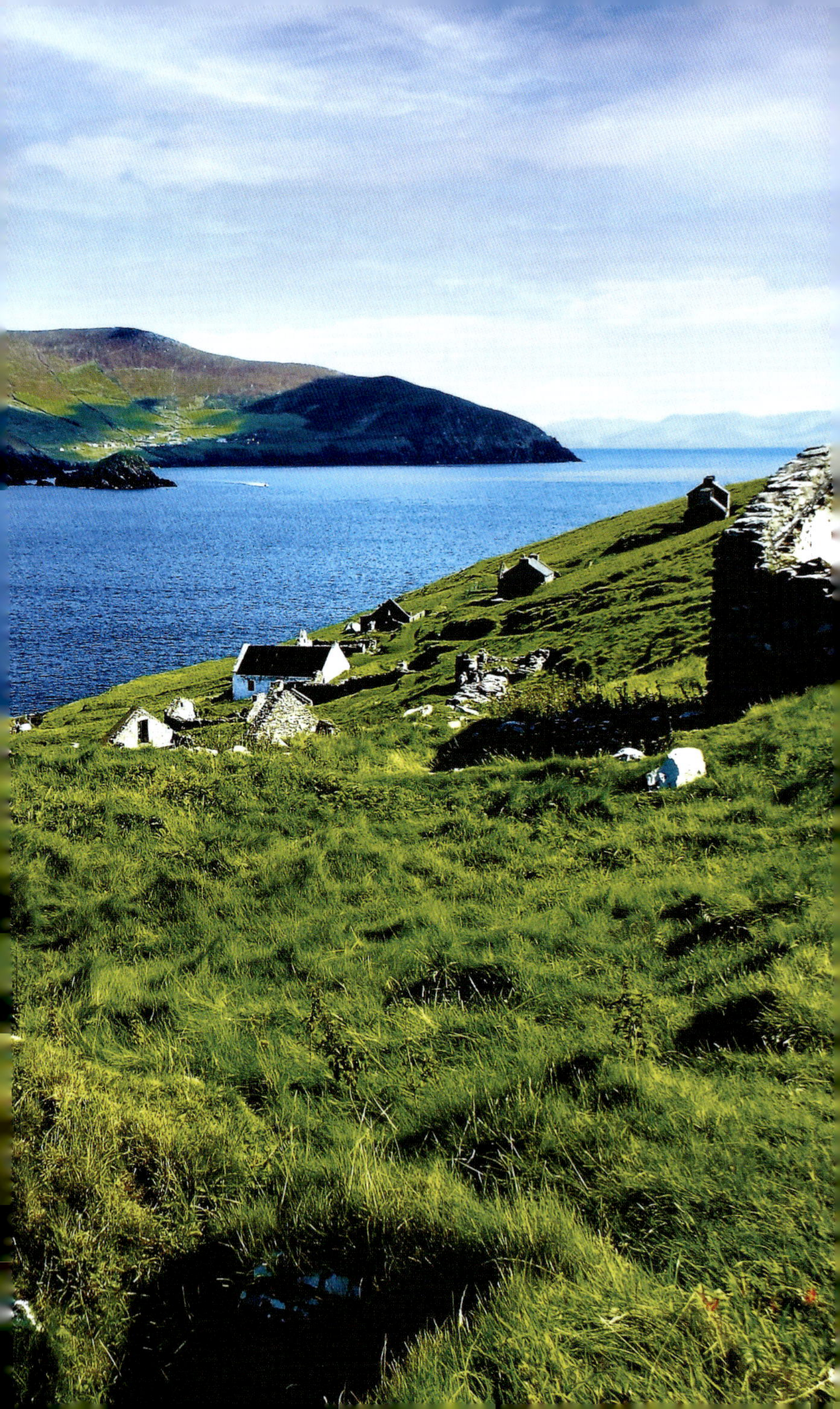

12

Great Blasket Island
Co. Kerry

An unmissable hike exploring a bygone time

Take the boat from Dunquin Pier to experience the unique isolation and beauty of the Great Blasket Island. This island is the largest of the archipelago known collectively as the Blaskets, which lie at the most westerly point of Ireland and Europe. This is a stunning hike where not only can you meet seals, whales, dolphins and puffins but you can also explore the deserted village and learn about the people who used to live there. The Great Blasket Island was home to some of Ireland's most celebrated literary figures, including Peig Sayers, Tomás Ó Criomhthain and Muiris Ó Súilleabháin. Free hourly guided tours are provided in the summer. This hike can only be attempted in fine weather as the island can be cut off in inclement weather. There are good paths throughout and hiking boots are essential.

LENGTH:	TIME:	DIFFICULTY:	OSI MAP NO:
2–9km	2–4 hours	Easy-Medium	70

⊙ NEED TO KNOW

From Tralee, head south on the N86 for 48km. Then take the R559 to Dunquin Pier. Check online to pre-book your ferry ticket. Make your way down to the pier. Then travel by boat and dinghy to the Great Blasket Island.

Coordinates: 52.1253 -10.46

◀ Abandoned dwellings on the Great Blasket Island

The Hike

1 After an exciting boat crossing of the notorious Blasket Sound, you will land at the harbour of Old Town. Exit the harbour and follow the path to the right as it winds its way up by the abandoned homes. With younger children, a very good time can be had by simply exploring the beach and old houses without progressing further.

2 For those who do want to go further, after around 250m on the right-hand path, take the grass path to the left and follow this track as it climbs uphill. This is quite steep but it does not last long. Soon you will enjoy stunning views of the island as well as the Kerry coastline.

Hiking on Great Blasket Island

3 After 3km, arrive at a junction of paths. For the easier 6km option, turn right back towards the village and harbour. For the 9km option, turn left and climb to Slievedonagh.

4 At 3.6km, arrive at Slievedonagh for more incredible views. If you have time and energy, continue down into the col before climbing to Croaghmore, from where you will have fabulous views of the rest of the Blasket Islands. When ready, return to point 3 and take the path on your left. Follow this path back to Old Town. If you have time, it is well worth listening to the guided tour of the village.

Myths and legends

The Great Blasket Island was home to a generation of renowned Irish writers. The Blasket Islands are an archipelago of seven islands. Inis Tuaisceart, the most northerly island, is also known as the Dead Man or the Sleeping Giant. The name of the island of Oileánnan Óg means 'Island of the Young' or 'Island of the Faeries', in other words the Sidhe, a remnant of the once mighty Tuatha Dé Danann that, depending on the tale, were banished or tricked or took to the underworld when the Milesians arrived in Ireland. Over time, and especially with Ireland's conversion to Christianity, the great gods and goddesses of the Tuatha Dé Danann were reduced to mere fairies, piseogs and nonsense. However, their names remain in the landscape, a legacy of a time when giants, witches, heroes and villains walked this beautiful land.

Dunquin Ferry crossing Blasket Sound ▲

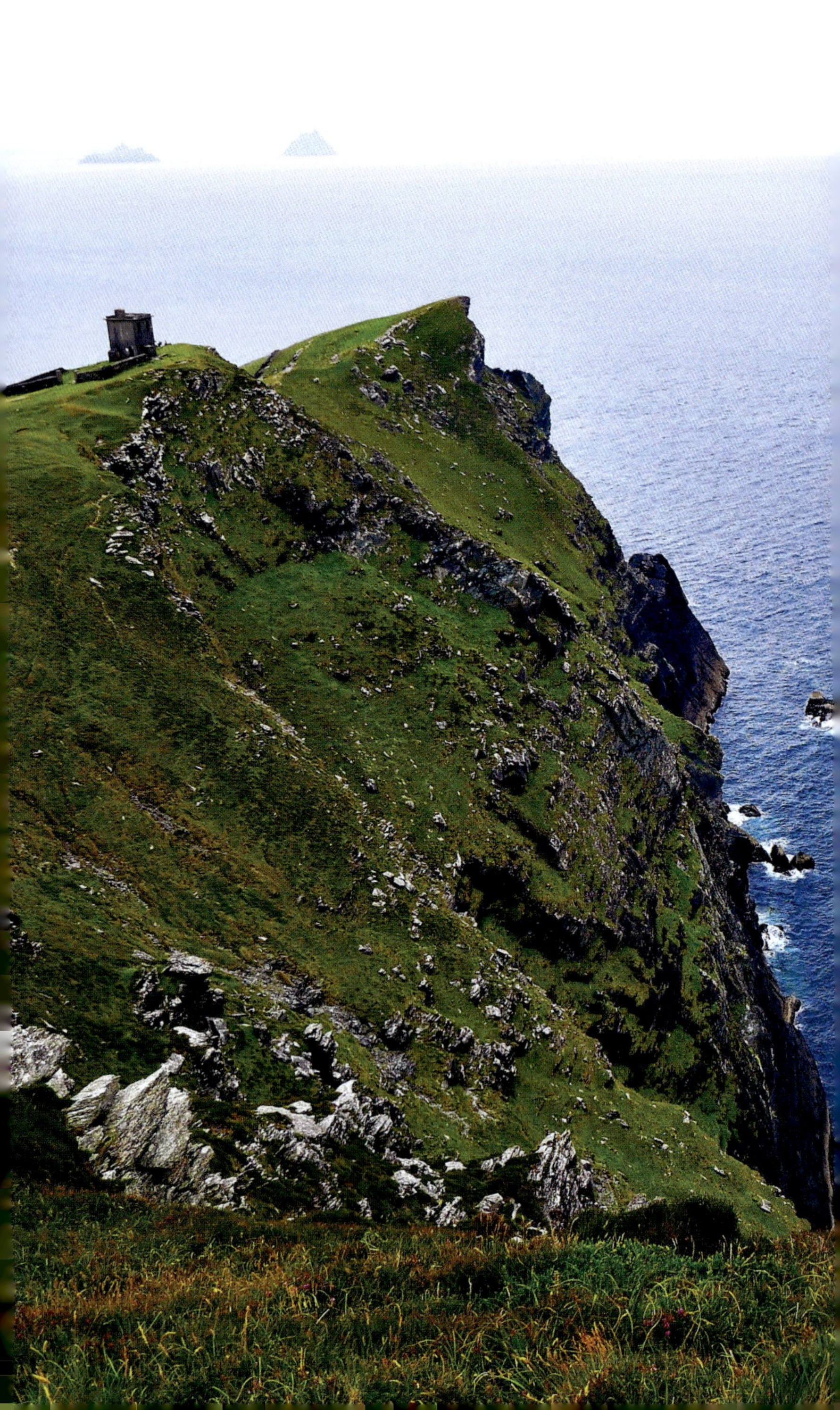

13

Bray Head
Valentia, Co. Kerry

A breathtaking headland hike with amazing views of the Skelligs

This exhilarating loop around Bray Head offers exceptional views of the Skellig Islands, the Dingle and Beara peninsulas and the Portmagee Channel. Explore a signal tower built by the British in 1815, during the Napoleonic Wars. It is one of over eighty similar structures built around the whole coastline of Ireland when England feared its Irish territories would be invaded by the French. More recently the tower was used as a naval signal station in 1907 and again during World War II. There are good paths throughout. Hiking boots recommended.

LENGTH:	TIME:	DIFFICULTY:	OSI MAP NO:
5km	1–2 hours	Medium	83

⊙ NEED TO KNOW

From Waterville, head towards Cahersiveen on the N70 for 11km. Then turn left onto the R565 and follow the road for 12km. Cross the bridge to Valentia Island. Turn left and follow the signs for Bray Head. The car park has a €2 charge.

Coordinates: 51.8919 -10.3968

The Hike

1 From the car park, head up the scenic track towards the headland for 2.3km until you reach the Napoleonic signal tower, where you will have spectacular views of the Skellig Islands.

2 After exploring the area around the signal tower, head up left towards the top of Bray Head using the informal grass path. This path is a cliff walk, so take extra care near the edge. As you reach the top, you will gain views of the Blasket Islands and the Dingle Peninsula on your left and MacGillycuddy's Reeks in front of you.

3 Continue downhill along the informal path. At 4km, rejoin the track you were on earlier. Turn left and after a further 1km reach the car park. This is a lovely place for a picnic.

Having fun on the path to Bray Head ▲

N

Bray
Head
293m

Atlantic Ocean

500m

Myths and legends

This hike is home to one of the most well-known myths in Irish mythology. It is from Valentia Island that Oisín left Ireland with Niamh as they travelled across the shimmering sea to Tír na nÓg (Land of Youth). Oisín was the son of the legendary Fionn Mac Cumhaill, and Niamh was a beautiful fairy from Tír na nÓg. When she arrived in Ireland, Oisín fell in love with her and they left Ireland together. They lived a wonderful life on Tír na nÓg and never grew old. However, after many years Oisín longed for the shores of Ireland. Niamh was very concerned and said he could go but on no account could he let his feet touch the soil. He rode off on Niamh's horse and when he arrived in Ireland he found a lot of things had changed and his friends had died. He met some men who were trying to move a giant stone. Oisín leaned down from his horse to help but his stirrup broke and he fell to the ground. He immediately turned into a very old man and never returned to Niamh and Tír na nÓg. He was brought to St Patrick but the saint could not save him. Before Oisín died, he told St Patrick of the wonderful stories of Fionn and the Fianna, Tír na nÓg and his beloved Niamh.

Long Island and Horse Island in the Portmagee Channel ▲

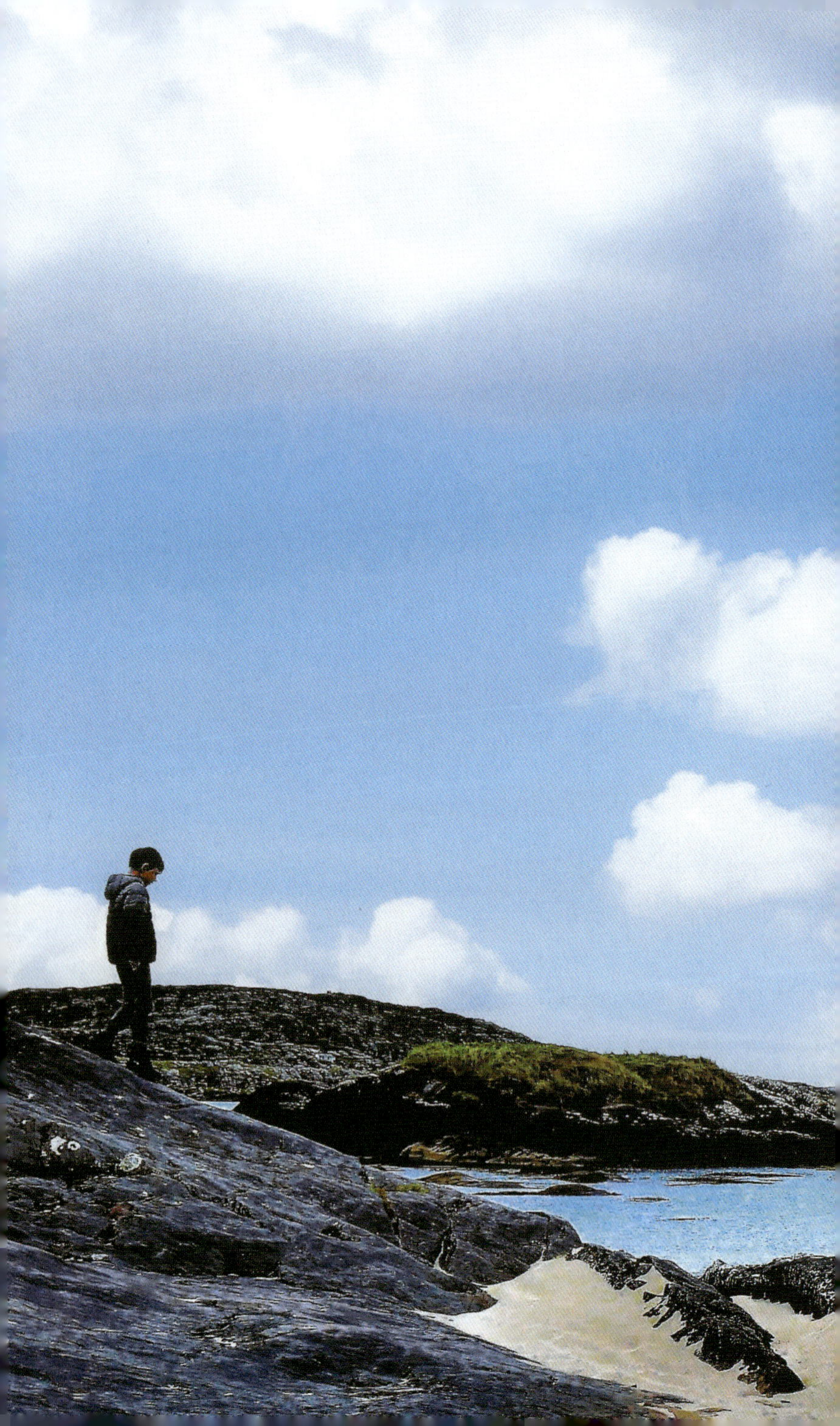

14

Caherdaniel Loop
Co. Kerry

An intriguing hike that takes in beaches, mass paths and the Kerry Way

This truly charming hike takes in beaches, woodland, abbey ruins, Daniel O'Connell's ancestral home and a mass path as it twists its way through the highways and byways of the Caherdaniel hinterland. There are gorgeous views of Kenmare Bay and the Beara Peninsula throughout. With its dunes, white sand and rugged rocks, Derrynane Beach at Caherdaniel is one of Ireland's most beautiful and enticing beaches. Hiking boots recommended.

LENGTH:	TIME:	DIFFICULTY:	OSI MAP NO:
8km	3–4 hours	Medium	83

⊙ **NEED TO KNOW**

From Caherdaniel, head north on the Ring of Kerry, N70, for a short distance. Then turn left and follow the signs for Derrynane House. Park in the free car park at Derrynane House.

Coordinates: 51.7634 -10.1288

The Hike

1 From the car park, take a left through a green gate with a sign reading 'Long Beach' onto a gravel path. Don't go towards Derrynane House at this point. (You can go later if you wish.)

2 Shortly afterwards reach a grassy area and go towards the beach. Turn right and walk across the beach.

3 After about 1km on the beach, at the lifeguard cabin, turn right up a path and go through a tree archway to the road. Turn left up the road. At 1.3km, turn left for Abbey Island.

4 At 1.6km, reach a car park, where you have an opportunity to explore the abbey ruin on Abbey Island if you wish. Otherwise continue on the path and after 100m follow an arrow to your right through a gap in the wall. This looks as though you're entering someone's garden shed! Follow the narrow path as it winds its way along the coastline.

5 At 2.3km, reach a stony cove. Look for a yellow sign on the rock face in front of you pointing diagonally upwards towards your right. Climb the steps carved into the rocks. Keep following the yellow signs along the path. At 2.8km, turn left onto a track, following the signs for the Derrynane Mass Path and the yellow signs. You can choose to stay on the lane or walk across the small beach at this point as both ways bring you to the same place. Then go right up the road. At 3.5km, take the road around to your right, continuing uphill, following the signs for the Kerry Way. This road walk has beautiful views overlooking Caherdaniel. However, road walking can sometimes be less interesting for children, so this may be a time to introduce games, stories or snacks if needed.

6 At 4.7km, turn right, following the Kerry Way sign. Continue on the lane straight down in front of you. Cross the stile at 5km and 25m later turn left up a steep path uphill, following the signs of the yellow walking person. As the path plateaus, enjoy a rest on the rocks overlooking Caherdaniel and the Beara Peninsula.

7 At 6.5km, turn right onto a road and continue downhill. Take care as there can be traffic on this road. At 7.5km, take the road downhill signposted Trá / Strand and Derrynane Harbour. At 7.6km, take the road signposted Derrynane House. Keep to your left and follow the signs for the car park, which you will reach at 8km. Derrynane Beach is ideal for a picnic, relaxation and exploration. Derrynane House, ancestral home to the Irish nationalist leader and Catholic emancipator Daniel O' Connell, is open to the public for a small charge.

Myths and legends

Caherdaniel – Cathair Dónall – means Dónall's stone ringfort and is located on the Iveragh Peninsula on the Ring of Kerry. The art of poetry is said to have originated in this region with the arrival of the great bard and judge Amergin of the Milesians from Iberia. The three queens of the Tuatha Dé Danann (Banba, Ériu and Fódla) gave permission for Amergin and his people to settle in Ireland. However, the druids of the Tuatha Dé Danann did not trust the Milesians and raised a storm at sea to keep them from reaching land. In response, Amergin sang an invocation known as 'The Song of Amergin' and was able to part the storm and bring the ship safely ashore. The two sides battled, with heavy losses on both sides, but the Milesians won in the end. Several of Amergin's brothers drowned in the attempt to reach land. His brothers Donn, Aireach and Érrannán are said to be buried on the islands off the shore of Caherdaniel, with his brother Ir buried on Skellig Michael. Amergin's brothers, Éber Finn and Éremón, went on to divide the country between them, with Éber Finn ruling in the north and Éremón ruling in the south.

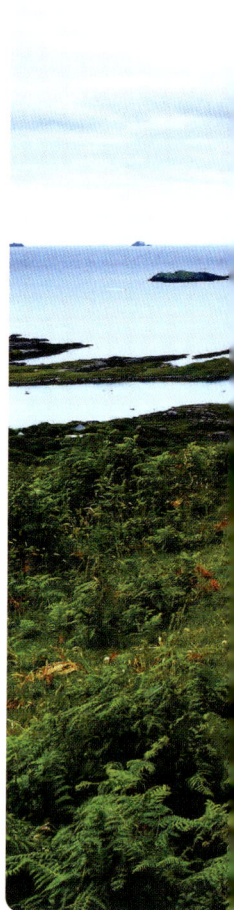

Having fun on the rocks at Caherdaniel ▲

15

Carrauntoohil
Co. Kerry

An awe-inspiring hike to Ireland's highest mountain

At 1,039m, Carrauntoohil is the highest mountain in Ireland. It is set in the heart of the rugged MacGillycuddy's Reeks, which contain nine of the ten highest peaks in Ireland. This challenging but stunning route involves trekking through the beautiful Hag's Glen and climbing the fearsome Devil's Ladder. Prior hiking experience in other mountain ranges is essential. The views from the summit are spectacular when not covered in cloud! Attempt only in dry, clear weather. Full hiking gear and navigational experience required.

LENGTH:	TIME:	DIFFICULTY:	OSI MAP NO:
9–15.5km	4–7 hours	Medium–Experienced	78

ADVENTURE SERIES: MacGillycuddy's Reeks & Killarney National Park
EASTWEST MAPPING: The Reeks
SUPERWALKER XT30: MacGillycuddy's Reeks

⊙ NEED TO KNOW

From Killarney, go west along the N72 for 5km and then left onto Gap Road. Continue for 11km until you arrive at Cronin's Yard, where there is a small parking charge. There are toilets and a tearoom here.

Coordinates: 52.0268 -9.6964

◄ Carrauntoohil summit

The Hike

1 From Cronin's Yard, leave through the gates along a path with a fence. This will then bring you over a bridge. Keep following the path and cross another bridge.

2 After 1.5km, you will be joined by a path from your right coming from Lisleibane. Keep going straight and further into the Hag's Glen. After another kilometre, cross another bridge. The Devil's Ladder and the Hag's Tooth will come into view. Continue between the two beautiful lakes of Lough Callee and Lough Gouragh.

3 At 4.5km, arrive at the base of the Devil's Ladder. For the medium 9km option, simply retrace your steps back to Cronin's Yard. For the experienced route, you may ascend by climbing the Devil's Ladder or via the Zig Zags path here if the ladder looks too difficult. The Devil's Ladder is a wet and rocky gully, often with steady water flows, and you have to pick a route through it. Scrambling is required throughout. Many keep to the left-hand side of the gully when climbing, but it is up to you to find what works best. There is a risk of stones falling from hikers above you. If you inadvertently knock a stone and it falls down the gully, shout 'Below!' immediately to warn hikers below you. This is a steep climb of 700m, taking almost an hour, but take your time and you will emerge at the top of the ladder.

4 Turn right at the top of the ladder and follow the path up a rocky landscape. This climb will seem relatively easy compared to the scrambling required on the ladder.

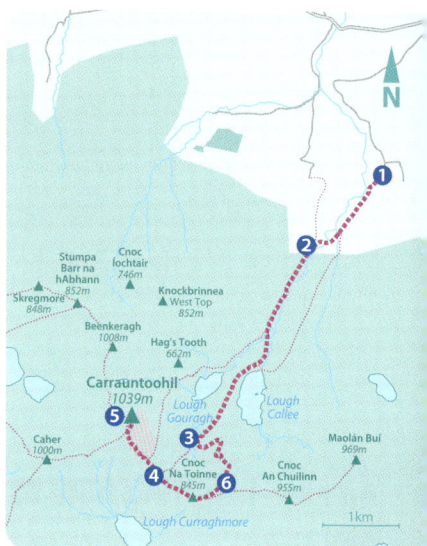

Entering the Hag's Glen with the Heavenly Gates shrouded in cloud ▲

5 Arrive at the summit of Carrauntoohil at 6.2km. You are now standing on the highest point in Ireland! A large cross and wind shelters are at the top. On a clear day, enjoy stunning views across the rest of MacGillycuddy's Reeks and across Kerry. Following a well-earned rest, retrace your steps to the top of the ladder (7.2km) at point 4 on the map. The descent down the ladder is difficult, so we recommend continuing straight in front of you and climb up Cnoc na Toinne instead. After climbing, the ground levels out as you swing to the left.

6 At 9.7km, just before a rock outcrop on your left, the Zig Zag path should be visible on your left. Descend this path carefully through a series of switchbacks. At 11km, arrive back at point 3. From here, turn right and retrace your steps with the Heavenly Gates high up on your left, leaving you with sense of wonder on your return to the car park.

Myths and legends

Carrauntoohil or Corrán Tuathail means 'inverted sickle or fangs', which is a wonderful description of the crescent of jagged rocks that face inward rather than outward.

Carrauntoohil and MacGillycuddy's Reeks are breathtaking but not always benign and several myths and legends swirl in their mists. One story tells of a fight that broke out among the three cailleacha (sometimes pejoratively called hags) that lived respectively on the summits of Carrauntoohil, Mullaghanattin and the Paps of Danú in Kerry. They were fighting over a shared hair comb. The cailleach at Carrauntoohil was at a disadvantage as she was nursing a baby. In order to keep her baby safe, she jumped from Carrauntoohil to the top of the Devil's Ladder. However, she and her baby slipped down the ladder and their four footprints can be seen imprinted today on Carraig na Lathí (Rock of the Enclosure). The cailleach then jumped off the rock into the lake and was never seen again. This lake is today called Lough Callee (Loch Callaí, Lake of the Witch). In Gaelic mythology, the Cailleach was a goddess, meaning 'veiled one', who shaped the landscape and was seen as ever-renewing, passing through many lifetimes from old age to youth in a seasonal, cyclical fashion. The Irish words 'cailín', to describe women at all ages, and 'cailleach' are closely related. Her grandchildren and great-grandchildren formed the tribes of Cork and Kerry and surrounding areas.

Carrauntoohil was also once the throne of the dark fertility god, Crom Dubh, whom we met earlier in his battles with St Patrick, who brought Christianity to Ireland. Crom Dubh ('black crooked one') derives from Crom

The Heavenly Gates, Carrauntoohil ▲

Cruach, an ancient god associated with harvest, plenty, sacrifice and lack of pity for human woes. Interestingly, in Irish, MacGillycuddy's Reeks are called Na Cruacha Dubha, which translates to 'the black stacks'. In late July and August, harvest festivals and pilgrimages related to the gods Lugh, Crom Dubh and St Patrick still take place in Ireland, including celebrations of Lughnasa, Crom Dubh Sunday and the Reek Sunday pilgrimage to Croagh Patrick. Another, darker incarnation of Crom Dubh is the headless horseman who roams the land looking for victims. He is also known as Dullahan or Gan Ceann, meaning 'without a head'. Even today, tales tell of people falling or jumping to their death from the summit of Carrauntoohil, underlining its somewhat malevolent atmosphere.

16

Torc Mountain
Killarney, Co. Kerry

Follow the footsteps of Fionn Mac Cumhaill to the best view in Killarney

Torc Mountain and Torc Waterfall are synonymous with Killarney. Rising up from the shores of Muckross Lake, the mountain looms over many of Killarney's famed beauty spots. This incredible hike includes stunning views of Torc Waterfall, the Lakes of Killarney and the brooding MacGillycuddy's Reeks. Good paths and boardwalks throughout. Arrive early as it is a very busy site, especially in the summer. Hiking boots recommended.

LENGTH:	TIME:	DIFFICULTY:	OSI MAP NO:
8km	3–4 hours	Medium	78

ADVENTURE SERIES: MacGillycuddy Reeks & Killarney National Park
EASTWEST MAPPING: Killarney National Park
SUPERWALKER XT30: MacGillycuddy's Reeks

◎ NEED TO KNOW

From Killarney, head south on the Ring of Kerry on the N71. After 5km, turn left and follow the road for a further 2km until you arrive at the free car park for Torc Waterfall. If this is full, park at the free Killarney National Park car park on Cloghereen Upper road and start the hike from point 2. However, you will miss Torc Waterfall from point 2.

Coordinates: 52.0058 -9.5067

The Hike

1 From the lower car park, take the path up towards the beautiful Torc Waterfall, which you reach after 220m. When ready, continue up the stone steps beside you.

2 After 780m, arrive at a junction and go left following the Kerry Way to Kenmare sign. After another 60m, reach a tarmac road beside the upper car park. Turn right here and follow the track.

3 At 1.2km, follow the yellow Kerry Way sign to the left and continue straight ahead. The Owengarriff River is beside you at this point.

4 At just over 2.5km, reach the turn off (right) for Torc Mountain. Follow the path and boardwalk to the summit. Incredibly beautiful views will emerge as you climb.

MacGillycuddy's Reeks from Torc Mountain

5 At 6km, arrive at the top of Torc Mountain. Enjoy the panoramic views of the Lakes of Killarney, MacGillycuddy's Reeks and nearby Mangerton Mountain. Notice the Kerry Way as it snakes its way into the mystical landscape. After a well-earned rest, retrace your steps down the mountain. Remember at just over 7km to turn right over the bridge. At 7.7km, just after the upper car park, remember to turn left and then turn right soon after. Now follow the path back past Torc Waterfall to your car.

Myths and legends

Boar stories are linked to Torc Mountain. The great Fionn Mac Cumhaill reputedly killed the magical boar of Torc Mountain with his golden spear. However, he may not have succeeded, because another more recent tale involves a local man who was cursed by the Devil to spend each night as a wild boar. When a local farmer learned about this nightly transformation, the boar burst into flames and disappeared into the Devil's Punchbowl, which can be found on nearby Mangerton Mountain. The boar-man then made his way back to Torc Mountain and the Owengarriff River and is believed to still hide today in the cave that lies beneath the torrential Torc Waterfall.

▲ Beautiful Torc and MacGillycuddy's Reeks

The magical Torc Waterfall ▲

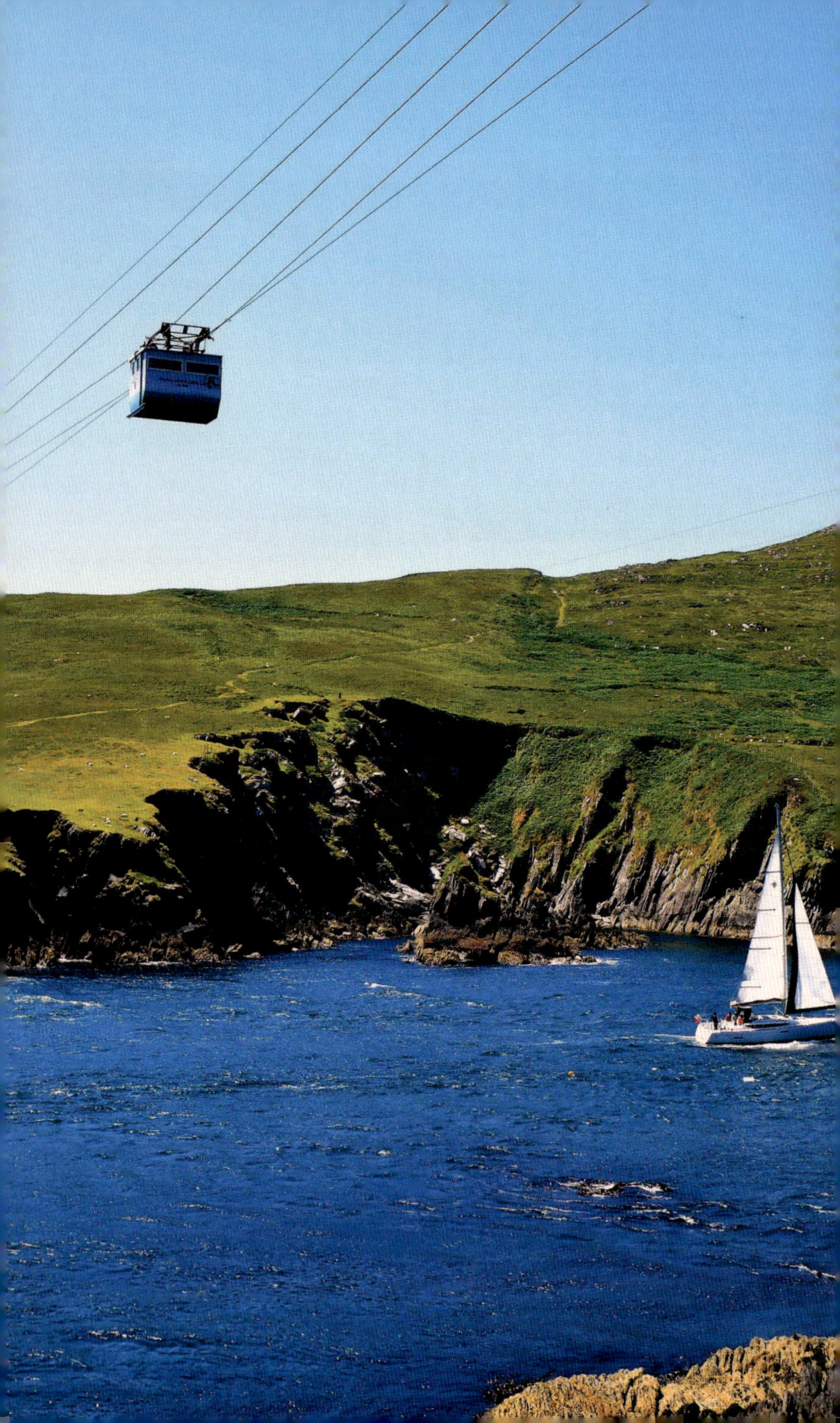

17

Dursey Island
Co. Cork

Take a cable car for a stunning island hike

Cross to Dursey Island via Ireland's only cable car. Dursey Island is located at the most western tip of the Beara Peninsula in Co. Cork and has only a few remaining inhabitants; most of the buildings are deserted, signifying a bygone time. The views of the Atlantic Ocean and the Kerry and Cork peninsulas are spectacular. Dolphins and whales are regular visitors to the waters that surround Dursey, in addition to a wide range of seabirds and butterflies. The Napoleonic signal tower is located at the island's highest point. Arrive early for the cable car as it operates on a first come, first served basis. Check online for operating times throughout the year. Good paths and signs throughout. Hiking boots essential.

LENGTH:	TIME:	DIFFICULTY:	OSI MAP NO:
3.5–11km	1.5–5 hours	Easy–Experienced	84

⊙ NEED TO KNOW

From Castletown-Bearhaven, take the R572 south and follow the road to the free car park at Dursey Island cable car. The cable car costs €10 for adults and €5 for children. There are no services on the island.

Coordinates: 51.6101 -10.155

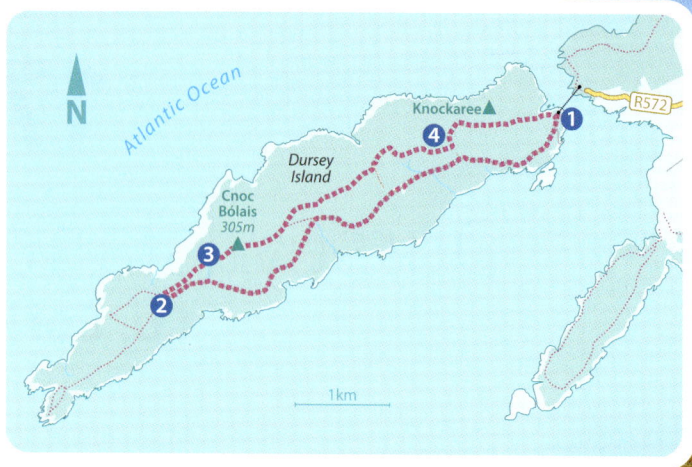

The Hike

1 Take the cable car across to the island. When you arrive on the island take the road on the left. After 400m, St Mary's Abbey and graveyard is down on your left and is worth a visit. When ready, regain the path. After 1.5km, reach Ballynacallagh, a small collection of houses. For the easy 3.5km route, turn right at Ballynacallagh, which will bring you to point 4 on the map, where you should then follow the path back to the cable car. For the experienced option, continue straight ahead through Ballynacallagh. You should also keep straight at the next junction, following the yellow walking person. Enjoy beautiful views across the Atlantic Ocean. After 3.2km, keep on the road and do not go up the grass path on your right.

2 At 5.4km, reach a signpost and take the grass path uphill to your right. This route takes you back to the cable car via the mountain loop. From here you will have a good vantage point to see the Cow, Calf and Bull islands.

Freewheeling on Dursey Island ▲

3 At 6.4km, reach the island's Napoleonic signal tower. This is the highest point of Dursey Island and is also known as Cnoc Bhólais (Hill of the Cow Pasture). There are magnificent views back towards the mainland. When ready, continue on the path as it takes you back to the cable car. At 7.4km, keep to the left as directed by the sign. At 8.2km, keep to the left again and follow the yellow posts. After 20m, cross a metal stile and follow the path.

4 At 9.2km, keep to the left again and follow the signs for the mountain loop. Fabulous vistas of Dursey Sound and the cable car open up. Follow the path downhill and make your way to the cable car. As the cable car can only carry six people, you may, depending on the number of visitors, have to wait to cross back, but what a lovely place to wait!

Myths and legends

The Beara Peninsula is steeped in myth and legend. The Cailleach Béara, or Hag of Béara, is synonymous with the region. One of her names is Boí and Dursey Island's Irish name is Oileán Baoi, meaning 'cow-like island'. In Irish mythology, the Cailleach was seen as the darker side of the goddess Brigid and ruled the land from Samhain (31 October/1 November) through the winter months, while Brigid ruled from the beginning of spring on 1 February (Imbolc or St Brigid's Day). Further up the Beara coast, there is a rock called the Hag of Béara. The Hag/Cailleach looks out over the Atlantic Ocean waiting for her husband Manannán Mac Lir to return. Manannán was a sea god and king of the Otherworld and one of the Tuatha Dé Danann.

The glistening Atlantic Ocean

Enjoying the wind at the signal tower

18

An Cailleach Béara
Co. Cork/Co. Kerry

A wild hike in the footsteps of the Cailleach Béara

The wild and exhilarating Cailleach Béara walk traverses the county boundaries of Cork and Kerry through the Shehy Mountains. Follow the well-marked path and set out from Molly Gallivan's traditional farm with its Famine cottage and Neolithic stone row. There are stunning views of Glengarriff, Bantry Bay and the jagged Caha Mountains up on the summit ridge with good signs throughout. Best hiked in drier seasons. Hiking boots essential.

LENGTH:	TIME:	DIFFICULTY:	OSI MAP NO:
10km	4–5 hours	Experienced	85

⊙ **NEED TO KNOW**

From Kenmare, take the N71 towards Cork. After 14km, arrive at Molly Gallivan's Visitor Centre. The trailhead is on the right-hand side of the road beside the centre. There is plenty of free parking here.
Coordinates: 51.8011 -9.5627

The Hike

1 From the car park, go to the information boards beside the centre and start the hike by passing through the gate on your left. You are following the Cailleach Béara loop walk with purple arrows. Shorter 6km hikes include the Fionn Mac Cumhaill Loop and Druid's Loop. Make your way uphill and pass through a charming traditional farm area. Cross the stile at the top of the path and turn to your right along the fence, aiming for a yellow post in the distance. Cross the next stile and continue on the informal path.

2 At 800m, cross a stile and turn right down the hill towards the main road. Cross the road, looking out for traffic. Go left on the road, perhaps getting behind the barrier for safety. After a very short distance, turn right down the lane and follow the signs. Cross another stile and follow the lane as it swings to your left. Keep going straight down the lane even if a gate seems to be in your way. Just go around the gate or climb it. At the end of the lane, cross a small footbridge and turn right up the hill.

3 At 2.2km, follow the Cailleach Béara Loop to the left up a lane.

4 After 3km, take the lane to your right and cross a stile. Continue uphill along a grassy track. After 800m, you will meet a post with the number 3 on it; turn right here across the boggy path. Continue across the mountain and follow the posts as they guide you. The informal paths and signs are an excellent navigational aid. Enjoy stunning views across the Shehy and Caha Mountains and down towards Glengarriff and Bantry Bay.

5 At around 5.6km, watch out for the posts as they swing to the left to bring you uphill. After 100m, ignore the stile to your left that leads to a Copper Mines walk. Continue to follow the posts for An Cailleach Béara.

6 After 6km, arrive at the summit of Turner's Rock. Continue to follow the posts, and at post number 24 the path descends to the right. There are incredible views here of the Turner's Rock Tunnel

A view towards Bantry Bay

that links Cork and Kerry on the N71. The descent is steep in parts, so take your time.

7 At 7km, cross another stile and turn to your left. Follow this lane for 800m. Then turn right and skirt around the field, following the signs. At 8.4 km, cross another stile and head down across the field. Cross the next stile and turn right down the lane, again following the signs.

8 At 8.7 km, go through a wooden gate and turn left up the road.

9 After 500m, emerge onto the N71. Turn right here, watching for traffic, and return to the car park. Enjoy a well-earned rest and picnic. Nearby Bonane Heritage Park is well worth a visit, with a wealth of archaeological sites from the Stone, Bronze and Iron ages up to pre-Famine times.

Myths and legends

The Cailleach Béara– also known as the Hag of Béara – was among the most ancient deities venerated in Ireland. She was a divine crone and creator deity, literally a 'hooded one' (*caille* translates as 'hood'). She was particularly associated with the Beara Peninsula in Co. Cork and was feared and revered as the Queen of Winter for her ability to bring winter to the land. She presided over life and death and was seen as a key shaper of the Irish landscape. Therefore, as well as denoting seasonal changes, she is also a likely personification of the ice ages and glacial erosion that created much of Ireland's topography. The Cailleach lived several lives, having several successive periods of youth, during which she birthed the ancestors of multiple clans in counties Cork and Kerry. In the medieval Irish poem 'The Lament of the Hag of Béara' in the Great Book of Lecan (1400 CE), the Cailleach laments how she used to drink 'mead and wine with kings' but now lives a lonely life amid 'the gloom of a prayer' and 'shrivelled old hags'. This may reflect how the old pre-Christian mythologies were slowly fading from Irish consciousness.

Making our way home ▲

19

Coumshingaun
Co. Waterford

A thrilling hike around Ireland's most stunning corrie lake

Coumshingaun is one of the finest examples of a corrie lake or coum in Europe and is surrounded on three sides by vertiginous cliffs. Our easier 4km route leads directly to the stunning lake. This hike is ideal for light scrambling, swimming and a picnic. The experienced option involves circumnavigating the thrilling amphitheatre of jagged cliffs overlooking the lake and descending to the lake towards the end of the hike. Scrambling and navigational skills are required. We'd suggest that while Carrauntoohil may be the Mount Everest of Irish peaks, the Coumshingaun ridge is arguably more difficult. The cliff walk should only be attempted by experienced hikers and in dry, clear weather. Hiking boots essential.

LENGTH:	TIME:	DIFFICULTY:	OSI MAP NO:
4–9km	2–5 hours	Medium–Experienced	75

EASTWEST MAPPING: Comeraghs

⊙ NEED TO KNOW

Take the N25 towards Cork from Waterford. After 17km, turn right and follow the road before turning right again onto the R676. After 5km, Kilclooney Wood car park is on your left. Parking is free. The park can get busy in summer months.

Coordinates: 52.2434 -7.5013

◀ High above Coumshingaun, Comeragh Mountains

The Hike

1 From the car park, enter the forest and head up the path. At 330m, turn right onto a broader, non-forested track and pass by the tall green mast on your left. You will see the Comeragh Mountains on your left. As a rough guide, the rocky outcrops on your left are where you will aim for if you are going on the cliff walk; the peaks on the right are where you will aim for if you choose the easier lake walk.

2 At over 600m, cross a metal stile and turn immediately left up by the fence on a rocky path. At about 850m, the fence line veers to the left and seems to beckon with a well-defined path; however, do not follow this path! You need to identify a low stone wall here on your right, cross it and find a narrow but defined path that winds itself up through gorse bushes. Walk up a steep, grassy, stony slope, aiming for the lowest point on the horizon.

3 Arrive at the top of the ridge. From here you have two options. For the medium route, take the path to the right to go straight to Coumshingaun Lough. On this route, just keep to the path as it climbs steadily uphill through the rocks. The lough will appear after 2km. For the experienced route, take the left path along the ridge towards the rocky outcrop on the left. As you progress upwards, the path towards the rocky outcrop becomes better defined. The ridge narrows at the first rocky outcrop and we advise going through the 'keyhole' in the rock rather than attempting to walk either side of it. Gain your first views of the lake. The path then takes you through and around several further outcrops as you aim for the plateaued top of the mountain. Take care at all times to take the safest route around the obstacles.

4 Before you aim to climb to the top of the mountain, the path is firmly on the south side of the ridge (i.e. not the lakeside). Care is needed here at approximately 3.5km to find the best route up to the plateau. We advise walking on the main path until it seems to run out as it leads to a climbable series of stepped rocks that lead to the plateau. Ignore earlier offshoot paths that appear to bring you up more quickly but could leave you exposed.

5 The terrain is boggy on the plateau, but shortly after gaining the top, at about 3.7 km, find a small, safe and defined stony path nearer to the edge, on the lakeside, which allows a very enjoyable circumnavigation of the lake along the cliff ridge. While the views of the surrounding countryside and the Atlantic Ocean are beautiful, the main thrills are the dramatic views of the lake from the 380m cliffs and looking back with amazement at the ridge you have just climbed!

6 At approximately 4.5km, reach the top of Stookanmeen at 702m. Then descend steeply – there are several intriguing rock formations along your path. Keep to the left and don't descend towards the lake too directly in order to avoid very difficult crags. Even on the left path, some scrambling is required for a short passage to negotiate large boulders. The path eases down towards the lake.

7 At 6.75km, arrive at Ireland's most impressive corrie lake with its cliff surrounds. Soak your feet in the cool water, swim or have a picnic. Then in order to return to the car park, take a path downwards on the non-cliff side, aiming roughly for a little lake you can see in the distance. At 7.8km, do not take the left path downwards but stay on the right path to carry you across the mountain. As you proceed, aim for the tall green mast that you passed earlier. At 8km, keep to your left and continue downhill. Retrace your path by the green mast and through the woods to the car park.

Vertiginously contemplating Coumshingaun Lough ▶

Myths and legends

Coumshingaun, which means 'the hollow of the ants', is one of the most beautiful and foreboding corrie lakes in Ireland. Many legends are associated with the area. One involves the ghost of William Crotty, the eighteenth-century highwayman who hid in caves in the Comeragh Mountains. When he was a youth, his family was evicted and he took to thievery as a means of survival. Crotty led a gang of highwaymen who stole from the rich to give to the poor. The police could not catch him because he knew the mountains so well, but he was ultimately betrayed by his most trusted companion, David Norris, who accepted a bribe from the police. Crotty was hanged and had his head cut off and spiked outside Waterford County Gaol as a warning to others. To this day, his ghost is known as the Dark Stranger who 'comes out of the mist, tall, dark-clothed, moving purposefully, his footsteps making no sound'. It is believed that his treasures lie hidden somewhere in the Comeraghs beneath a rock with a hoof mark.

Another legend in the area involves the Cloch Labhrais, or Speaking Stone, in the nearby townland of Durrow. This stone is reported to speak if somebody tells a lie beside it. In one story, a man brought his wife there because he suspected her of being unfaithful. His wife's lies were such that the stone not only contradicted her but split in two! The split rock can be seen to this day.

Arriving at Coumshingaun Lough ▲

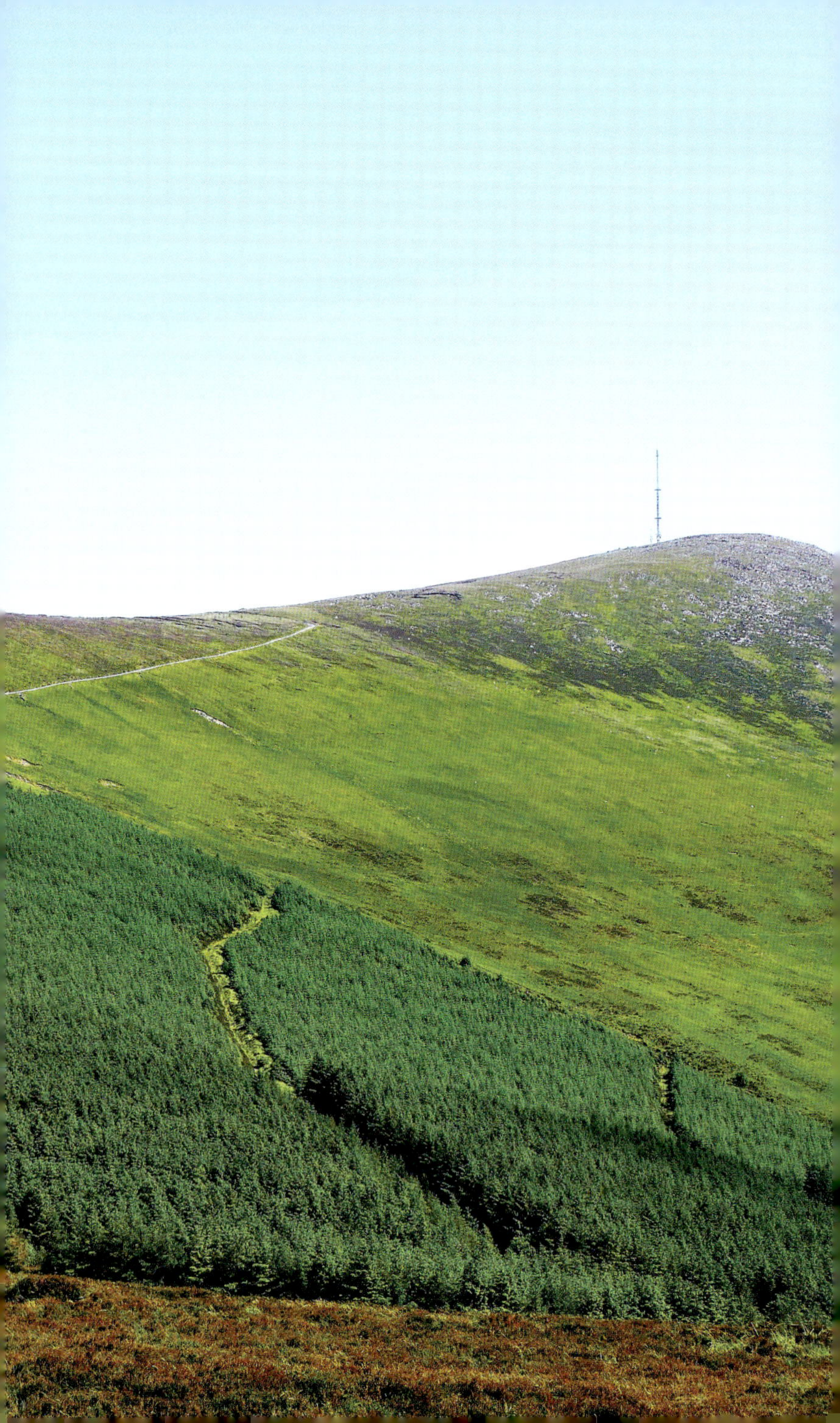

20

Mount Leinster and Slievebawn
Co. Carlow/Co. Wexford

A panoramic hike to the highest point in counties Carlow and Wexford

At 794m, Mount Leinster straddles the border between Carlow and Wexford and is the high point of both counties. Access to Mount Leinster is via a tarmac road, while nearby Slievebawn provides a grassy bog track. Stunning panoramic views of the surrounding countryside can be enjoyed from both, including the Blackstairs, Wicklow, Comeragh and Galtee mountains, as well as across the midlands plain. The easy 2km option is simply to climb to the summit of Slieve Bawn from the car park. There are clear paths throughout. Hiking boots recommended.

LENGTH:	TIME:	DIFFICULTY:	OSI MAP NO:
2.5–13km	1–5 hours	Easy–Experienced	68

EASTWEST MAPPING: Blackstairs and Mount Leinster

⊙ NEED TO KNOW

From Carlow, take the N80 south. There are numerous turns on this route, but your final destination is the Nine Stones car park. Parking is free but it can be busy in summer months.

Coordinates: 52.6369 -6.7938

The Hike

1 After parking at the Nine Stones car park, proceed past the metal gates on the other side of the road. Walk up this steep road and wonderful views of Carlow and Wexford begin to open up.

2 After 3km, reach the top of Mount Leinster. Walk around the transmitter station and find the trig pillar that signifies the summit. Enjoy stunning views of the Blackstairs Mountains, the Wicklow Mountains to the north and across the midlands plain. Off to the north-east, there is a path to Black Rock Mountain, which is a lovely hike to be enjoyed another day (unless you feel energetic today!). When ready, retrace your steps to the car park.

3 After having a break, the gentle Slievebawn Hill on the other side of the car park looks inviting. This is the hill with the well-worn turf path on it.

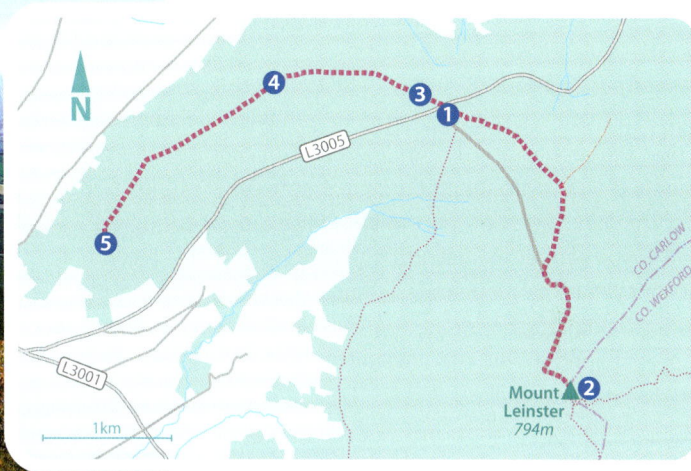

◄ A view from Mount Leinster across the midlands plain

4 After 1.3km, reach the top of Slievebawn and enjoy expansive views of Mount Leinster, the Blackstairs Mountains and the midlands. To extend the walk, follow the path down to Tonduff Hill.

5 After 2km, arrive at the unmarked summit of Tonduff Hill. When ready, retrace your steps to the car park.

Easy 2.5k option: Start at point 3 from the car park up towards Slievebawn hill with its turf path. Retrace your steps to the car park once you reach the top.

Myths and legends

The car park at Mount Leinster is called the Nine Stones car park and there is some mystery as to its name. One story has it that the stones are the resting place of nine shepherds who died on the mountain during a storm. Other stories say that they are the site where rebel fighters died during the 1798 insurrection against British rule. Yet another legend recounts that the nine stones came about as a result of St Moling being refused bread by a traveller. St Moling was not impressed and turned the traveller's bread into nine stones. *Creid é nó ná creid é!*

T-posing on Slievebawn ▲

A view of Mount Leinster from Slievebawn ▲

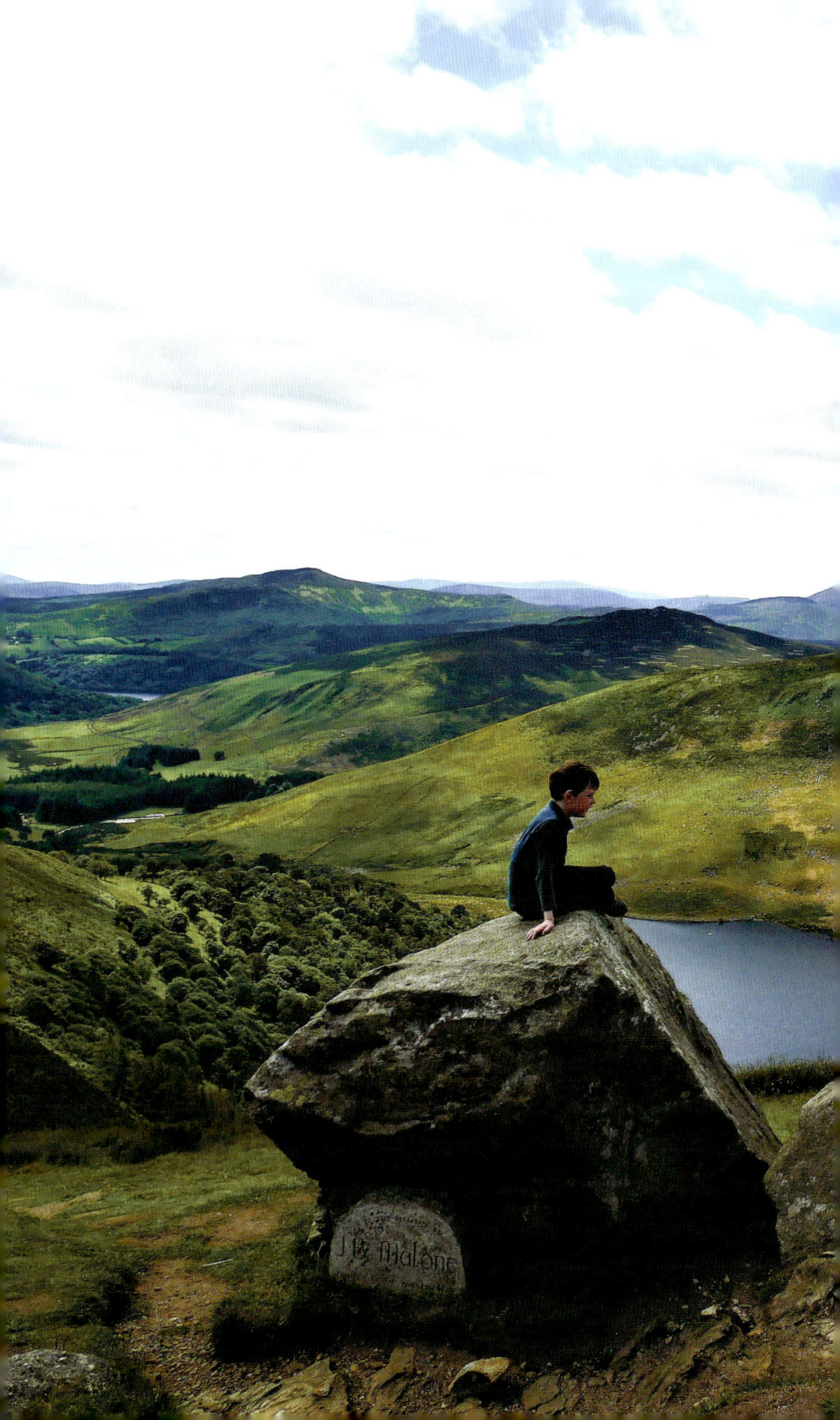
J B Malone

The East

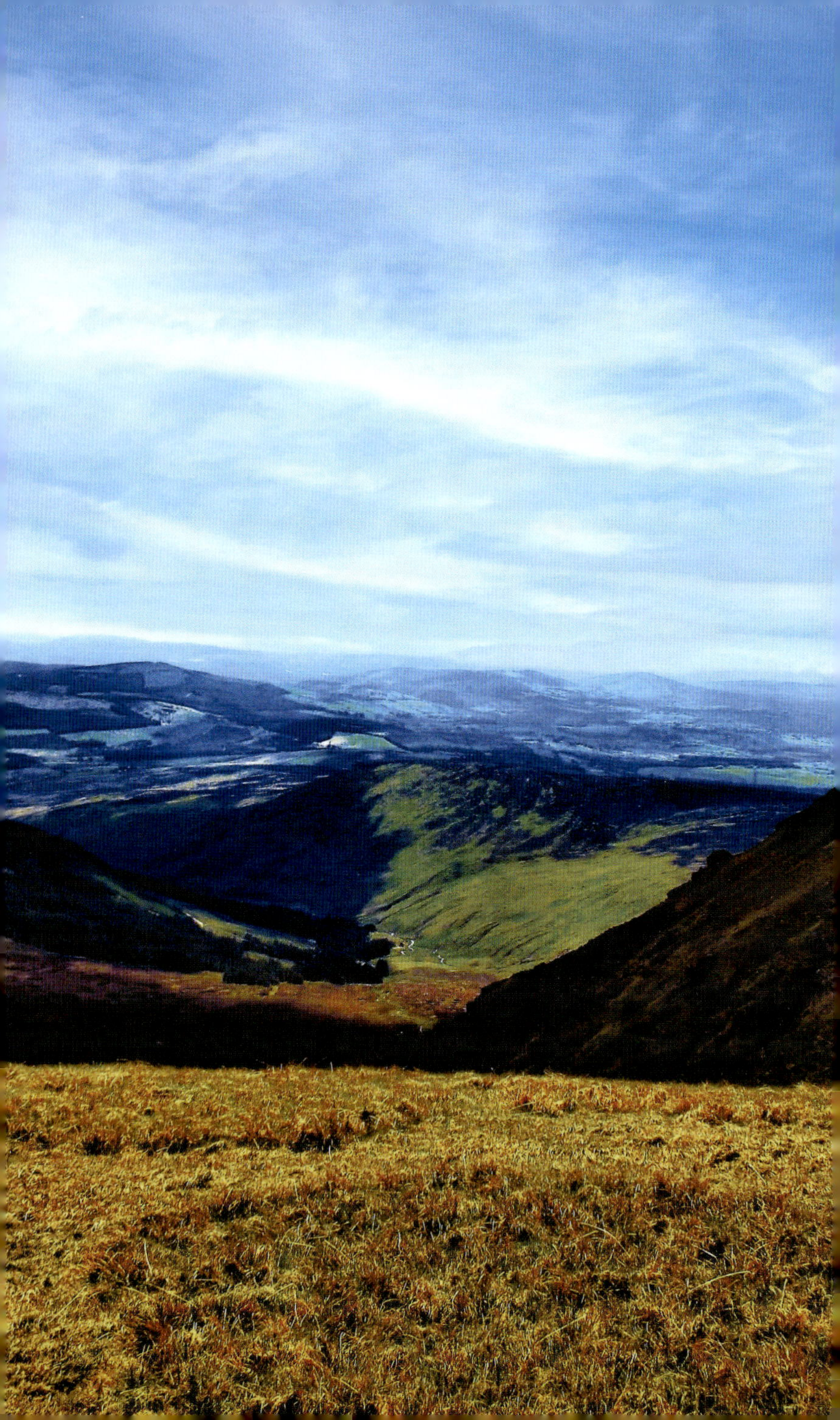

21

Lugnaquilla
Co. Wicklow

A spectacular hike to Leinster's highest peak

This is a long but very rewarding hike to Leinster's highest summit. At 925m, it's the highest mountain in Ireland outside Kerry, set in the heart of the Wicklow Mountains. On this hike, enjoy wonderful views in every direction. Navigational skills and prior hiking experience are required. The hike should be undertaken in clear, calm weather. Hiking boots essential.

LENGTH:	TIME:	DIFFICULTY:	OSI MAP NO:
14km	5–6 hours	Experienced	56

EASTWEST MAPPING: Lugnaquilla and Glendalough
HARVEY SUPERWALKER XT30: Wicklow Mountains

⊙ NEED TO KNOW

From Dublin, take the N11 south to Kilmacanogue. From there, take the R755 for 23km. Then turn left to stay on the R755. After 1.5km turn right for Glenmalure and after almost 8km turn right onto a narrow road. Follow this road for 5.5km and park in the large Baravore car park. Parking is free.
Coordinates: 52.9881 -6.4128

◄ A view across the valleys from Lugnaquilla

The Hike

1 From the car park, head for the noticeboards, cross the stream and turn right. After less than 100m, turn left uphill onto a more minor path. You will shortly pass a stone building on your right. At 850m, turn left uphill on to a wider track. At 1.5km, pass through a metal gate and continue uphill ahead. Views of the Faughan Glen, the Avonbeg River, Benleagh and Mullacor mountains start to open up.

2 At 2.6km, keep on the track to start climbing on the right-hand side of the waterfall. The path becomes more informal as you climb and some light scrambling may be required at times. Aim for a small group of evergreen trees for an approximate route but rest assured that all paths will lead to the top. Take as many rest breaks as required as this part is steep.

3 At 3.3km, at the top of the waterfall, the landscape opens to a bog plateau. Find any informal path and aim westwards for the horizon that rises gently before you. The sound of rushing water is from the myriad of bog streams that weave their way between upper and underground worlds. As you progress, aim for the col – the lowest point – on the horizon. Lugnaquilla slopes down from your left. If the weather has been rainy, parts of the ground may be boggy, so pick the best path forward.

4 At almost 5km, keep to your left up the mountain. Wonderful views of many peaks of the Wicklow Mountains start to reveal themselves, including Mullaghcleevaun and Tonelagee (second and third highest peaks after Lugnaquilla), Turlough Hill with its reservoir, Camaderry, Mullacor and the Great Sugarloaf. At 5.7km, reach a plateau with a small cairn/group of stones. Turn left up the wide informal grassy path. Keep on the informal path as this is the most direct route to the summit of Lugnaquilla. Do not be distracted by the posts to your right: they appear to offer a quicker route but actually involve more climbing!

Summit of Lugnaquilla ▲

5 At 6.7km, reach the summit trigpoint of Lugnaquilla. Enjoy the 360-degree panorama across the Wicklow Mountains and the midlands. When ready, aim roughly eastwards with the Irish Sea in front of you. Walk downhill around the perimeter of the South Prison, a gorge that drops precipitously on your right. Do not go down this gorge but stay on top. Keep going east and aim for Cloghernagh Mountain in front of you until you see a post and gain a more defined rocky path.

6 At 8km, a sign indicates that access is denied for the walk. However, pass this sign and keep to the left path toward Cloghernagh. This sign is only relevant if you intended to exit by the zig-zag path, but you will be exiting by Art's Lough.

7 At 9.6km, reach the summit of Cloghernagh. Descend via the informal path to your left with the Fraughan Glen and Mullacor Mountain in front of you.

8 At just over 10km, turn left at a small stone cairn down towards Art's Lough, which will come into view as you descend. (Access is denied to the other zig-zag path.)

9 At 11km, reach Art's Lough. Keep to the right of the lake, where there is an informal muddy path between the lake and a fence. Descend towards the Avonbeg River.

10 At 12.35km, on your descent, aim for the right-hand corner of the fence and cross it. Cross the river at the point where a track leads down to it as it connects to a track on the other side. Take your time crossing as, while there are stepping stones, some are covered in slippery moss. At times, to gain purchase, it may be wise to stand on stones somewhat submerged in water and to risk getting a bit wet rather than fall. Alternatively, if worried about slipping, take boots and socks off and walk through the water at its lowest point. Children will need help to cross. At 12.5km, reach the track that you were on earlier. Go through the gate and retrace your path back down to the car park, remembering at approximately 13km to turn right onto a small downhill track (signalled by two rocks on the ground and a post). You will add another two kilometres to your walk if you miss this track. At 14km, arrive back at the car park.

Myths and legends

The name Lugnaquilla is thought to come from the phrase 'log na coille', meaning 'hollow of the wood'. The mountain's name puts us in mind of one of the most important Celtic gods, Lugh, who represents sun and light. Lugh was all-wise and all-seeing and was skilled in many arts and crafts. He led the Tuatha Dé Danann to victory against the seafaring Fomorians and defeated his grandfather, Balor of the Evil Eye, with his magic spear. The landscape is also linked to Fionn Mac Cumhaill. When Fionn saw pigs eating the oats he had sown on Lugnaquilla, he threw a great rock at them to scare them off. This rock is known as the Knickeen Ogham Stone and can be found close to the nearby village of Donard.

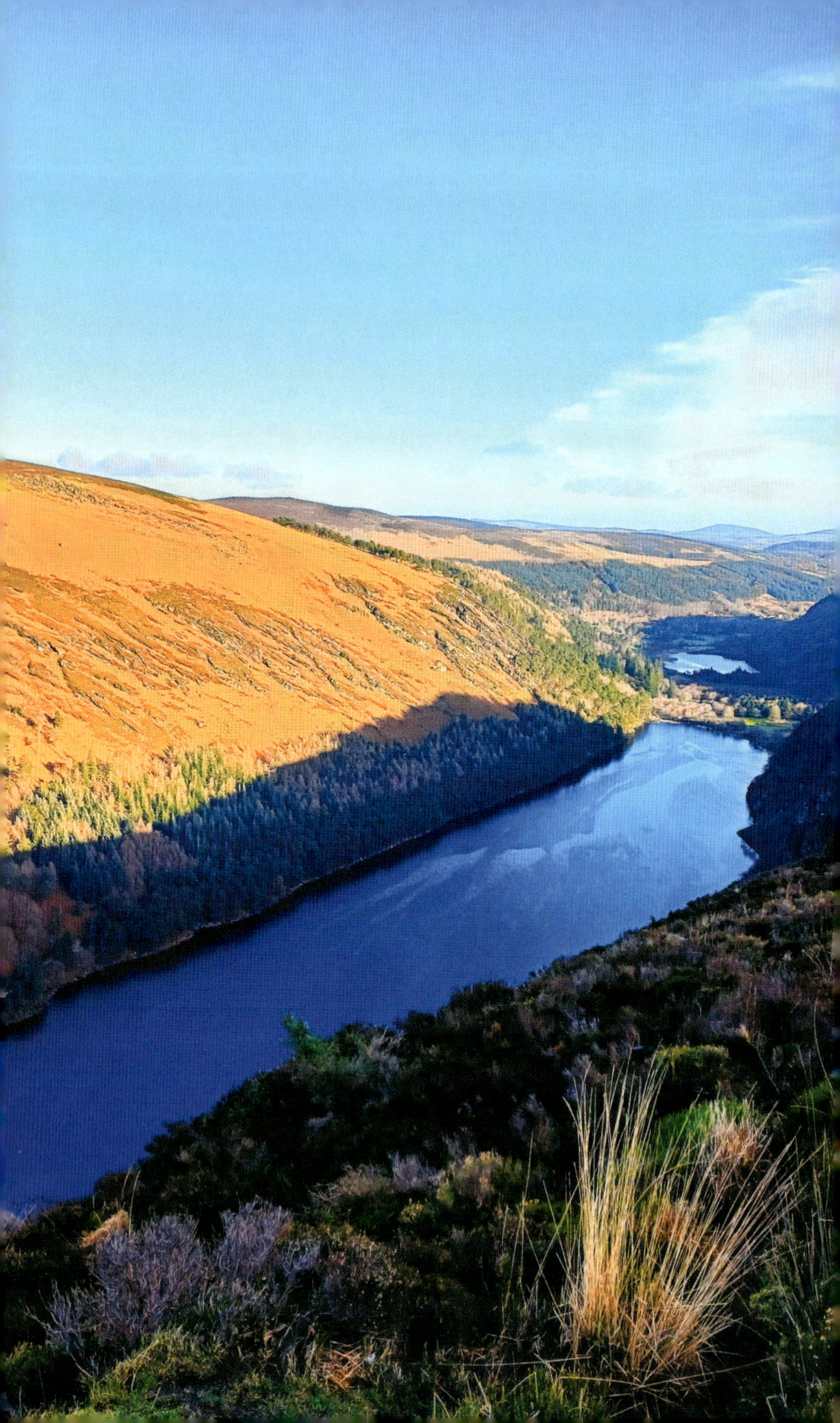

22

Spinc Mountain
Glendalough, Co. Wicklow

Walk in the footsteps of St Kevin

The Spinc ridge overlooks the spectacular Glendalough valley and monastic city while also providing breathtaking views of the surrounding Wicklow uplands. The valley of Glendalough was carved out by glaciers during the Ice Age, and the two lakes, from which Glendalough gets its name (Gleann dá Loch, meaning 'valley of the two lakes'), were formed when the ice eventually thawed. The walk includes the Poulanass Waterfall and miners' deserted village and descending by the rushing Glenealo River. Deer can regularly be sighted here. The terrain is mixed and includes forest tracks, rock steps and boardwalks. The path is well defined throughout with good signage. Hiking boots essential.

LENGTH:	TIME:	DIFFICULTY:	OSI MAP NO:
9km	4 hours	Medium	56

EASTWEST MAPPING: Lugnaquilla & Glendalough
HARVEY SUPERWALKER XT30: Wicklow Mountains

⊙ NEED TO KNOW

From Dublin, take the N11 south to Kilmacanogue. From there, take the R755 for 24km to Laragh. Then proceed on the R756 for 3.5km to Glendalough. Take the narrow road to the end, to the Upper Lake car park. Parking costs €4 a day, and closing times vary by season. There are toilets and refreshment stalls.

Coordinates: 53.0071 -6.3447

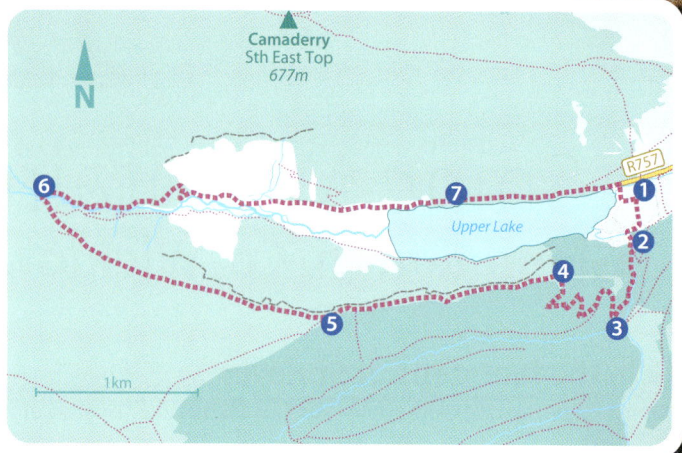

Camaderry
5th East Top
677m

N

R757

Upper Lake

1km

The Hike

1 From the car park, head towards the Upper Lake, but keep slightly to the left.

2 Find a broad path where several of the walking trails in Glendalough start. Follow the signs for the white walk. Turn left and begin to climb up alongside the beautiful Poulanass Waterfall.

3 After 500m, emerge onto a broader path and follow it left until you meet a crossroads of paths. Turn right here and follow the rising path, which involves a series of switchbacks for over a kilometre.

4 After this tough climbing section, arrive at a viewing point with spectacular views over the monastic city and the Upper Lake. The path now continues on a boardwalk, offering incredible views of the Upper Lake and Camaderry Mountain on your right hand side.

5 At 3km, arrive at a junction of paths. Keep to the right (the left path leads to Lugduff and the magnificent Mullacor Mountain

Along the Spinc ridge ▲

– see Hike 23). Reach the high point of Spinc and as you descend downhill towards the Glenealo River you may catch sight of the beautiful deer herd.

6 After 5km, cross the bridge over the Glenealo River, where there are several nice spots for a break and a well-earned rest. When ready, continue straight ahead and enjoy invigorating close-up views of the river as it thunders down the valley. Continue for 3.5km on a lovely path through forest, which brings you back towards the car park.

7 Turn right at the road gate and cross the stream. Then turn left and you will arrive at the car park. If you have time, it is well worth visiting the Upper Lake to see the ducks and engage in some stone skimming and relaxation. In addition, the wonderful monastic city with its round tower is well worth a visit. The Office of Public Works provides a guided tour of the monastic site for a small charge.

Myths and legends

Glendalough has several legends involving St Kevin, the hermit founder of the monastery. One of the most beautiful is about Kevin and the blackbird. As Kevin was deep in meditation, he held his upturned palm so still that a blackbird landed on it, nested and laid her eggs there. Kevin chose to stay motionless like a tree until the fledglings had been safely hatched and flew the nest. This story is immortalised in art and literature, including in a poem by Seamus Heaney called 'St Kevin and the Blackbird'. Kevin's deep love of nature embodied a belief in the sacredness of the natural world, a conviction that was rooted in the early Irish Christian tradition and in Celtic pre-Christian religions.

▲ Enjoying the Glenealo river in Glendalough

Looking down the valley of Glendalough ▲

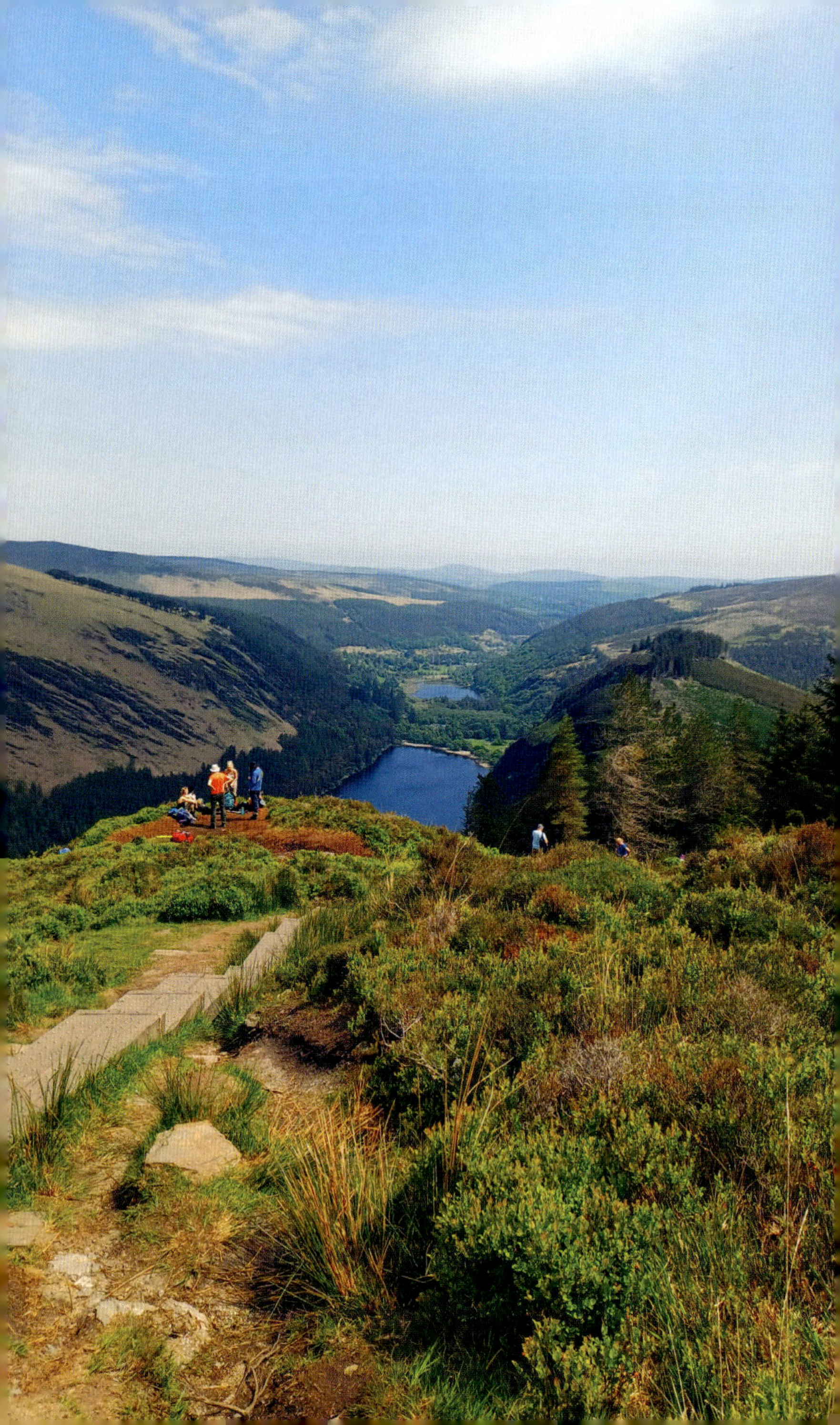

23

Mullacor and Derrybawn
Glendalough, Co. Wicklow

Follow the Miners' Way across the stunning Wicklow Mountains

This hike includes stunning views of the monastic city of Glendalough, the two lakes and the surrounding Spinc and Camaderry Mountains. The route takes the miners' route up Lugduff Mountain, crosses to Mullacor Mountain and returns to Glendalough via the stunning Derrybawn ridge. The hike is set deep in the heart of the Wicklow Mountains, and the views at all times are spectacular. Paths include forest tracks, boardwalks and informal grass, bog and rock paths. As the ground can become soft in wetter seasons, this walk is best enjoyed in the drier months. Hiking boots essential.

LENGTH:	TIME:	DIFFICULTY:	OSI MAP NO:
12km	5 hours	Experienced	56

EASTWEST MAPPING: Lugnaquilla and Glendalough
HARVEY SUPERWALKER XT30: Wicklow Mountains

⊙ NEED TO KNOW

From Dublin, take the N11 south to Kilmacanogue. From there, take the R755 for 24km to Laragh. Proceed on the R756 for 3.5km to Glendalough. Take the narrow road to the end to the Upper Lake car park. Parking costs €4 per day. Closing times vary per season. There are toilets and refreshment stalls here.

Coordinates: 53.0071 -6.3447

◄ On the way to Mullacor

The Hike

1 Leave the car park and head towards the Upper Lake but keep slightly to the left.

2 Arrive along a broad path where several of the walking trails in Glendalough start. Follow the signs for the white walk. Turn left and begin to climb up alongside the beautiful Poulanass Waterfall.

3 After 500m, emerge onto a broader path which you follow left until you meet a crossroads of paths. Turn right here and follow the rising path, which involves a series of switchbacks for over a kilometre.

4 After this tough climbing section, arrive at a viewing point with incredible views over the monastic city and the Upper Lake. The

On the boardwalk to Mullacor ▲

path now becomes a boardwalk along the Spinc ridge offering fantastic views of the Upper Lake. At 2.7km, ignore a path to your left with a blue arrow and continue straight, following the red and white arrows.

5 After another 200m, arrive at a junction of paths. Keep to the left and follow the red arrows or the Miners' Way signs (the right path leads to the looped Spinc trail – see Hike 22).

6 Follow this rough path uphill, and after 1.3km follow the path around to the left. You are now at Lugduff East top. Enjoy the stunning views and, when ready, continue on the path towards Mullacor Mountain.

7 At 5.4km, meet a path which is part of the Wicklow Way. Turn right here and after a few metres turn left onto a grassy path leading up towards Mullacor.

8 Follow this path uphill for around 700m to arrive at the summit of Mullacor. As you climb, look to your right for incredible views of the majestic Faughan Glen that leads toward the magnificent Lugnaquilla. After enjoying the summit, continue straight ahead and aim towards a path that is clearly visible in front of you. There is a large forest away to your left. Follow the path and at 7.5km cross a stile over a fence and follow the path in front of you, keeping the fence on your right.

9 After another 600m, turn left towards Derrybawn. Do not continue up the mountain in front of you. Continue along the Derrybawn ridge with stunning views all around. Reach the summit of Derrybawn at 10.1km. When ready, continue straight ahead and start to descend.

10 After thirty metres, turn down a small path to your left. This provides a thrilling descent. After 500m, continue straight ahead when you meet a grassy path. After another 500m, emerge onto the Wicklow Way but continue straight ahead on the small path descending in front of you. The path descends for another 200m until you meet another wide path.

11 Turn left here and follow the yellow walking man and cross the bridge in front of you. After another 200m, cross the next bridge and turn right. You are now on the same path you started on earlier. Keep following the arrows downhill and after a few hundred metres arrive back at the bottom of Poulanass Waterfall and from there retrace your steps to the car park.

Traversing the sensational Derrybawn Ridge ▶

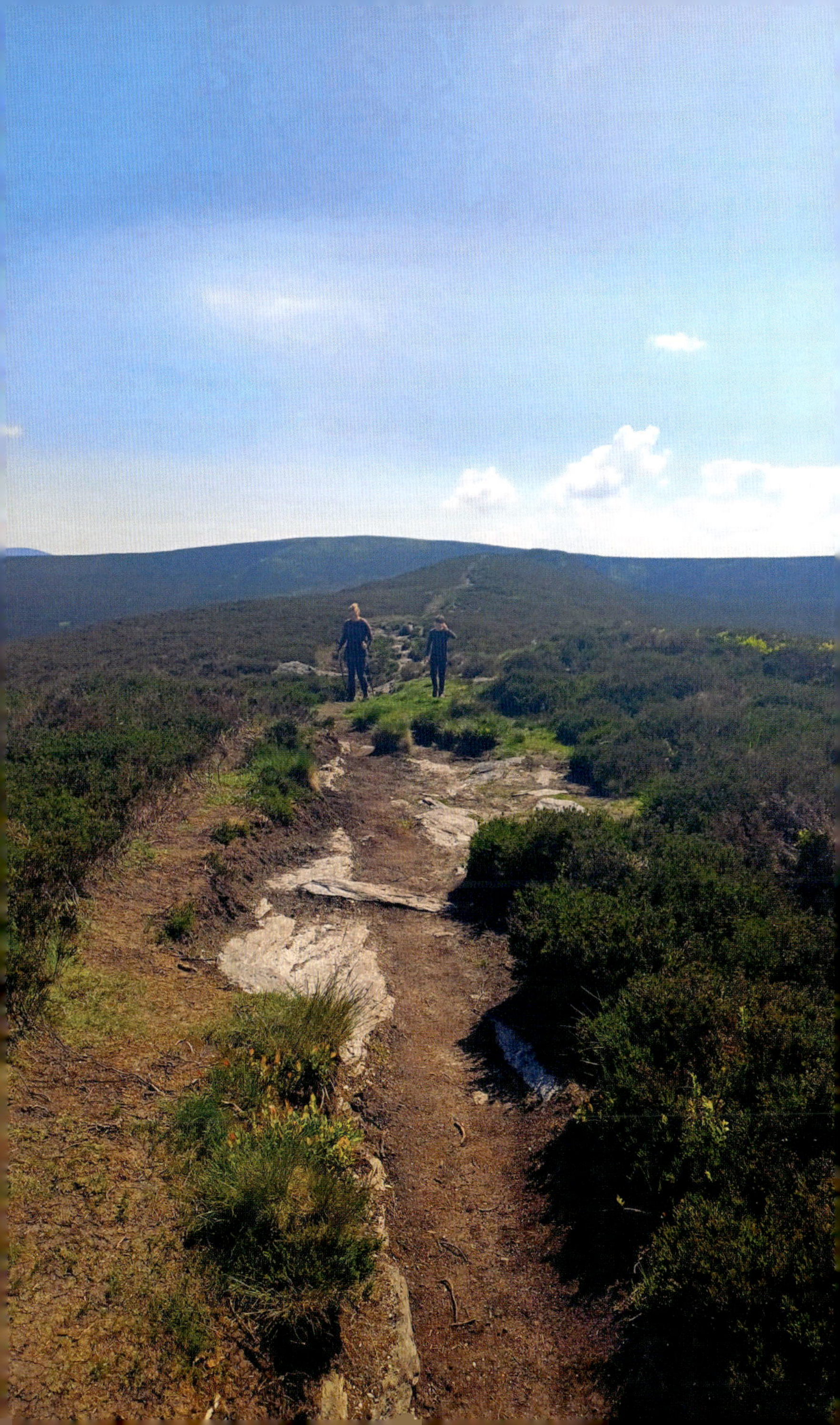

Myths and legends

The Upper Lake at Glendalough is said to have no bottom and to be home to more than one female pursuer of handsome St Kevin. One story tells of a local woman, Kathleen, who loved St Kevin and drowned in an act of unrequited love. Another tells how St Kevin whipped her with nettles and pushed her into the Upper Lake. It is said that a ghostly form of a woman in a red dress, believed to be Kathleen, has appeared in photos taken in the area. St Kevin is also said to have banished a serpent monster to the Upper Lake. This is similar to other myths from around Ireland in which Christian saints vanquished serpents and demons, usually the pagan gods and goddesses associated with the older pre-Christian Irish religions.

Descending Derrybawn to Glendalough ▲

24

Great Sugarloaf
Co. Wicklow

An adventurous hike around one of Ireland's most iconic mountains

With its distinct conical shape and proximity to Dublin, the Great Sugarloaf is one of Ireland's most iconic mountains. While the standard 2.5km route starts at Red Lane car park, this looped hike offers a more adventurous circumnavigation of the mountain while also taking in the rocky climb to the summit. Enjoy spectacular panoramic views of the Dublin and Wicklow mountains and the Irish Sea. On a clear day, it is possible to see all the way up to the Mourne Mountains in Co. Down down to Mount Leinster in counties Carlow/Wexford. Navigational skills are needed for the first part of the walk (points 2–3) as it is very overgrown with bracken. Hiking boots recommended.

LENGTH:	TIME:	DIFFICULTY:	OSI MAP NO:
6km	3–4 hours	Medium	56

EASTWEST MAPPING: Wicklow East

⊙ NEED TO KNOW

From Dublin, take the N11 south to Kilmacanogue. From there, take the R755, shortly afterwards turning left onto Quill Road, and continue straight onto Glencap Road. Continue for just over half a kilometre and park outside Fitzsimons Park, Kilmacanogue GAA club.

Coordinates: 53.1632 -6.1413

The Hike

1 Go down the road you drove in on and find a small path to your left at the edge of the playing pitch. This path has bracken on it.

2 From points 2–3, aim to go between the Sugarlump and Great Sugarloaf mountains. As a rule of thumb, when in doubt, keep left. At 370m (point 2), turn left uphill through the bracken. At 550m, keep left. Terrain can be tricky with the bracken, but keep going. Stunning views of the Irish Sea start to open up. At both 800m and 1.2km, keep left. At 1.4km, arrive at a wider grass path. Turn left. The Wicklow Mountains are in front of you.

3 At almost 1.5km, take the left path uphill, where you will climb the shoulder of the Sugarloaf. You are aiming for the summit. Do not take the wider path with the red sign. Some clambering is required near the summit, so hiking poles are less useful at this point.

4 At 2.5km, reach the summit of the Great Sugarloaf and enjoy spectacular views across the Irish Sea and the Dublin and Wicklow mountains. On a clear day, you can see up to the Mourne Mountains in Co. Down and down to Mount Leinster in Carlow/Wexford.

5 Descend the mountain, clambering for the first while. About halfway down, hiking poles are useful again! At 2.9km, take the path down to your left.

6 At 3.25km, turn left onto a smaller path through the gorse. (This path is about 20m before where the Great Sugarloaf Way meets you on your right. Do not take that path.) Continue on the gorse path down around the side of the Great Sugarloaf Mountain.

7 At 3.9km, take a small path left (just before a rock outcrop). This path takes you downhill for some time. At 4.6km, the path swings to your left around the base of the mountain. Go through a wooded area.

8 8. At 5.7km, reach a leafy tarmac road and continue straight back for 300m to the car park.

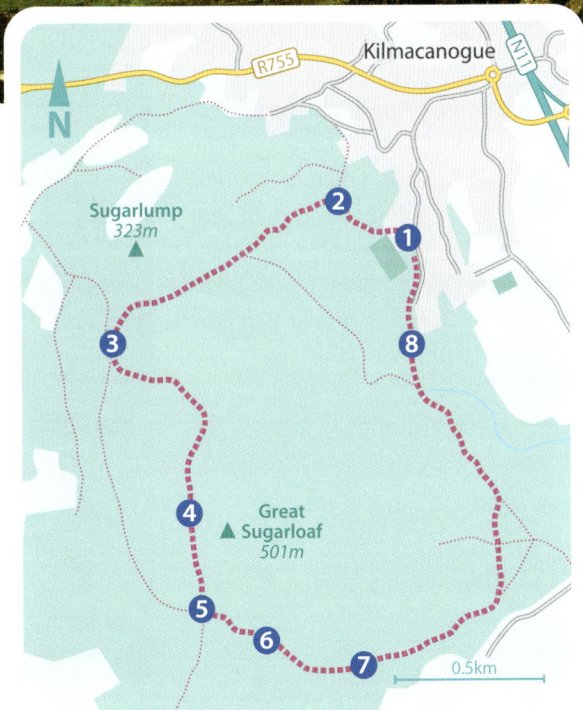

In peak position

Kilmacanogue

R755

N11

N

Sugarlump
323m

Great
Sugarloaf
501m

2
1
8
3
4
5
6
7

0.5km

Myths and legends

In the first century BCE, the ferocious British pirate Ingcel, whose single eye had three pupils, led a band of reavers/raiders across the Irish Sea to attack Conaire Mór, King of Ireland, who was foredoomed to a tragic death. As part of their travels, the reavers climbed Howth Hill and the Great Sugarloaf in order to reconnoitre the landscape and spied Conaire's fortress at Downshill Hillfort, close to Glen of the Downs (near the Great Sugarloaf). Togail Bruidne Dá Derga (The Destruction of the Hostel of the Red God) tells of Conaire's death and is considered one of the finest Irish sagas of the early period, comparable to the better-known Táin Bó Cúailnge. The Sugarloaf is also called Cú Chulainn's Spear. The mountain is in the heart of the ancient territory of Cuala, an area roughly co-extensive with modern Co. Wicklow. The area takes its name from the Cualainn, an early people who lived there around 200 CE.

The view from the Sugarloaf to the Irish Sea ▲

25

Djouce
Co. Wicklow

An incredible hike to the fortified mountain

This is a very enjoyable and accessible hike in the heart of the Wicklow Mountains. From initial stunning views of Luggala ('Fancy' Mountain) and Lough Tay, move on to panoramic vistas of the Wicklow Moutains, the Irish Sea and Dublin city. The scenery from the summmit is particularly striking. The return route from Djouce brings you across a wonderful winding path, part of the Wicklow Way. There are clear paths and boardwalks throughout. Hiking boots recommended.

LENGTH:	TIME:	DIFFICULTY:	OSI MAP NO:
3–9 km	1–3 hours	Easy–Medium	56

EASTWEST MAPPING: Wicklow
HARVEY SUPERWALKER XT30: Wicklow Mountains

⊙ NEED TO KNOW

From Dublin, take the N11 south to Kilmacanogue. From there, take the R755 for 11km. Then turn right onto the R759 and after around 4km arrive at the car park that overlooks Luggala and Louth Tay. If full, there are several other car parks nearby. All car parks are free. Do not block access points for emergency vehicles.

Coordinates: 53.1046 -6.2548

◂ A view from Djouce towards the Irish Sea

The Hike

1 After parking above Lough Tay, walk up through the car park towards a barrier and go around the barrier. After 200m, turn left onto a path with a yellow walking person sign. After another 200m, go straight through a crossroads of paths and continue uphill. After another 300m, arrive at a dramatic viewing point overlooking Lough Tay. There is a commemorative stone to J.B. Malone here, who was a founder of the Wicklow Way. When ready, continue uphill on the boardwalk.

2 After climbing steadily for 1.5km, reach the top of White's Hill and enjoy stunning views of the Great Sugarloaf and the Vartry Reservoir. For the easy 3km option, retrace your steps to the car park. For the medium option, continue on the boardwalk towards Djouce.

3 At 2.8km, do not follow the boardwalk as it turns sharp right. Instead, continue up the stony and grassy path in front of you.

4 At 4km, arrive at the impressive trig pillar that marks the summit of Djouce. Drink in the amazing views towards Dublin Bay and of other great peaks in the Wicklow Mountains. This is a good place for a break and there are plenty of big rocks for young hikers to

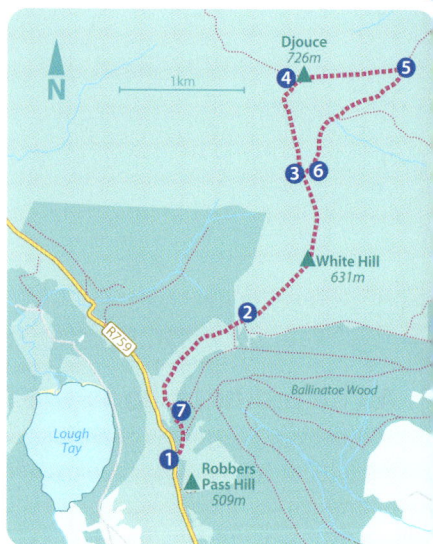

Returning from Djouce ▲

clamber on. When ready, continue down the wide path to your right just after the summit. This is a steep descent with stunning views in the direction of the Great Sugarloaf.

5 After descending for 800m, arrive at a T-junction. To the left lies the Wicklow Way heading north. You will turn right here and follow an intriguing winding path that hugs the edge of Djouce.

6 At 6.4km, arrive at the end of the boardwalk at point 3 above. Turn left and follow the same path back to the car park. The return trip from here is largely downhill and there are breathtaking views all around.

7 After hiking for almost 2km, pass the viewing point with the J.B. Malone commemorative stone and bear left at a fork in the path. Follow the path back to where your car is parked. At Luggala car park there is a lovely grass bank overlooking Lough Tay that provides a picturesque spot to picnic.

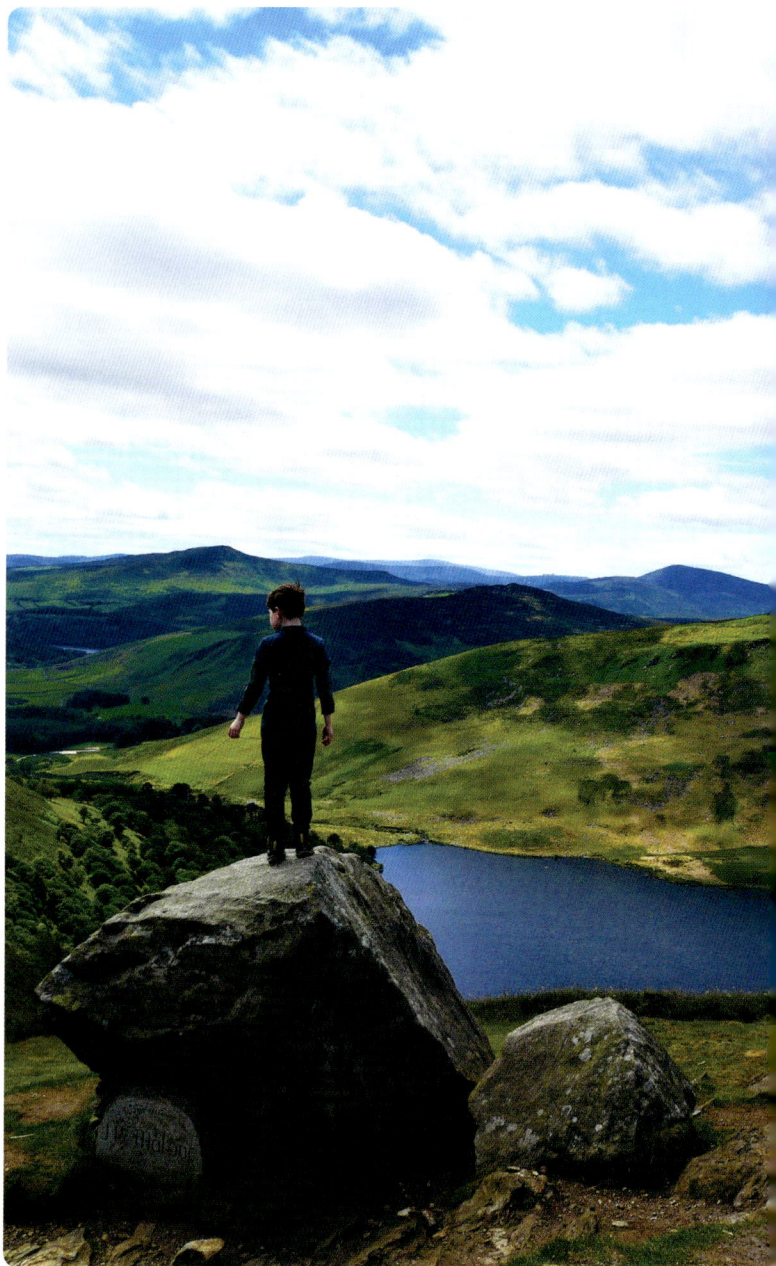

Myths and legends

Djouce – Dioghais in Irish – means 'fortified height' and the summit certainly has a commanding view over Wicklow and Dublin. Diarmuid and Gráinne are believed to have hidden in the Wicklow Mountains in so-called 'Diarmuid and Gráinne beds' – caves, nooks, dolmens, Neolithic tombs and glacial erratics – where the couple supposedly spent a number of nights while on the run from Fionn Mac Cumhaill. The name Wicklow is of Norwegian origin – 'Vikingr-lo' or 'Wykinglo' – and translates as 'meadow of the Vikings'. The Vikings invaded Ireland in 795 CE and the earliest written evidence of Viking activities in Wicklow dates to 827 CE. The Irish name for Wicklow is Cill Mhantáin, meaning 'church of the toothless one'. The story goes that Maintáin was with St Patrick when they tried to land on the Wicklow coast to convert Ireland to Christianity in the fifth century CE. They were strongly resisted by the King of Leinster, and as Patrick attempted to come ashore, one of the king's men threw a stone that struck Maintáin and left him toothless. Patrick failed to land and left a curse on the shore so that few or no fish would be caught there.

◀ The verdant Wicklow Mountains

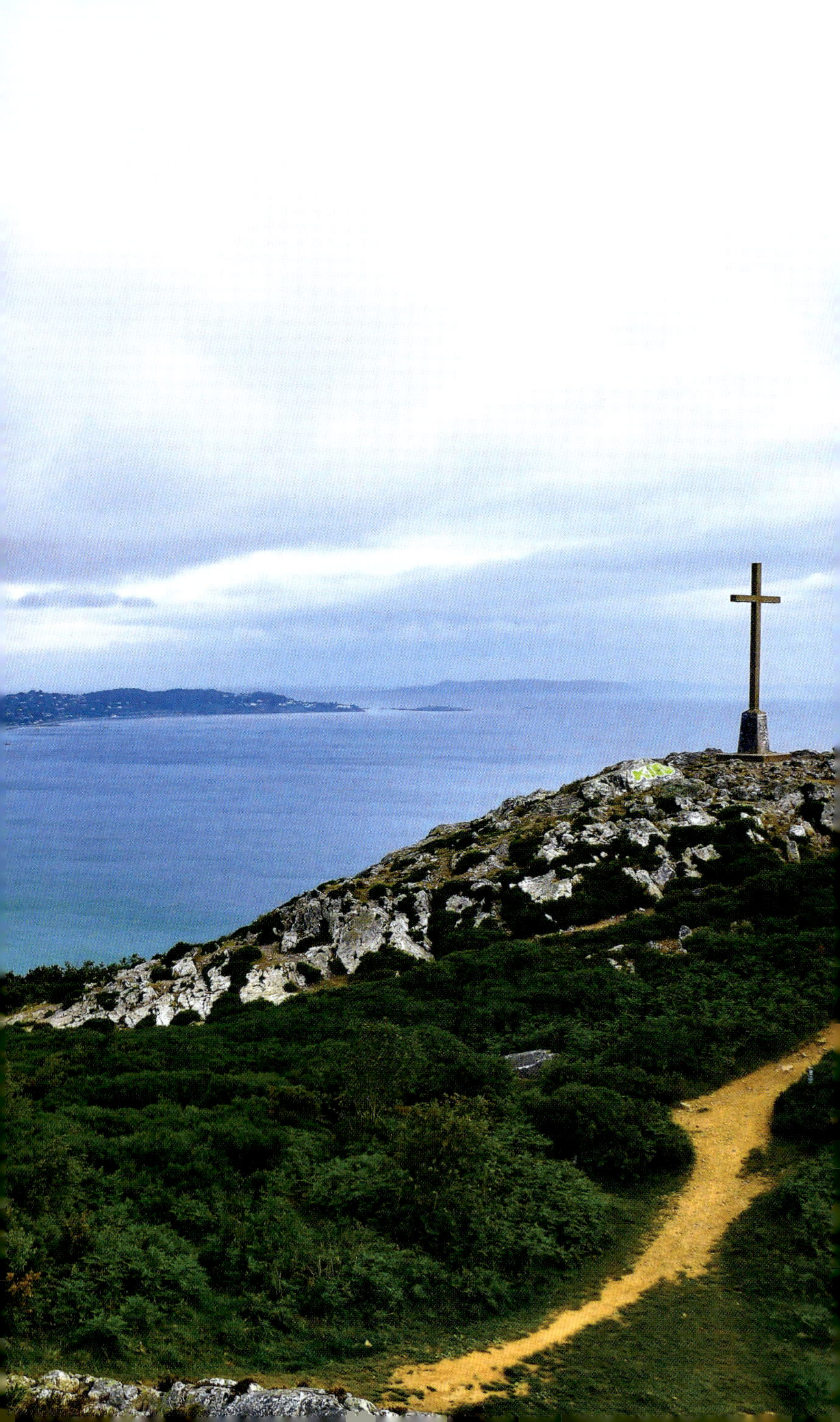

26

Bray Head
Co. Wicklow

A wonderful headland walk on the Irish Sea

This stunning looped hike around Bray Head offers breathtaking views of Co. Dublin, Bray town, the Irish Sea and the Wicklow Mountains. See the iconic cross on Bray Head. Paths are generally well kept, although the path down through the gorse may require some care. Check online and local notice boards before starting as parts of the cliff path can be prone to closure at times. Hiking boots essential.

LENGTH:	TIME:	DIFFICULTY:	OSI MAP NO:
7km	2–3 hours	Medium	56

EASTWEST MAPPING: Wicklow East

⊙ NEED TO KNOW

From Dublin, leave the M50 at junction 7 for Bray. At the first roundabout, take the third exit and stay on the R768. Go straight through the next five roundabouts. At the sixth roundabout, take the first exit onto the R761. Continue straight through the next two roundabouts. Take the next right down Newcourt Road and then take the third right onto Raheen Park and follow the road to the free car park at the end.

Coordinates: 53.1951 -6.0888

The Hike

1 Check the notice board at the top right-hand corner of the car park for any notices about the hikes around Bray Head. When ready, ascend the steps that are marked De Buitléar Way. The path will become rockier as you climb but continue uphill, ignoring paths to your left and right. As you climb you will see the large cross on Bray Head above you and this is your target.

2 After 850m of steep climbing, arrive at the cross on Bray Head. There are amazing views of Dublin Bay, the Irish Sea and the Wicklow Mountains, including the Great Sugarloaf (see Hike 24). When ready, take the path to your right that leads through a metal gate and out further along the headland. At 1.5km, follow the path around to your left and ignore the grassy track to your right.

3 At 2.5km, arrive at a beautiful viewing point overlooking the Irish Sea and down towards the town of Greystones. There is a metal gate here which leads to a downhill path that you will take later – but not just yet! We recommend continuing along the path; soon after, you will see a grass path to your left. Take this and follow the path to the stunning rocky summit of Bray Head Hill.

4 When ready to leave Bray Head Hill, return to the metal gate at point 3 above. Go through the gate and take the brilliant path

Running through the gorse on Bray Head ▲

downhill through the bracken and gorse. Enjoy expansive views of the Irish Sea in front of you but be mindful as the path can be tricky underfoot in places. We would advise slipping on your coat here as the gorse and brambles can be overgrown and snag in places. At a black post 100m from the gate, keep to the right down the hill. After continuing downhill for 1km, emerge onto a path that swings to the left. Take this and ignore the path to the right that has a farm gate. After walking for 100m, you will meet three paths: continue straight ahead down the middle path.

5   After the next 100m, arrive out onto the cliff path. Turn left back towards Bray. Simply proceed along this splendid path for around 3km until it brings you back to the car park. Along the way you can marvel at the wonderful engineering of the tunnels and rail line you can see below. Depending on the time of year, there are also wonderfully coloured flowers along the path.

Myths and legends

A local tradition has it that St Kevin lived near Bray before he went to Glendalough. Before Christianity came to Ireland, nature worship was likely, given the presence of Bronze Age settlements in the Bray area (2300–600 BCE). The Book of the Dun Cow indicates that Bray was on one of the five main roads that led from Tara across the country in the Bronze Age, the Slighe Cualann that ran south-east through Dublin to the Bray coastline. Fifty years ago, a part of this road was still plainly traceable between Dublin and Bray. These roads were made of stone and wood, were open to chariot and horse traffic and were well maintained, as outlined by the Brehon Law regulations.

Sunrise at Bray Head ▲

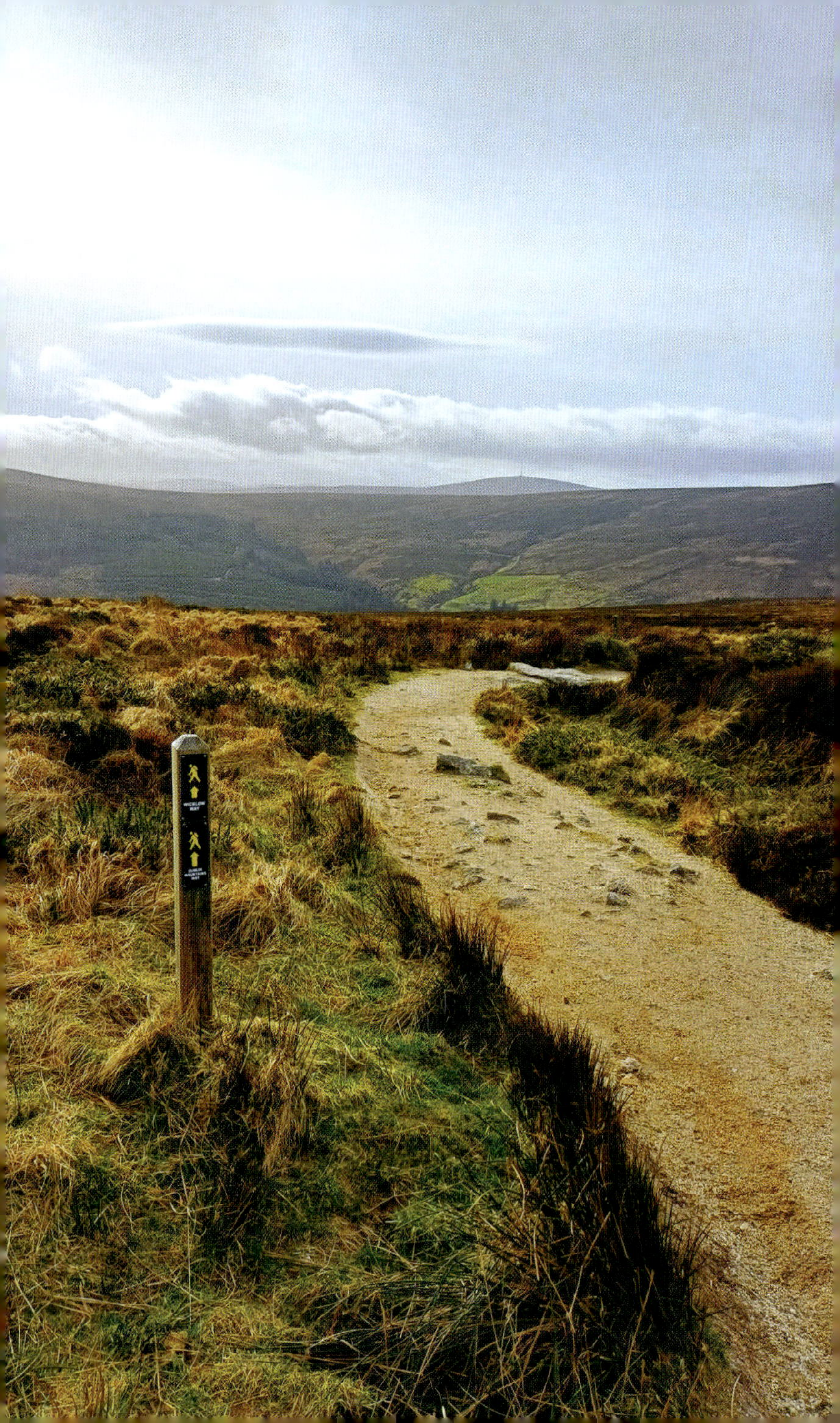
WICKLOW WAY
DUBLIN MOUNTAINS WAY

27

Tibradden via Ticknock
Co. Dublin

Follow the ancient cairns for a welcome in Tigh Bródáin

This hike offers a great day out in the Dublin Mountains. At Three Rock Mountain, there are stunning views across Dublin city and bay, while at Two Rock Mountain, you can visit a prehistoric cairn and enjoy panoramic vistas across the Dublin and Wicklow mountains. The cairn at Tibradden – Tigh Bródáin (Bródáin's house) – offers spectacular views of Howth Head, Ireland's Eye and Lambay Island. Good paths and boardwalks throughout. Follow the Dublin Mountain Way signs. Hiking boots recommended.

LENGTH:	TIME:	DIFFICULTY:	OSI MAP NO:
10–16km	3–5 hours	Medium–Experienced	50

EASTWEST MAPPING: Dublin Mountains

⊙ NEED TO KNOW

From Dublin, leave the M50 at junction 15 Carrickmines and follow the road to Kilternan. Take a left and then the next right onto R116. Follow the R116 into the village of Glencullen. Pass Johnny Fox's pub and after the crossroads, turn right into Glencullen Adventure Park (The GAP). You will need a €2 coin or to buy a token from the onsite shop in order to exit the car park.

Coordinates: 53.2228 -6.2248

◄ The Wicklow and Dublin ways near Tibradden

Tribadden
Mountain
466m

Tribadden
Wood

Three Rock
Mountain
536m

Two Rock
Mountain
536m

Ballyedmonduff
Forest

L3020

R116

1km

Glencullen

The Hike

1 From the car park, walk up the path towards the adventure centre. Pass by the GAP café and continue along the Dublin Mountain Way (DMW) around the car parks and up alongside the adventure park cycle tracks. As you climb upward, turn around to enjoy the first view of the Sugarloaf in the distance. Keep on the DMW walk track and not on the bike tracks.

2 Enter the forest briefly and then move alongside a gravel roadway. After 1.5km, enter the forest again. Signage for the DMW is poor here but keep to your right and after a few metres you will pick up the main path once again. Follow this path up through the forest.

3 At 2km, exit the forest and follow a wide path right for another 1.5km to bring you to the top of Three Rock Mountain.

4 At Three Rock Mountain, enjoy stunning views over Dublin Bay over to Howth and taking in Dollymount Strand and the iconic

Playing on Three Rock Mountain ▲

red Poolbeg Lighthouse. There are some very climbable rocks at the top which children will enjoy. When ready, turn left up the path; you will reach the top of Two Rock Mountain (Fairy Castle) at 5km. For the medium 10km option, simply retrace your path to the car park.

5 If you have more energy, continue downhill for 500m, where the Wicklow Way joins the Dublin Mountain Way. Turn left here and continue for 1.5km to where the Wicklow Way and the Dublin Mountain Way separate.

6 Turn right and follow the path through the woods until you reach the top of Tibradden Mountain at 8km. Ancient cairns and more stunning views make for an intriguing mountaintop.

7 When ready, return to the car park by retracing your steps.

Myths and legends

The cairn at the top of Tibradden is said to be the burial place of Niall Glúndub, High King of Ireland 916–919 CE. Niall was the first High King to be killed by the Vikings. Two Rock Mountain has a Bronze Age cairn dating from 2500–2000 BCE and the summit is also known as Fairy Castle. Fionn Mac Cumhaill and his war band, the Fianna, are said to have roamed the Dublin Mountains. There is a large passage tomb dating from 4000–2500 BCE at nearby Seefin, which is one of the peaks in the Dublin Mountains. Seefin, 'the seat of Fionn'.

▲ Running towards Fairy Castle with Dublin Bay and city in the background

Near the summit of Two Rock (fairy) Mountain ▲

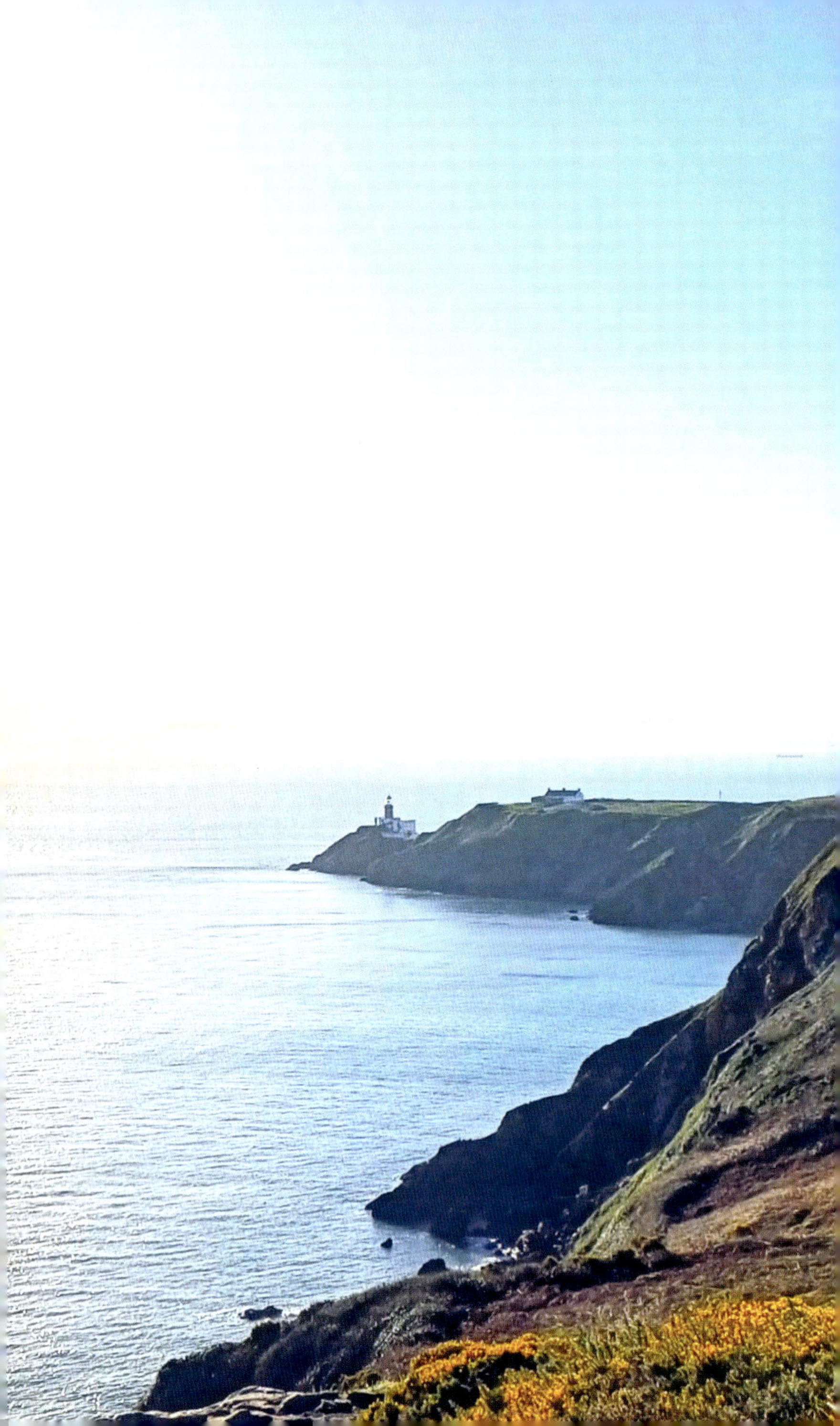

28

The Bog of Frogs Loop
Howth, Co. Dublin

A stunning coastal cliff walk around Howth Head

Setting off from the pretty harbour village of Howth, the Howth coastal cliff walk boasts panoramic views of the Irish Sea, the Wicklow Mountains, Dublin Bay and Dublin city. The adventuresome Bog of Frogs walk takes in the Baily Lighthouse, and O'Pint Beach, crosses a golf course and winds its way past the mansions of the rich and famous. There are well-defined paths throughout, although parts can become muddy after wet weather. Hiking boots essential.

LENGTH:	TIME:	DIFFICULTY:	OSI MAP NO:
11.5 km	4 hours	Medium	50

⊙ NEED TO KNOW

From Dublin, take the M50 north and use the right lane to take the R139 exit to Malahide. Continue on the R139 for 4km until it changes to the R809. Continue on the R809 for 3km and enter Howth village. There is a large free public car park on the harbour.

Coordinates: 53.389524 -6.071667

◄ Howth Head coastline

The Hike

From the car park, head south along the harbour and follow the road up the hill to another smaller car park. Go through this car park and onto the coastal path. You will mainly follow the purple arrows for this hike. Follow the path along the coast and get your first views of the impressive Thulla Rocks.

2 Continue along the coastal path high above the Irish Sea. After 2km and on a clear day, the mighty Lugnaquilla can be seen in the distance surrounded by the Wicklow Mountains.

3 At 3km, arrive at a junction of paths. For this route, continue straight ahead and follow the path downhill for another kilometre to a small road.

4 Cross the road and if you look to your left you will get a good view of Baily Lighthouse. Cross the road and join the narrow path on the far side, which is slightly to your left. Continue along this pathway as you pass beneath some very impressive houses high to your right.

5 At 6.5km, arrive at the delightful O'Pint Beach. This makes for a great picnic spot or a little rest. When ready, rejoin the path and make your way further along the coast as some wonderful views of the iconic Poolbeg Lighthouse and Dollymount Strand come into view.

6 Follow this path for approximately another kilometre, and at the end, climb up the edge of the rugged coast to meet a junction of paths. Follow the purple arrows to the right and go uphill. At 8km, keep to the left across a field and then follow the purple arrows across the field and up the hill until you come to a road, which you should cross with care.

7 At the next junction you have a choice of two routes. You can follow the purple arrows to the left, which will bring you around Shielmartin Hill. Or, for a glorious panorama of Dublin, we would recommend taking the steep uphill path in front of you, which brings you directly to the top of Shielmartin Hill.

8 After a sharp but short climb of 400m, arrive at the summit cairn

A view from O'Pint Beach, Howth

of Shielmartin Hill at 8.4km. After enjoying the expansive views, descend by the steep path, which brings you to Howth Golf Course, where you may cross the fairways on the path provided. From here, continue your hike by keeping to the purple arrows at any junction you come to. As you descend back into Howth, enjoy the last views across the bay.

9 At 11.5km, arrive back into the main street of Howth. Turn right and follow the road back to the car park. There are several eateries here to extend your day in Howth. You can take a boat from Howth to Ireland's Eye, where there is a Martello tower that was built in 1803 as a lookout for a Napoleonic invasion.

Myths and legends

Several legends are linked to the Howth region. A local folktale recounts how Conall Gulban from Howth travelled to many far-flung places, such as Scandinavia, Greece, Spain and Turkey, to battle giants, terrible warriors, hounds and fearsome cailleacha (hags) and to rescue his bride, Eithne.

The Baily Lighthouse was built on the fort of Crimthann Nia Nár, High King of Ireland at the time of Christ. In the first century BCE, the one-eyed British pirate Ingcel and his army climbed to the top of Howth Hill in their quest to find and destroy Conaire, the King of Ireland. Interestingly, Howth Head was an island around 5,500 years ago. However, the waves left an isthmus of sand and gravel about five metres above sea level which today links the promontory of Howth to the mainland. From the top of Shielmartin Hill, there are clear views of nearby North Bull Island and Dollymount Strand. Incredibly, these landmarks only developed in the last 200 years as a byproduct of building the South and North Bull Walls in order to deepen the waters of Dublin Bay and facilitate the expanding trade of Dublin Port.

Winter sunlight on Howth Head ▲

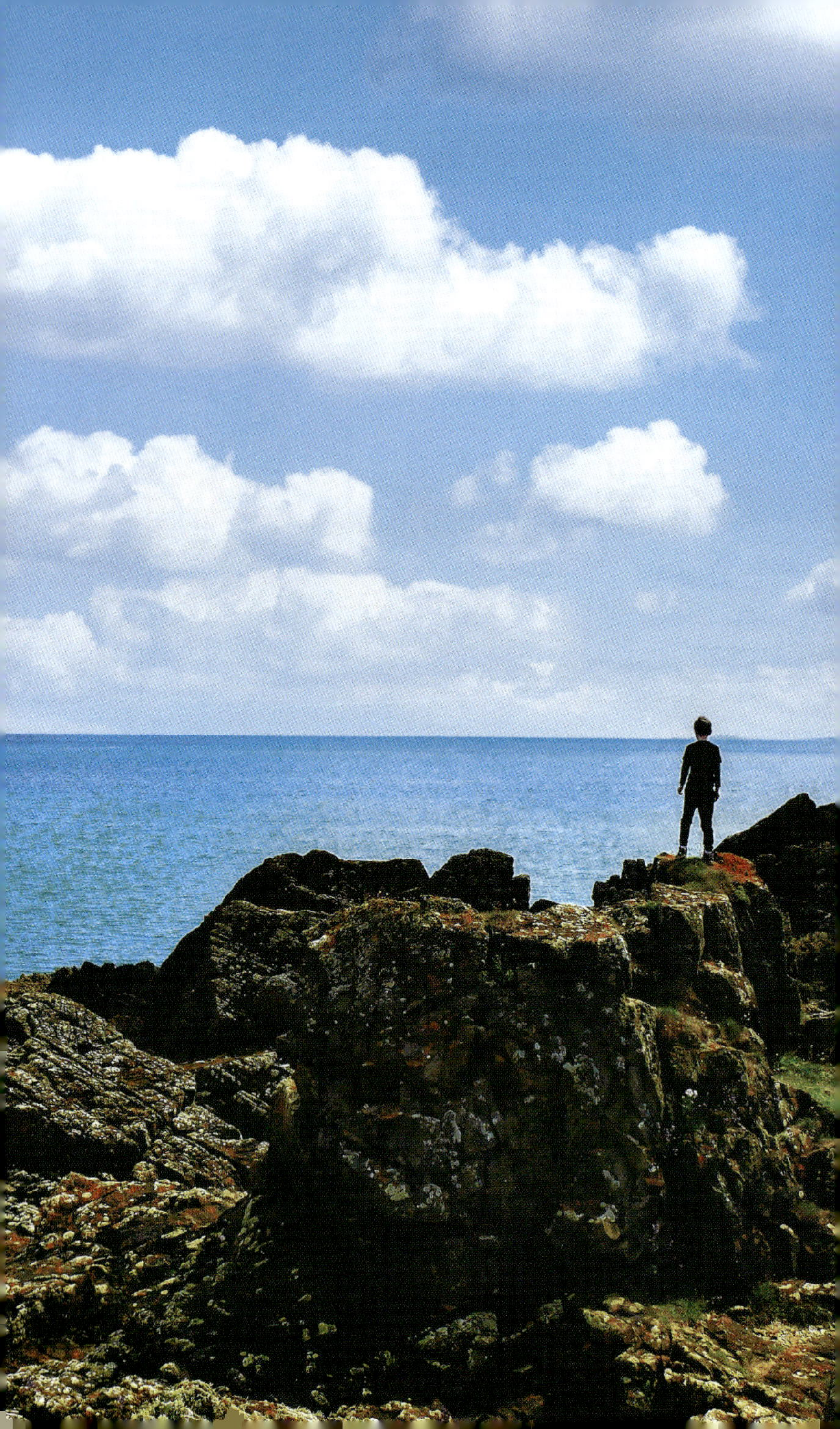

29

Clogherhead Walk
Co. Louth

A beautiful hike along a rocky headland leading to a delightful beach

This is a short but beautiful hike along the only rocky headland in Co. Louth. Indeed, Clogherhead means 'rocky headland'. Children will enjoy clambering on the rocks and exploring rock pools. Cormorants and gannets can be sighted here. There are views of Ireland's east coast, from the Mourne and Cooley Mountains in the north down to Lambay Island off Dublin. Find a glorious sandy beach at the end of the headland, a beach that stretches all the way down to Drogheda at low tide. The walk can become muddy after wet weather. Hiking boots are recommended for rock climbing and if the ground is wet. And don't forget the beach wear!

LENGTH:	TIME:	DIFFICULTY:	OSI MAP NO:
4km	2–3 hours	Easy	36

⊙ NEED TO KNOW

From Drogheda, take the R166 north and keep following the signs for Clogherhead. When you arrive in Clogherhead, turn right and follow the signs for Port Oriel. Turn left into a large free car park. Park on the upper level for stunning views across the Irish Sea.

Coordinates: 53.7963 -6.2216

◄ Exploring the rocks on Clogherhead

Port Oriel

N

Irish Sea

Clogherhead

500m

The Hike

1 Walk down the car park a little and pass through a broken metal gate on your right. Follow the informal grass path. There are interesting rocky areas here to explore on the left, but we are going to continue straight on.

2 After 400m, cross a wooden stile and continue on the path through the gorse. After another 400m, reach an area where it is possible to explore and walk on the rocks. When ready, continue on the grassy path.

3 At 1.2 km, pass through a metal stile, and after 300m reach a gravel track.

Walking on Clogherhead ▲

4 Turn left on the track and keep over to the right-hand side where a narrow path hugs a fence. Follow the path and turn right. This will lead you to Clogherhead Beach.

5 This wonderful stretch of sand extends for 2km and at low tide you can walk along it all the way down to Drogheda. Spend as long as you like on the beach and retrace your steps when ready. If you have time, visit Port Oriel pier at the bottom of the car park. In summertime, the local fish and chip shop is open and well worth a visit.

Myths and legends

A chilling legend is told about Clogherhead. There are some rocks at the side of the headland known as Red Man's Cave or Dead Man's Cave. The story tells of a captain and six Spanish sailors who arrived at Clogherhead after the rest of the crew had died of scurvy. The remaining sailors camped at Clogherhead but for three nights a crew member mysteriously died. The remaining three crew were suspicious of the captain so they killed him and placed his head on a stick at the entrance to the cave. It is said that if you are near this area at evening time it is possible to hear the Red Man whistling and singing.

▲ The Irish Sea and Mourne Mountains from Clogherhead

Clogherhead Beach ▲

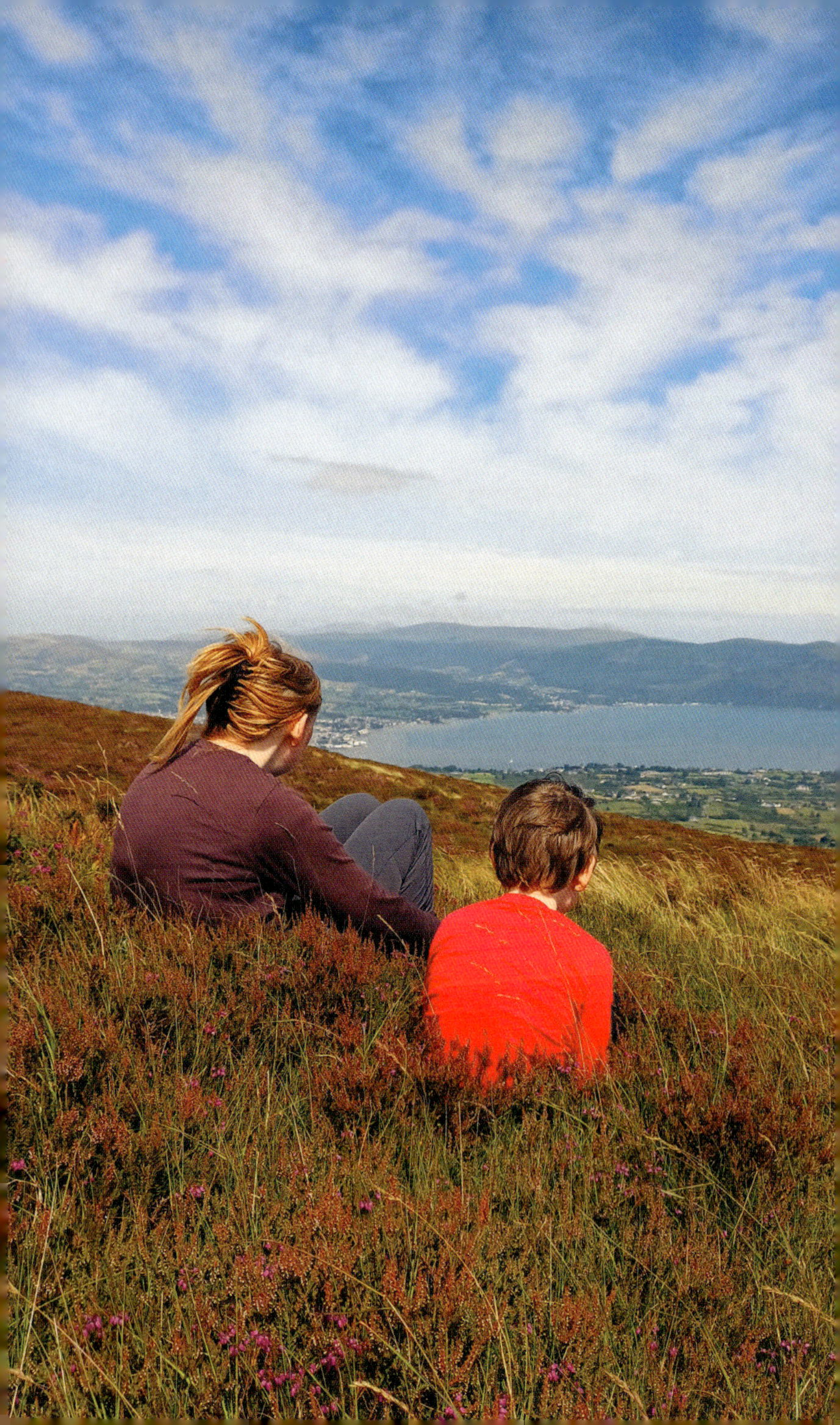

Carnavaddy
Cooley Mountains, Co. Louth

A splendid hike in the footsteps of Cú Chulainn

The Cooley Mountains in Co. Louth offer a paradise for those who like to enjoy stunning views far from the madding crowd. The landscape is one of unspoilt rolling countryside with beautiful seascapes and panoramas in all directions, with several passage tomb cairns and a standing stone circle en route. The views include Carlingford Lough, the Cooley and Mourne mountains, the Ring of Gullion, Dundalk Bay, the Irish Sea and, on a clear day, the Isle of Man. The experienced hike option finishes with a walk through Ravensdale Forest. Paths are generally clear but some navigation is required on the experienced route in terms of paying attention to taking the right junction. While the ground is generally firm, parts can become boggy after rain or in winter. Hiking boots essential.

LENGTH:	TIME:	DIFFICULTY:	OSI MAP NO:
5–17km	2–6 hours	Easy–Experienced	36

EASTWEST MAPPING: Cooley

◄ Enjoying Carlingford Lough amidst the blooming heather

From Dublin, take the M1 to Dundalk. As you pass Dundalk, take the N52 exit towards Dundalk North/Carlingford. At the roundabout, take the fourth exit. At the next roundabout, take the first exit onto the R132. Stay on this road, going straight through the first roundabout. After 4km, at the next roundabout, take the first exit onto the R147. After 400m, turn left onto the L7092 and park carefully along the edge of the road near the Ravensdale Forest.

Coordinates experienced option: 54.0693 -6.3457
Coordinates 5km option: 54.0805 -6.3207

The Hike

1 Start walking back the road you drove in on, the L7092. Continue straight onto the road ahead, the R174. This is quite a long walk on a busy road, so take care.

2 After 1.8km, turn left up the road marked L30906. After 300m, turn left again near a stone wall and proceed uphill.

3 At 2km, take the stony track to your right between two houses that goes in the direction of the mountain. After a hundred metres, pass through a farm gate, remembering to close it behind you. A lovely broad grass path winds its way upward. At 2.7km, visit a stone circle on your left. When ready, proceed uphill using the yellow painted stones that are used for the annual Poc Fada (Long Puck) competition as a guide.

4 At 4.3km, arrive at a junction of paths and turn right here (the left is the path you will take later towards Clermont Carn). Follow the yellow stones as you aim directly for Carnavaddy Mountain in the distance. This part of the walk has some descents and ascents but the views on either side are among the finest in Ireland. As you make your way across, ignore any paths to your right that go downhill and keep moving toward Carnavaddy, which has a large cairn on top of it.

5 After 6.5km, arrive at the large stone cairn on Carnavaddy. If you continue a little, you will see the small stone summit marker for Carnavaddy. It is well worth stopping here and letting the superlative views seep into you. When ready, retrace your steps back along the same path towards Clermont Carn with its tall aerial tower as a guide. At 7.5km, the path forks but it doesn't matter which path you take as both lead you back in the correct direction.

6 At 8.7km, arrive back at the path you left at point 4. Head directly uphill towards the large aerial in front of you.

7 After 400m of steady uphill climbing, reach the top of Clermont Carn. There are beautiful views here of the Mourne Mountains and the Ring of Gullion. When ready, head past the aerial on your left and start going downhill. There are some picnic tables and information boards at this point. Continue down the tarmac road, which may have traffic on it. At 11km, ignore the road to your right and continue on the road to the left.

8 At 12.5km, turn left into a forest entrance with a yellow barrier across it. Continue straight in front of you and ignore the path to the left. You are now following signs for the Ring of Gullion Way. At 13.8km, keep to the left at a junction and keep going downhill. At 14.5km, follow the signs for the Ring of Gullion Way downhill onto a smaller grass path.

9 After walking down this path for 300m, there is a small turn to your left that leads down steeply into the woods. Ignore the signs for the Ring of Gullion Way and take this little left path. You will hear the river beside you. Cross a lovely old bridge before emerging on the far side. Go up the steep little path and arrive out on a large path with a yellow walking person sign; this is the Táin Way. Turn right here and follow it downhill. At 15.9km, take a slight right onto a grassy path, following the yellow walking person signs. After another 200m, continue through the crossroads. Keep going downhill and after 600m follow the path around to your right. After 300m, reach another path and turn left to take you back to your car. At this point it is worth driving further down the L7092 for about a kilometre, where there is a larger car park with picnic tables.

Easy 5km option

Park near the picnic tables at point 7 on the map and walk in the direction of Carnavaddy Mountain for as long as you want, i.e. towards points 4 and 5 on the map. When ready, simply retrace your steps to the car park. There are stunning views along this ridge of Carlingford Lough and the Mourne and Cooley Mountains.

Stone circle en route ▲

▲ Following the footsteps of Cú Chulainn up the Poc Fada route

Myths and legends

The Cooley Peninsula is a land steeped in the mythical tale of the *Táin Bó Cúailnge*. On this particular hike, you walk in the footsteps of the mighty Cú Chulainn himself. Nearer the start of the hike, there are yellow marker stones leading up the valley and across to Carnavaddy. These stones are used for the annual Poc Fada (Long Puck) competition. This is where hurlers try to hit a *sliotar* (leather ball) up and down the mountain in as few strikes as possible. The competition evokes the spirit of the young Setanta (later known as Cú Chulainn). As a teenage boy, Setanta wanted to join the Macra, a select group of boys who were trained in sports and fighting and overseen by Conor MacNessa, the King of Ulster. If the boys were good enough they could become a warrior in Conor's legendary army, the Red Branch Knights. Setanta convinced his mother to let him walk to the king's fort in Eamhain Macha (near the town of Armagh) from his home outside Dundalk. In order to entertain himself on the long hike towards Eamhain Macha, he decided to strike the sliotar as far as he could around the mountains. How Setanta became Cú Chulainn is another story. Suffice to say that Cú Chulainn went on to become the greatest warrior in the Red Branch Knights.

31

Slieve Foye
Cooley Mountains, Co. Louth

Where Queen Maeve fought the King of Ulster for the Brown Bull of Cooley

Looming high behind the pretty medieval town of Carlingford, Slieve Foye is the highest point in Co. Louth with a summit elevation of 589m. From the start of the hike, stunning vistas of Carlingford, Carlingford Lough and the Mourne Mountains reveal themselves. On gaining elevation, the Irish Sea and the Cooley Mountain range come into view and on a clear day one can see all the way down to the Wicklow Mountains. The views from the summit are simply stunning, so make sure you choose a clear day. The summit ridge also offers splendid clambering opportunities for children (and adults!). Paths are mostly clear but some navigational skills are required near the summit. The ground can be soft, especially in winter. Hiking boots essential.

LENGTH:	TIME:	DIFFICULTY:	OSI MAP NO:
10km	4–5 hours	Experienced	36

EASTWEST MAPPING: Cooley

⊙ **NEED TO KNOW**

From Dublin, take the M1 to Dundalk. As you pass Dundalk, take the N52 exit toward Dundalk North/Carlingford. At the roundabout take the fourth exit onto the R173. Proceed for 14km and then turn left to stay on the R173. After 2km, turn left onto Rooskey Road and after 2.5km turn left. After 100m, keep right. After 500m, arrive at the parking space at the edge of the road. Park with consideration for other road users. If there is no room to park, continue into the village of Carlingford, where there is plenty of parking; but this will add a couple of kilometres to the overall hike.

Coordinates: 54.0343 -6.1937

The Hike

1 Head up the path to the left with the fence on your left. Follow signs for Commons Loop, Slieve Foye Loop, Barnavave Loop and the yellow hiking person. After a couple of hundred metres, pass through a gate and follow the grass path straight in front of you towards the summit of Slieve Foye, which towers above you.

2 After 900m, turn left following the yellow hiking person sign and head back towards the col between Slieve Foye and Barnavave. Enjoy spectacular scenery of the Irish Sea. Ignore any faint paths to your right and continue on the main path, following the yellow person signs. After a kilometre, follow the path as it bends to the right.

3 At 2km, turn right towards Slieve Foye in front of you. There is a green path winding up towards the mountain. Do not follow the gravel path downhill. If you look to your left you will see Barnavave. As you make your way towards Slieve Foye, enjoy stunning views all around. As you near the mountain, aim towards the small col on the left. The nearer you get, the sharper the path rises and it becomes stonier. You will now come across some purple signs; follow these initially.

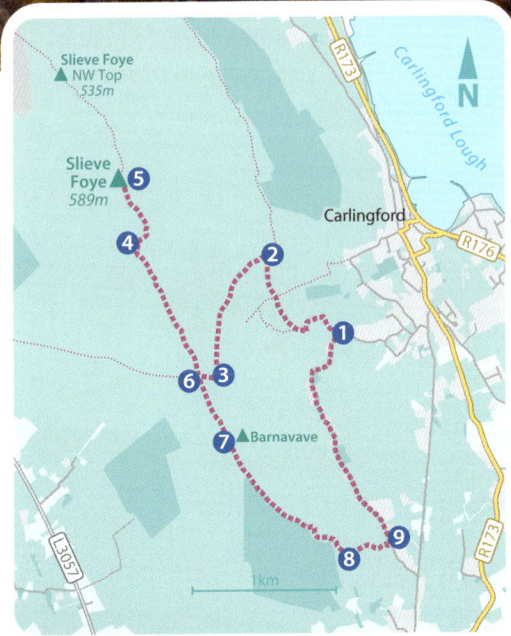

Slieve Foye NW Top 535m

Slieve Foye 589m

Carlingford

R173

R176

R173

L3057

Carlingford Lough

Barnavave

1km

N

1
2
3
4
5
6
7
8
9

4 At 3km and at the second purple sign, turn to the right and start to climb steeply again. After climbing for 200m, keep to the left path just past a large stone outcrop that looks like it has a small cave inside it. Navigation is slightly tricky at this point, but just keep following the path even though it is faint at times. After another hundred metres, you will see the summit of Slieve Foye in the distance. You will now turn to the right across some rocks and pick up the path again as it winds its way towards Slieve Foye. There are several faint paths all going in the same direction, so just keep heading for the summit.

5 At 3.6km, reach the summit. Take plenty of time to enjoy the views, relax and allow children to explore and scramble. When ready, descend the way you came, keeping Barnavave as your guide. Keep towards the right as you descend from the summit. Once you have found your path, continue for just over a kilometre and return to the crossroads of paths at point 3 on the map.

6 You could turn left at this point and follow the path back to your car. However, if you have energy, we encourage you to head straight towards Barnavave, which is now directly in front of you. Follow the Barnavave Loop Walk signpost. Aim towards a large cross you can see on top of a hill.

▲ Overlooking Carlingford Lough on the way to Slieve Foye

Exploring Slieve Foye ridge ▲

7 At 5.7km, you have several options. You can decide to ascend to the hill with the cross via the small gate on your right or turn left to reach the top of Barnavave. Or neither! Whatever you decide, when ready, continue straight through the gap between the hills and descend the grassy track. At 6.3km, keep to the left as you round the bends with a stone wall on your right. Keep following the red arrows as they direct you through a gap in the wall. After another 200m, arrive at the ruins of old Famine cottages.

8 At 7km, follow the purple arrows for the Rooskey Loop to Grange. Do not follow the red arrow to the right. Continue along this path and at 8km pass through a metal gate. After another 200m arrive into a car park.

9 Turn left onto the road and ignore any arrows for any of the walks that point to the right. Continue for 1.8km along the road until you reach your car.

Myths and legends

The area around the Cooley Mountains is where the fearsome warrior Cú Chulainn was the only Ulster fighter able to resist the curse of Macha and stay awake to fight the Queen of Connacht's men when they raided here to steal the mighty Brown Bull of Cooley. It was on Slieve Foye that Cú Chulainn killed many of the Connacht men in single combat over a period of several months. Ultimately, however, he was not successful and they took the bull. You can see in the landscape at Barnavave where the Connacht men carved out a passage through which they brought the Brown Bull back to Connacht. What happened next is told in full in the legend of Táin Bó Cúailnge.

Taking a moment on Slieve Foye summit ▲

The Midlands

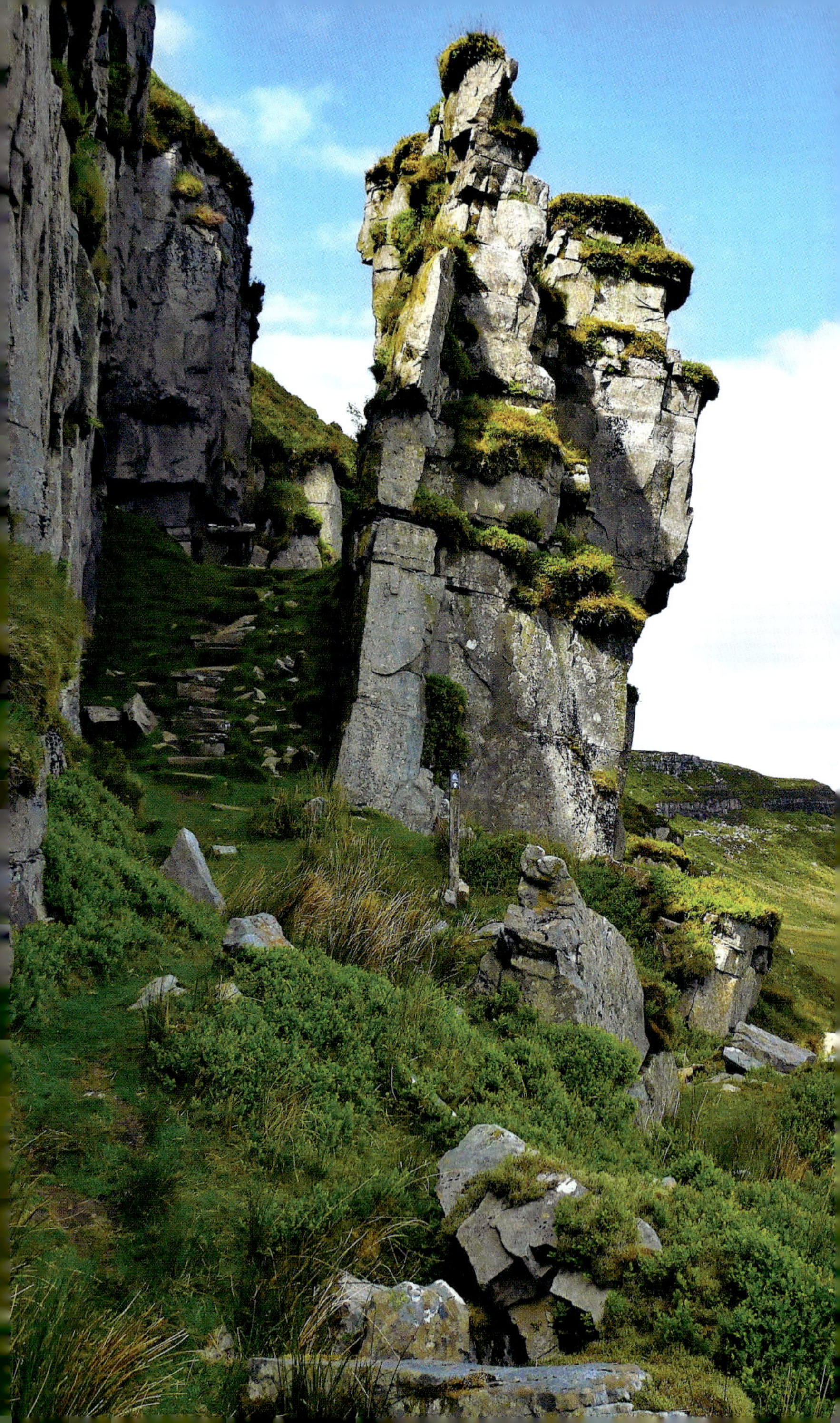

32

Iron Mountain
Co. Leitrim

An evocative and wild hike in a remote landscape

Iron Mountain is a remote and rugged mountain in Co. Leitrim, located on the eastern shore of Lough Allen. This wild, adventuresome hike climbs up to a hidden mass rock where Catholics practised their faith in secret during Penal times in the seventeenth and eighteenth centuries. The hike includes a cliff walk before an ascent to the otherworldly peat-hagged summit of Iron Mountain, and breathtaking panoramic views over the west and midlands of Ireland. There are regular sightings of foxes, hares, rabbits, badgers and peregrine falcons. While initial paths are well defined, navigational skills are required for much of the medium hike option. Dry, clear weather conditions are best. Hiking boots essential.

LENGTH:	TIME:	DIFFICULTY:	OSI MAP NO:
3–6km	1.5–4 hours	Easy–Medium	26

◉ NEED TO KNOW

From Fenagh in Co. Leitrim, take the R202 north for 2.3km and then turn left onto the R208. After 2.8km, turn right. After around 6km, pass the post office at Aghacashel and then turn right and follow the road as it climbs steadily to the car park for the Mullaghgarve Mass Rock. This is a free car park with stunning views across the midlands plain.

Coordinates: 54.0813 -7.9511

◀ The Mullaghgarve Mass Rock, Iron Mountain

Iron Mountain
585m

500m

The Hike

1 From the car park, head up the road to the noticeboard. This contains excellent information about the Mullaghgarve Mass Rock and the flora and fauna you can find on the mountain. Continue up this broad path that climbs steadily uphill and passes through a couple of gates with stiles.

2 After just over a kilometre, come to a footbridge that turns left. The grassy path in front of you will be your return path later in the hike. Cross the footbridge and follow the signposts for Mullaghgarve Mass Rock.

3 At 1.5km, arrive at the base of the mass rock. You can access it by climbing the steep path above you or you can continue on for a few metres past the pinnacle and enter the mass rock by stone steps on the other side. This is an evocative site highlighting the lengths that Catholics went to practise their faith in secret during

View across the midlands from Iron Mountain ▲

Penal times. For the easy 3km option, retrace your steps to the car park. For the medium 6km route, continue along a path with the cliff face beside you on your right. This path is tricky in places, so take your time.

4   This path continues for 500m until it runs out. Scramble up the escarpment to the top of the cliffs at a suitable point. When you reach the top, turn right, back in the direction you came from and proceed straight ahead. Make your way up the hill towards some rocks you will see. There are no defined paths here but the ground is firm. You will encounter some peat hags along the way, but the going is easier if you can keep closer to the right-hand side of the cliff top. You will see below you the path on which you started the hike. Noting this path is an important navigational aid for the return route.

5 Keep going straight until you arrive at a wire fence at 3km. Cross this fence at a low point. Put a coat across the wire to help you get over it if needed. Once you cross the fence, head up towards the summit of Iron Mountain in a two o'clock direction, i.e. keeping somewhat to your right.

6 After climbing for 500m, reach the top of Iron Mountain. Your hiking app will be a help here in locating the exact summit as it is a very broad flat top. The summit is on a plinth on top of a peat hag surrounded by soggy bog. It is likely that only the lightest people in your group will be able to get safely to the summit! When ready, return to the point where you crossed the fence (point 5 above). Cross back over the fence so that it is now on your left

as you make your way downhill. Stay close to the fence as a navigational aid as you descend. This path is very steep in places, so take your time. A mountain stream accompanies you along the way and there are some beautiful small waterfalls and rock pools en route. As you descend, notice below the path on which you started the hike and aim in that direction. After 300m, emerge into some rushes.

7 Continue through the rushes until the path eases out into a grassy track. After a further 300m, arrive back at the footbridge you crossed earlier (point 2 above). Retrace your steps to the car park.

◄ Returning through the rushes on Iron Mountain

▼ Our first time reaching the summit of Iron Mountain

Myths and legends

Iron Mountain is steeped in history and mythology. Iron found on the mountain was used in building the famous Ha'penny Bridge in Dublin over two hundred years ago. It was an important religious site during Penal times. In Irish mythology, Iron Mountain was where Goibhniu, the metalsmith for the Tuatha Dé Danann, had his forge. It was here that Goibhniu forged the weapons used in the famous Second Battle of Moytura that was fought between the Tuatha Dé Danann and the Fomorians at nearby Lough Arrow (Co. Sligo). The Second Battle of Moytura is an epic tale of combat between the forces of light and darkness, with the Tuatha Dé Danann associated with light and the Fomorians with destruction and chaos. Goibhniu also supplied the slingshot that Lugh used to kill Balor of the Evil Eye on Mount Errigal in Donegal (see Hike 42).

▲ A view across to the Cuilcagh Mountains

◄ The peat-hagged summit of Iron Mountain

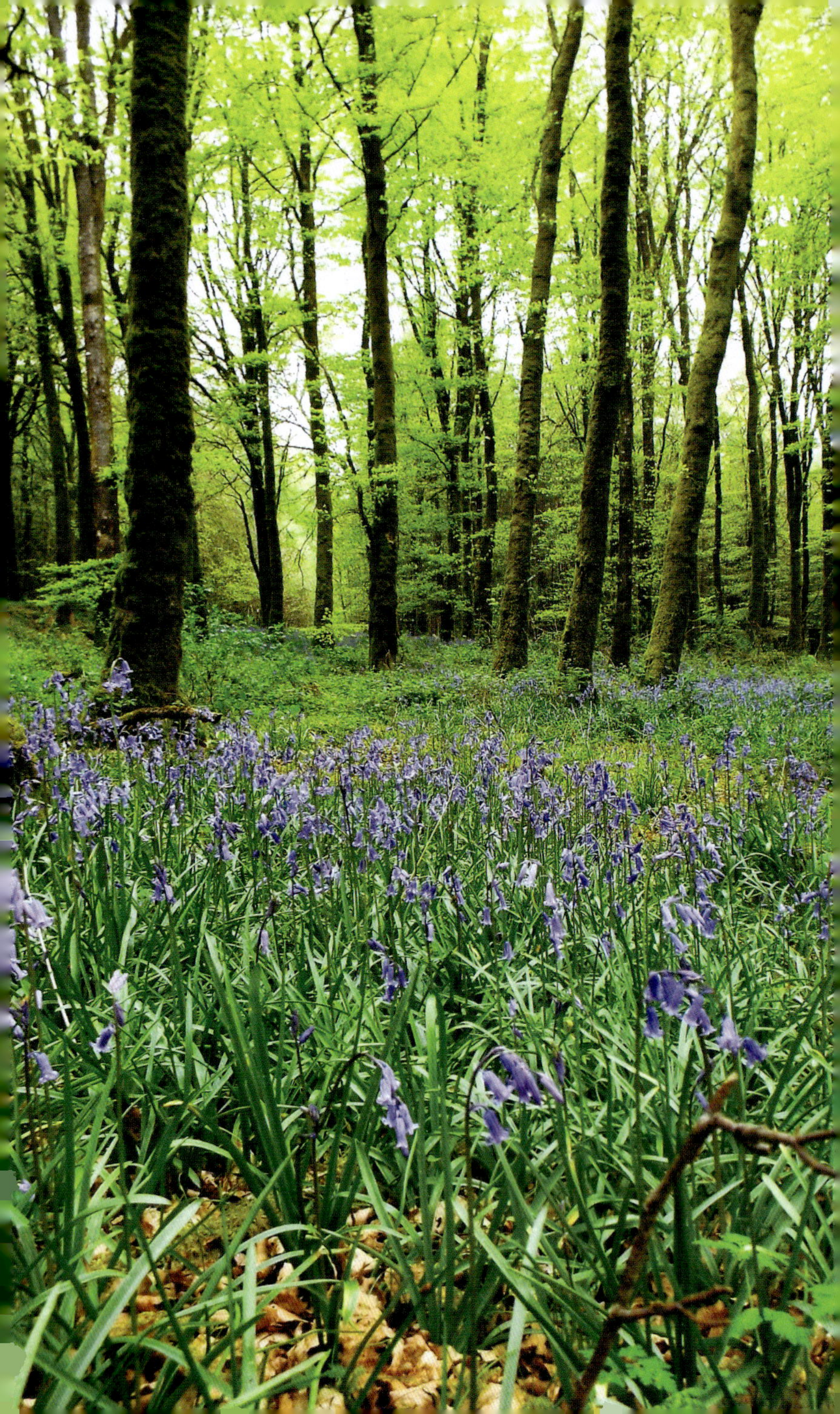

33

Mullaghmeen Forest
Co. Westmeath

A magical hike through the largest beech forest in Europe

Mullaghmeen Forest is the largest planted beech forest in Europe and includes the high point of Co. Westmeath. The summit reveals beautiful views north across Lough Sheelin and into the neighbouring county of Cavan. On a sunny day, the dappled light through the beech leaves is mesmerising, while in late spring the forest floor is covered with a carpet of bluebells and other wild flowers. There are good paths throughout. Hiking boots recommended.

LENGTH:	TIME:	DIFFICULTY:	OSI MAP NO:
3.5–7.5km	1–3 hours	Easy–Medium	41

◎ NEED TO KNOW

From Mullingar, take the road to Castlepollard. Take the first left at the roundabout and then take the first turn to the right. At the next junction take the road to the left onto Water Street. Continue on this road for 8km. There are a few sharp bends on this road. After 8km, arrive at the forest entrance on your left. Drive down the narrow road where there is free parking.

Coordinates: 53.749 -7.2737

◄ Bluebells in spring

The Hike

1 From the car park, head up the main wide path. There is an information board that will tell you about Mullaghmeen and the different walks available. For the first part of this hike you will follow the white path. The path rises gently and there are banks alongside the path for children to explore. At 210m, ignore a path to the left and keep going.

2 After a further 200m, turn left and enjoy a beautiful path that winds up through the trees. If you are here in late spring, you will see hosts of stunning bluebells.

3 After just over 1km the path descends and rejoins the main path you left earlier. Near this point is a signed arboretum of native trees and exploring these is well worth the small detour. When you emerge again, turn right and continue up the broad path.

Winter colours ▲

4   At 1.6km, turn left and follow the signs for the white walk. Continue
    on this path past a strange hollow in the ground on your left. After
    another 500m, the path turns sharply to the left, still following the
    white walk signs. At 2.7km you will get a view of the Hill of Mael to
    your left and the path starts uphill.

5   After another kilometre, reach a junction of paths. Continue
    straight ahead directly to the fence in front of you. You should
    get a view of Lough Sheelin at this stage. At the fence turn right
    as the path climbs quite steeply uphill for four hundred metres.

6   At 4.1km, arrive at the main path again and turn left. Very shortly
    after, turn left again. There are a few trunks of old trees that are
    fun for children to try to balance on. Continue down this path
    for 400m. You now have an option to continue straight on the
    white walk or turn sharply uphill on the blue path to your right.

For this walk, we take the path to the right and follow the blue walk signs.

7 This path rises sharply. At 5km, reach the summit of Mullaghmeen, the highest point in Co. Westmeath, although it is the lowest county top in Ireland. Enjoy the views towards Lough Sheelin and across the midlands. Unfortunately, every year the views are being increasingly blocked out by the growing trees.

8 Continue straight down the hill, dropping sharply into the woods. Follow the path for another kilometre to a crossroads and continue straight ahead.

9 This is a very enjoyable section of the woods with its ups and downs and play of light and shadow. Pass an old booley hut, where shepherds used to take refuge in bygone years.

10 At 6.7km, come to a path and turn left.

11 After a couple of hundred metres, turn right at the next path. If you have time, turn left at this point and follow the path uphill, where you will come across a sign for the Famine fields on the right. However, if you are not interested, follow the path downhill and back towards the car park.

12 As you reach the car park, the forest opens for a brief view to the east where you can see Slievena Calliagh (Hill of the Witch) in the distance. This is the highest point in Co. Meath. There are tables for a picnic at the car park.

Easy 3.5km hike

At the noticeboard in the car park, follow the signs for the red walk that are well posted within the forest. Start by heading up the main wide path beside the noticeboard.

Myths and legends

The forest and surrounding land is shrouded in mythological lore. Queen Maeve brought her fearsome Connacht army through these lands on her way to acquire the Brown Bull of Cooley. In addition, the nearby town of Castlepollard bears the Irish name of Cionn Toirc and is named after a boar that gored Diarmuid when he was out hunting with Fionn Mac Cumhaill.

The nearby Slieve na Calliagh – Hill of the Witch – is associated with An Cailleach Béara – the divine crone of Béara. It is said that she tried to attain rule over the land by jumping from one hill to the next, dropping stones (the cairns across the landscape) as she went. She needed to complete this for four mountains but could only manage three before falling to her death. It is said that she is buried on Slieve na Calliagh beneath the Hag's Chair at Cairn T, the biggest passage tomb on the hill. Legend has it that the Cailleach may grant your wishes if you sit on her chair as the sun sets. On the spring and autumnal equinoxes, the beams of the rising sun shine down the passage of Cairn T, highlighting the megalithic art within.

The dark and deep woods ▼

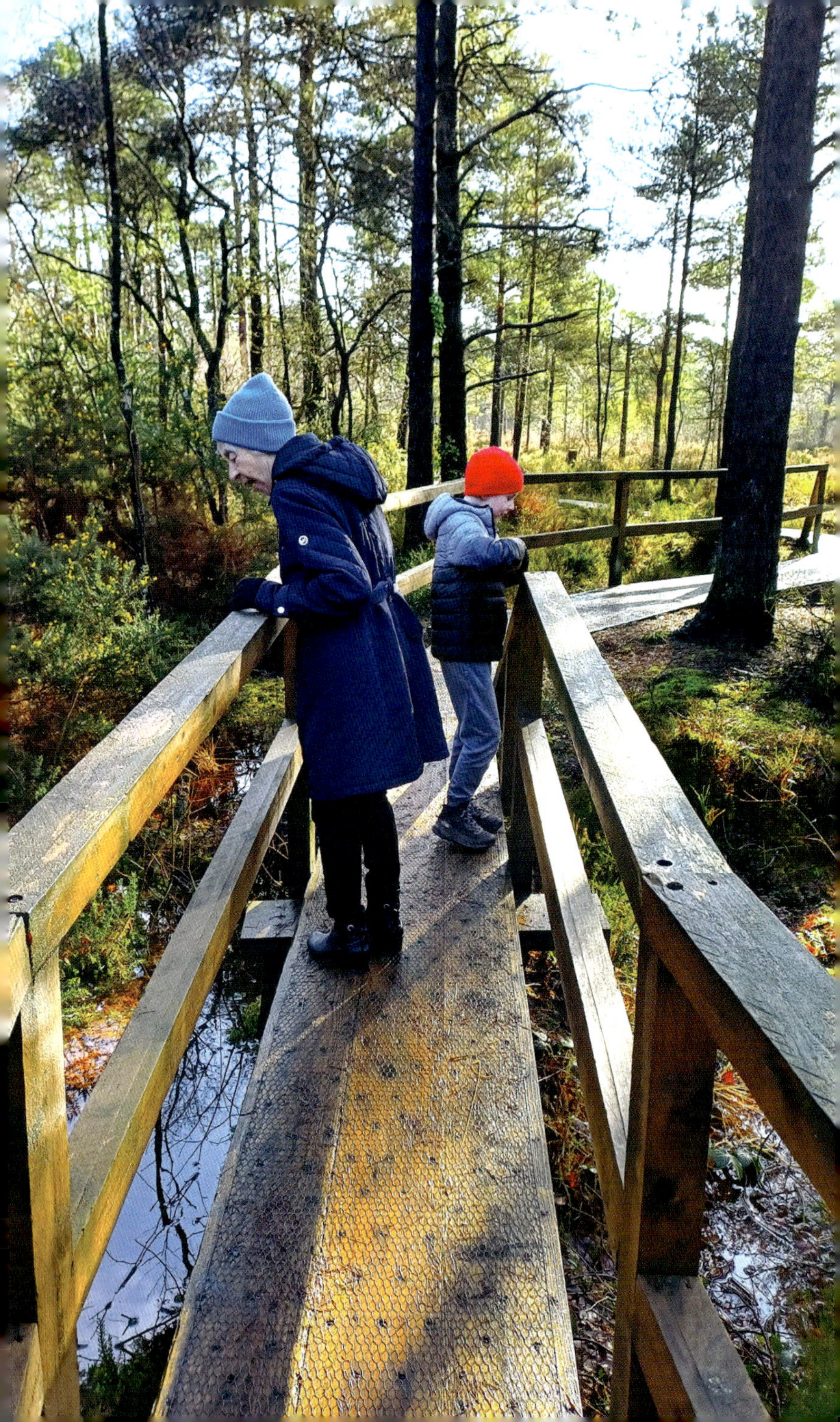

34

Lakeland Trails
Co. Westmeath

These are neighbouring trails on or near the shores of Lough Owel in Co. Westmeath. They include woodland, bog and shoreline walks and each can be completed in about 1–2 hours.

TRAIL 1 Captain's Hill

A sublime view across Lough Owel

An exciting short walk to the summit of Captain's Hill overlooking Lough Owel. The lakeshore, surrounding rolling hills and railway line can also be explored. Hiking boots recommended.

LENGTH:	TIME:	DIFFICULTY:	OSI MAP NO:
1–3km	Up to 1 hour	Easy	41

⊙ NEED TO KNOW

From Mullingar, take the N4 north towards Longford. Just before 3km and with Lough Owel on your left, turn left and park at a layby on your right. Do not block the little road and park with consideration for others.

Coordinates: 53.5677 -7.3618

The Hike

1 From the layby, head up the small road beside you. After 50m, reach a pedestrian railway crossing. Cross safely to the other side and continue up the stony track.

2 After 200m, cross a stile over a fence on your right. Follow the narrow path through the bushes and it will open out into a field. Go through the farm gate and follow the rough path to the top of the hill.

3 Arrive at the summit of Captain's Hill and enjoy stunning views over Lough Owel and surrounding lands. You have an option at this point for further exploration by continuing down the hill on the far side and making your way across the field and down to the lake. When ready, retrace your steps to your car. Why not go to the nearby intriguing Scragh Bog next?

Sunset over Church Island, Lough Owel ▶

TRAIL 2 Scragh Bog

A rare journey from fen to bog

A short and intriguing ramble through one of Ireland's rarest environments – a fen habitat. Observe the transition from fen to bog and find unusual trees and vegetation. Good paths and boardwalks throughout. Hiking boots not necessary.

LENGTH:	TIME:	DIFFICULTY:	OSI MAP NO:
3km	Up to 1 hour	Easy	41

⊙ NEED TO KNOW

From Mullingar, take the N4 north toward Longford. Just before 3km, with Lough Owel on your left, turn right up a narrow road. After almost a kilometre, the entrance to Scragh Bog is on your left. Parking is free.

Coordinates: 53.5719 -7.3498

The Hike

1 From the car park, head through the wooden gate on your left. Proceed down the woodland trail. Children may enjoy exploring off the main track.

2 After 500m, you will see a path into the forest on your right. It is worth exploring this. There is a natural amphitheatre here where wigwams and

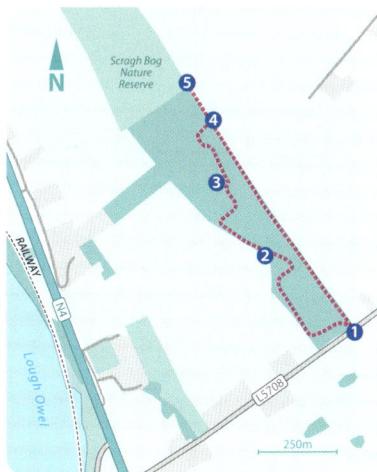

the scorpion tree await you. When ready, rejoin the path, which leads onto a boardwalk. The landscape changes into fen and bog here.

3 At 1.2km, meet a junction of paths. Turn left at this point, where there is an information post about birch trees. After a couple of hundred metres there is a small detour to a seating area where it is pleasant to sit and listen to the sounds of the bog. When ready, rejoin the path you were on.

4 After another 200m, the boardwalk ends. Turn left here and go to the end of the path, where there are some steps up to a viewing platform.

5 Enjoy the views over the bog. When ready, walk straight down the path in front of you. After 600m, reach an information board about the formation of Scragh Bog. When ready, proceed past the gate and go straight ahead. After another 600m, arrive back at your car. Why not go on to the beautiful Ballinafid Lake and woods next?

Exploring swampy Scragh Bog ▲

Enjoying Ballinafid Woods ▲

TRAIL 3 Ballinafid Lake and woods

An enchanting hike through a fen and woods

A short and restful trail through a diverse habitat showing the transition from open lake and reed swamp to fen wetland and bog. Paths and boardwalks throughout. Hiking boots not necessary.

LENGTH:	TIME:	DIFFICULTY:	OSI MAP NO:
3km	Up to 1 hour	Easy	41

⊙ NEED TO KNOW

From Mullingar, take the N4 north towards Longford. After 3km, pass the Lough Owel viewing point on your left. After another kilometre, turn left towards Ballinafid Lake and take the next left into the free car park.

Coordinates: 53.5958 -7.3834

The Hike

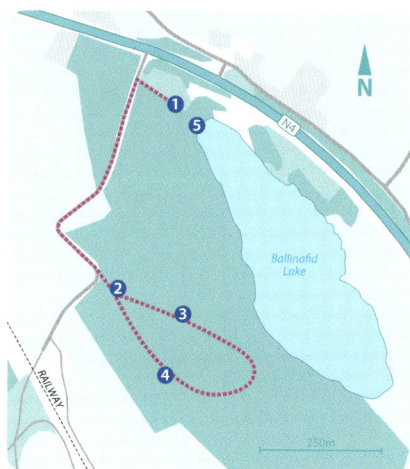

1 Head to the car park entrance towards the road. Turn left and walk along the quiet country road.

2 After 500m, you will see the entrance to the forest on your left. There is a gate with an emergency access sign. Go past the sign, using the stile on your right. There is an information board here about Ballinafid.

3 After 120m, turn left onto the boardwalk for a restful walk through the woods. After 400m, there is a small path to your left that you can take for a closer look at the lake.

4 At 1.6km, come to the end of the boardwalk. An apparently shallow river/stream prevents you proceeding further. Do not attempt to cross this body of water as it is deeper than it looks. When ready, head straight up the path, which will lead you back towards the entrance. Then retrace your steps on the road to the car park.

5 At the back left of the car park, a short path brings you out onto Ballinafid Lake. Here you can enjoy the rushes and lily pads and with a bit of luck, some swans will grace you with their presence. Why not go next to the beautiful wild woods of Kilpatrick, set on the shore of Lough Owel?

Kilpatrick Woods

A charming woodland trail beside the lakeshore

Kilpatrick Woods is a beautiful wild woodland on the shores of Lough Owel. The dramatic shoreline changes throughout the year. In warmer weather, people swim in the lake. There are a number of unusual trees here that need to be seen to be believed and plenty of places for children to explore and use their imagination. Some paths are well defined and others are more informal. Hiking boots recommended.

LENGTH:	TIME:	DIFFICULTY:	OSI MAP NO:
3km	Up to 1 hour	Easy	41

⊙ NEED TO KNOW

From Mullingar, take the N4 north towards Longford. After 5km, take a left onto the L5818. After 500m, park in the free car park on your left.

Coordinates: 53.6008 -7.4085

Hanging about in Kilpatrick ▲

The Hike

1 From the car park, head down the track past the black and yellow barrier. Follow the path downhill and you will soon get your first glimpse of Lough Owel below you.

2 After 200m, turn left.

3 After another 150m, turn right as the path winds downhill into the woods. Turn right where the path approaches the lake. There is a lovely area here with a rope swing and trees with exposed roots. It is also a good spot for skimming stones. Depending on the water level of Lough Owel, walk right along the lakeshore or just inside the shoreline among the trees. There is also a broader path here to the right, but it is less interesting.

4 After continuing right by the shoreline, arrive into an open area with a bench. This is a spot that people use for swimming in the lake. Pass through this area and continue right along the informal path through the trees. Along the way you will encounter many otherworldly trees that droop over the lakeshore with exposed, upturned roots.

5 At 1.9km, reach a fence that marks the end of the woods. There is a small stream here that makes its way down to the lake. When ready, retrace your steps to the bench (point 4). At this point, turn left and follow the path all the way straight back to the car park, ignoring any offshoots to the right.

Skimming stones on Lough Owel ▲

Myths and legends

The huge lake of Lough Owel provides Mullingar with its drinking water and has many stories attached to it. One tells of an old woman from the west of Ireland who came to Mullingar. On entering one of the houses, she burned her shin on a hot pot. She was so angry that she scolded the landlady for leaving the pot on the ground, and she decided to take revenge. The old woman was actually a cailleach (witch) and in her fury picked up a lake and tied it up in her shawl. She threw the lake into the centre of Mullingar and soon the waters covered all the houses and formed the present site of Lough Owel. When the cailleach saw her destruction, she was saddened and a tear fell from her eye, creating nearby Ballinafid Lake.

You are not far here from Lough Derravaragh, where the Children of Lir resided for their first three hundred years after being turned into swans by their malevolent stepmother, Aoife.

35

Croghan Hill
Co. Offaly

A wonderful short hike to an ancient site of ritual sacrifice

Croghan Hill is the remains of an extinct volcano and the site of an ancient burial ground associated with ritual sacrifice. Though only 232m high, it commands extensive views of the surrounding midland counties and across the low-lying expanse of the Bog of Allen. The body of Old Croghan Man was found here in 2003 and he has been dated back to the Iron Age. There are good paths and signs, but parts can become muddy in winter months. Hiking boots recommended.

LENGTH:	TIME:	DIFFICULTY:	OSI MAP NO:
2.5km	Up to 1 hour	Easy	48

⊙ NEED TO KNOW

From Rhode in Co. Offaly, take the L1010 west for 6km. Park in the village of Croghan with consideration for others.
Coordinates: 53.3408 -7.2794 (Please note: If you put Croghan Hill into Google Maps you will be brought to a hinterland 25km away from where you need. Therefore the instructions here are essential).

◂ The summit of Croghan Hill

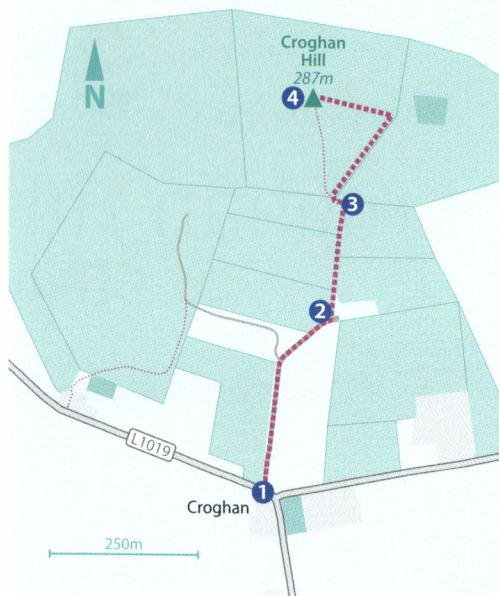

The Hike

1 Park in the village and head up a tarmac lane beside a white house. There is an information board, beside which you should start. Follow the signs. After 300m, ignore signs for 'Croghan Hill Mass' and keep going up the tarmac lane.

2 Soon after, come to a tree in the middle of the lane. Keep up to your left and pass through a metal gate, remembering to close it behind you. Follow the steep yet charming path uphill and pass through a wooden gate.

3 At 640m, pass through another wooden gate and turn left. Soon after, follow the signs and turn right. You will now meet two paths, either of which will bring you to the summit of Croghan Hill.

A view from Croghan Hill across the Bog of Allen ▲

For this hike, take the path to the right and follow it until you see an old graveyard on your right. Then turn left and ascend the hill to the summit.

4 After 1km arrive at the summit and enjoy panoramic views all across the midlands, the Bog of Allen and the Slieve Bloom Mountains. The summit trig pillar is beautifully engraved. When ready, descend the hill and visit the evocative Bishop Mac Caille's graveyard. Retrace your steps back to your car.

Myths and legends

People have journeyed to the ancient burial mound on Croghan Hill for millennia. Seen from the nearby sacred Hill of Uisneach, the midwinter sun rises over Croghan Hill. The hill is also known as Brí Éile, meaning 'prayer' or 'praise', said to be a goddess who dwells within the mound. The Boyhood Deeds of Fionn recounts that the men of Ireland went to the hilltop to woo Brí Éile at Samhain each year and that someone was always mysteriously killed to mark the occasion. In 2003, peatworkers found a body in the nearby bogland who has been named Old Croghan Man. Radiocarbon dating shows that Old Croghan Man was actually a young man in his twenties who lived between 362 and 175 BCE, during the height of the Celtic Iron Age. He is believed by experts to have been ritually sacrificed. The body is now in the National Museum of Ireland. It was so well preserved that it was possible to test for fingerprints. Old Croghan Man shows evidence of overkill: he has a defensive wound on his upper left arm that may have been caused when he tried to protect himself; he had been bound by hazel branches threaded through holes in his upper arms, was stabbed in the chest, struck in the neck, decapitated and cut in half. Researchers have found evidence that indicates wealth and special status. He stood almost six-and-a-half feet tall, exceptionally tall for a man of his time (or any time). Analysis of his hair and nails showed that he regularly ate meat, an expensive luxury. In contrast, his last supper was buttermilk and cereals, believed to be a ritual meal.

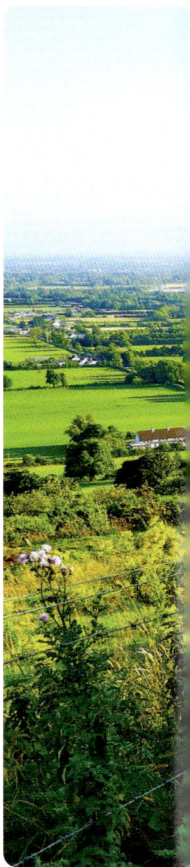

Descending through the gorse from Croghan Hill ▲

The cutting of his nipples may signify that he was a failed king or a failed candidate for kingship. Sucking a king's nipples was a sign of submission in ancient Ireland; therefore cutting them off would have rendered him incapable of kingship. Experts suggest that his body may have served as an offering to the goddess of the land to whom the king was wed in his inauguration ceremony. Therefore, the goddess was not only one of land and fertility but also one of sovereignty, war and death.

36

Glenbarrow Loop
Slieve Blooms,
Co. Laois/Co. Offaly

THE MIDLANDS // THE 50 BEST FAMILY HIKES IN IRELAND

A captivating trek by the source of the River Barrow

Glenbarrow is the source of the River Barrow, the second longest river in Ireland. It is one of the most scenic parts of the Slieve Bloom Mountains with its waterfalls, rivers, woodlands and panoramic views across the midlands of Ireland. Paths are generally in good condition but can become muddy in winter months. While the hike is suitable all year round, it is at its best in early spring when waterfalls and streams seem to gush from everywhere! Hiking boots essential.

LENGTH:	TIME:	DIFFICULTY:	OSI MAP NO:
3–14km	1.5–5 hours	Easy–Experienced	54

⊚ NEED TO KNOW

From Dublin, take the M50 to junction 9 and take the N7 and then M7 to junction 15. Pass through Emo and Mountmellick on the R422. As you leave the village of Rosenallis, keep to the left up the hill and after 1.5km turn right. After a further 2km, turn left and follow the road to the end, where there is a large free car park.

Coordinates: 53.12298 -7.45134

◄ Site of the Old Mill on the River Barrow

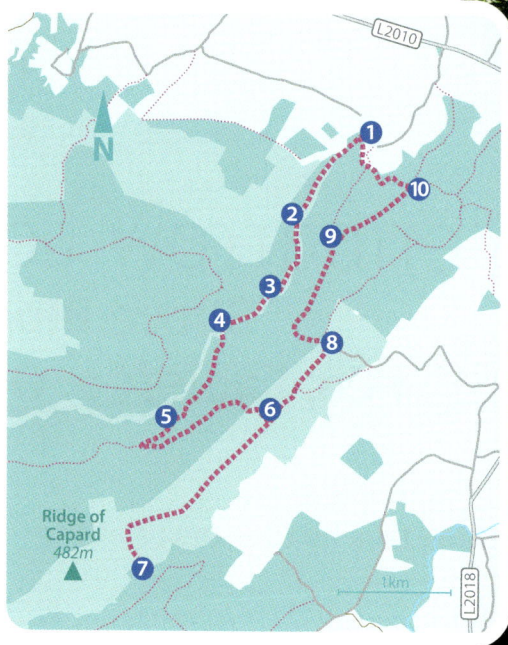

The Hike

1   From the car park, head past the coffee station and keep to the
    right-hand path, which goes downhill. The path winds left as you
    pass through a fence. There is a waterfall near the start of the path
    on the left that you can make your way up to if you want. After
    exploring, continue on the path for 1km and arrive at a small hut
    where large stone slabs stretch out into the River Barrow, which
    children might like to explore up close. There are also 'fairy show-
    ers' and a climb up through the 'altar' on the way to the waterfall.
    After another 400m, arrive at the beautiful Clamp Waterfall. For the
    easy 3km option, simply retrace the path to the car park.

2   For the medium (10km) and experienced (14km) options, follow
    the path upwards along the edge of the waterfall and along the
    narrow path high above the river gorge.

Having fun on the trees ▲

3 At 2.5km, arrive at a junction of paths. For this route, cross the steps straight in front of you into the forest. Do not follow the blue arrow up the steep steps to the left. Keep to the rough path which runs along the tree line closest to the river. After 300m, continue on the path over a stream and keep to the rough path along the tree line. Follow this for 200m until you come to the end of the forest. Ignore the slight path to the left, go straight to the end of the trees and turn right. You will now emerge into the light close to where a charming bridge for the Slieve Bloom Way crosses the Barrow. Do not cross this bridge (even though it looks very inviting), but keep to the left as the path winds through small trees and vegetation, all the while serenaded by the sound of the Barrow beside you.

4 At 4.5km, watch out for a charming place to rest close to the Barrow at the site of the Old Gallagher Mill before continuing uphill to a large forest track.

5 After 200m, arrive at a large track and turn to the right. At 4.9km, meet another junction of tracks and turn left onto the wide uphill track that passes by the ruins of the Cones deserted village. The last person to live here was Ann Clear, who left in 1962. Continue uphill, which can be slightly tough going, and after 1km you will reach the top. Turn right onto the boardwalk.

6 After 200m, meet a roundabout area on the boardwalk. Turn right for the Stony Man option here. (Turn left if you do not wish to visit the Stony Man and continue as per the instructions at the asterisk below in point 7. The hike without the Stony Man is 10km in total.) The Stony Man path has some boardwalk but can be very boggy in places after wet weather. It takes 2km to get to the Stony Man, so this detour would add 4km to your journey, bringing your hike to 14km in total. The trek to the Stony Man is evocative of times past when people walked to the high uphill cairn to resolve long-standing problems.

7 At just over 8km, arrive at the large stone cairn referred to as the Stony Man. It is well worth spending some time here letting the atmosphere seep into you and enjoying incredible views across the midlands. When ready, return to the roundabout indicated in point 6 above and go straight through it. After half a kilometre, exit the boardwalk and turn right down the path. *After only 100m, turn left back onto the boardwalk and ignore the path that continues to the right. After another 400m, turn right and aim for the Ridge of Capard viewing point at the top. There are amazing views of the midlands, Wicklow Mountains and Cuilcagh Mountains. When ready, descend the steps and enter the car park at the Ridge of Capard.

8 From the car park, turn left, follow the tarmac road downhill and enter the forest in front of you. Follow the path downhill through a wonderfully atmospheric part of the forest. This ends all too soon and you will emerge onto a wide forest track and crossroads.

Heading to the Metal Man on the Ridge of Capard boardwalk ▲

Turn right and follow the wide track. This section can be a little hard going for younger children so it might be a good idea to introduce games such as I Spy or Animal, Vegetable or Mineral or tell some stories or fairy tales. That packet of sweets might also come in handy!

9 After 1km on this track, there is an option to follow the path straight ahead down to the car park. However, we recommend one final highlight if you have the energy. Take the track to the right at the yellow and blue signs and follow the signs uphill.

10 After 9/13km, there is a small path marked with a blue arrow to the left, which brings you on an exhilarating boardwalk down through the dark forest. This provides a memorable ending to your adventure as you emerge from the forest after 800m and follow the path back to the car park.

Myths and legends

Known as Sliabh Bladhma in Irish, the Slieve Blooms are named after the mythical Connacht warrior Bladhma. Legend has it that a battle was fought here in 3000 BCE and Bladhma was killed and a cairn of stones – the Giant's Grave – was raised to his memory. Bladhma is also the Irish word for 'of flames' and so the Slieve Blooms can be translated as the Mountains of Flames. This name comes alive if you traverse the Ridge of Capard as the sun blazes upon it. It is also among the Slieve Blooms that the great Fenian warrior Fionn Mac Cumhaill spent his early years. Following the death of his father, Cumall, at the hands of the fearsome Goll Mac Morna, Fionn's mother, Muirne, took her child and herself into hiding. To give Fionn the best chance of survival, Muirne left him with two druidess-warriors known as Bodhmall and Liath Luachra, or the Grey One of Luachair. These two warrior women could survive in the wild and travelled all around the Slieve Blooms teaching Fionn all the skills he would need to one day take revenge on Goll Mac Morna and become leader of the Fianna.

A view across the Ridge of Capard to the Stony Man ▲

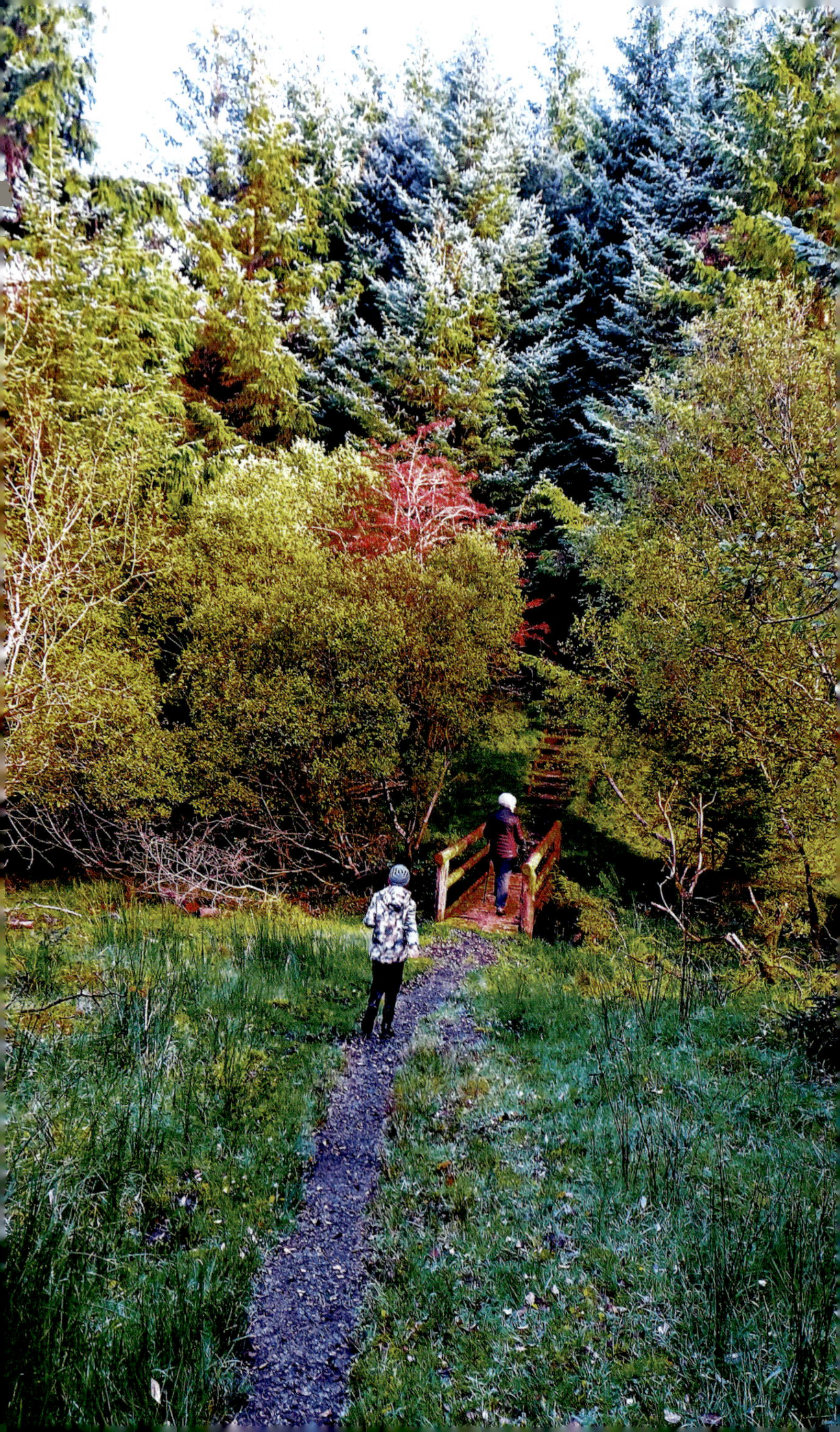

37

Giant's Grave to Silver River gorge
Co. Laois/Co. Offaly

The final resting place of the warrior Bladhma

This fascinating hike features woodland, evocative old lanes, the Giant's Grave (remains of a megalithic tomb where the warrior Bladhma is said to be buried), open mountainside and the exhilarating Silver River gorge. There are expansive views across the midlands, while other sections of the walk provide a more immersive experience. We also include two shorter 5km options that provide worthwhile alternatives. There are good paths throughout, although parts can become muddy in wet weather. Hiking boots essential.

LENGTH:	TIME:	DIFFICULTY:	OSI MAP NO:
5–13km	1.5–4 hours	Easy–Experienced	54

⊙ NEED TO KNOW

From Dublin, take the M50 to junction 9, then take the N7 and then M7 to junction 15. Pass through Emo and Mountmellick on the R422. Drive through the villages of Rosenallis and Clonaslee until you reach Cadamstown. Turn left in the village to the trailhead car park (no charge). At the car park, there is a barrel containing walking sticks that you can use and return. There are picnic tables that have lamps on them just in case you arrive back late from your walk!

Coordinates: 53.1268 -7.6601

◄ Crossing the bridge to the Giant's Grave

The Hike

1 From the car park, head up the little road between two houses. Follow the signs for the Giant's Grave Megalithic Tomb Loop Walk and red arrows. You will follow these signs throughout the hike.

2 After 750m, turn right off the road. This is Paul's Lane – a wonderfully leafy and evocative lane with charming groves alongside it. After 1.3km, keep to your left, following the red arrows and the Slieve Bloom Way yellow walking person. However, if you want an easier 5km option, take the right for Paul's Lane Loop – see more instructions below for this option.

3 If staying on the longer 13km hike, after a further 600m and soon after crossing a stile, follow the arrows on a post going left across a field. After 200m, cross a stile and enter a lane. Do not cross the next stile, which would take you on the Slieve Bloom Way. Instead, go left down the lane.

The Giant's Grave, Slieve Bloom Mountains ▲

4   After following the road for 600m, arrive at a T-junction. Turn right here and follow the road, which then turns into a forest track. Keep following the red arrows. This can be a long part of the walk for children. We have found that a game of kicking a stone down the road, passing to each other while trying to stop it falling off the edge of the track, is a good way to pass the time!

5   At 3.7km, turn left onto a grassy path off the main track. There are signs for the Giant's Grave Loop. This is a charming path that passes over a wooden bridge and stream and enters a dark and atmospheric forest entrance to the Giant's Grave. There is an information board and some picnic tables at the Giant's Grave, where the warrior Bladhma is said to be buried. When ready, continue past the site and meet a large track. Turn right here and follow the red arrows again. At 4.5km, keep to your left and follow the track uphill. After 500m, turn right at a crossroads and follow

the red arrows again downhill. At 5.2km, turn left at the next junction following the red arrows. This is a tricky section in terms of navigation so make sure to follow the instructions.

6 At 6.4km, pass through a metal gate and arrive at the top of Spinc Mountain. There are wide-ranging views of the midlands plain, including nearby Wolftrap Mountain. Continue down the mountain and at 7.8km ignore a track to the left and continue straight ahead following the red arrows.

7 At 8.7km, take a narrow path to your left. This is a delightful downhill trail which can be very boggy in winter. After 400m, turn left on the next track you meet and follow the arrows. Follow this lane downhill and pass through a gate. Arrive at Purcell's Brook. Follow the path to the right, pass by a beautiful weir and then embark on an exhilarating 2km forest walk along the edge of the Silver River gorge. This is a section not to be missed and it has a couple of viewing points that are well worth stopping at.

8 Emerge from the woods and turn left down a field path. Pass through a gate at the end, and at the end of the lane turn left down the road back to your car. Picnic in the shaded grove with the sound of the Silver River filling your senses.

Easy 5km option 1: Silver River gorge

From the car park, go up the road and find a farm lane on your right. Cross a field and after a few hundred metres, find a stile on your right that leads down to the exciting Silver River gorge. Follow the path to Purcell's Brook/weir (point 7 above). Retrace your steps to the car park.

Easy 5km option 2: Paul's Lane Loop

Follow the instructions above to point 2 but take the right for Paul's Lane Loop. Follow the blue arrows throughout until you come to Purcell's Brook and the forest walk along the Silver River gorge. Then follow the instructions for point 8 above.

Myths and legends

According to legend, the Giant's Grave is the resting place of the warrior Bladhma. Bladhma came from west of the Shannon, where he killed an important chieftain called Bregmeal. He fled to the Slieve Bloom Mountains but was slain in a revenge killing. The tomb is Neolithic, dating from between 4000 and 2500 BCE. During this period people were buried in the foetal position.

The weir on the Silver River ▲

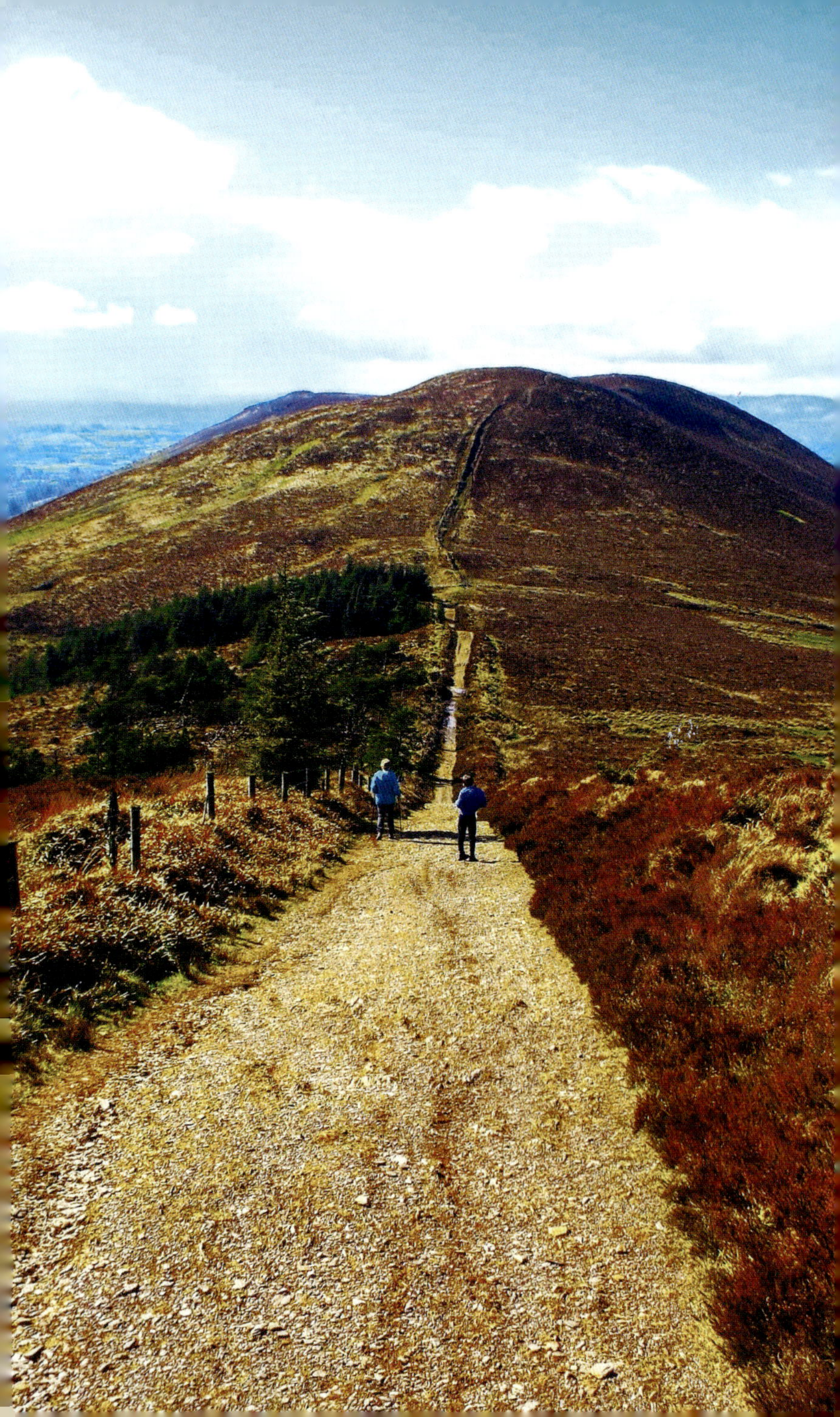

38

Silvermines Ridge
Co. Tipperary

A wonderful hike along the ridge of the world

Given its midlands position, the Silvermines Ridge walk offers tremendous views across Ireland, including Keeper's Hill, Clare Hills, the Galtee and Blackstairs mountains, the midlands plain, the River Shannon, Lough Derg and, in the far distance, the unmistakably angular MacGillycuddy's Reeks in Kerry. Paths are well defined but can be boggy in parts in wet weather. Hiking boots recommended.

LENGTH:	TIME:	DIFFICULTY:	OSI MAP NO:
6km	2–3 hours	Medium	59

⊙ NEED TO KNOW

From Nenagh, take the R500 south. After just over 6km, turn left onto the R499. After 200m, take a small turn to the right for Knockanroe car park. Follow the road for almost 3km until you arrive in Knockanroe car park. Parking is free.

Coordinates: 52.7759 -8.2313

The Hike

1 From the car park, head along the stony track that has a low yellow-and-black barrier across it.

2 After 250m, arrive at a slightly disjointed crossroads of paths. You should take the path that goes straight in front of you, i.e. a slight right and then left. This path will then climb.

3 After 1km, keep following the path as it swings more to the right and brings you up onto the Silvermines Ridge. Some incredible views emerge here. Hike across the ridge. There are a number of steep drops and climbs, but it is worth the effort to reach the Silvermines West Top.

4 At 3km, arrive at the summit of Silvermines West Top. The views are stunning and on a clear day you can see the River Shannon and MacGillycuddy's Reeks to the west and the Blackstairs Mountains to the east. It is possible to continue on the ridge further if you want a longer hike. Just follow the path in front of you until you wish to turn back. After a well-deserved break, retrace your steps to the car park.

A view of the midlands plain ▶

Silvermine Mountains
W Top *489m*

4

Silvermine Mountains
E Top *479m*

3

2

1

N

Silvermine Mountains
Far E Top *410m*

L2116

500m

Myths and legends

The oldest records of silver being mined here date from the thirteenth century, and the latest mines were closed in the 1990s. The original Irish name of the Silvermines is Béal Átha Gabhann, which means 'the river mouth of the ford of the blacksmith'. This indicates that the area is long associated with different forms of mining. Nearby Keeper Hill is also known as Sliabh Coimeálta and it is here that Sadb, daughter of Conn of the Hundred Battles, raised her two children, Éogan and Indderb, after they had been rejected by their father, Ailill Ólom, King of Munster.

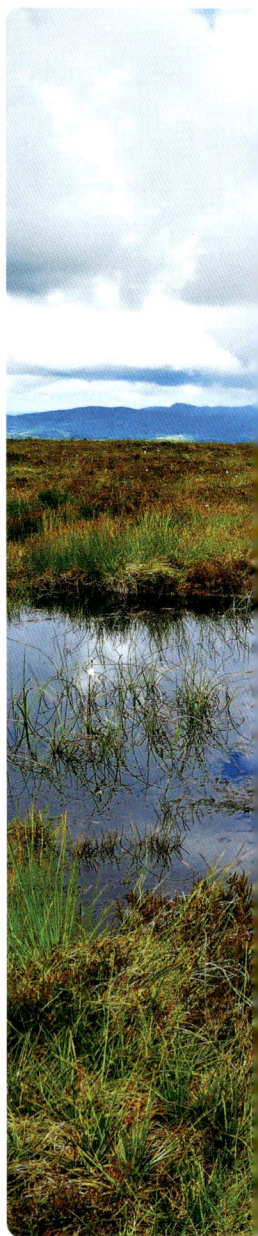

Boghole on the summit of Silvermines West Top ▲

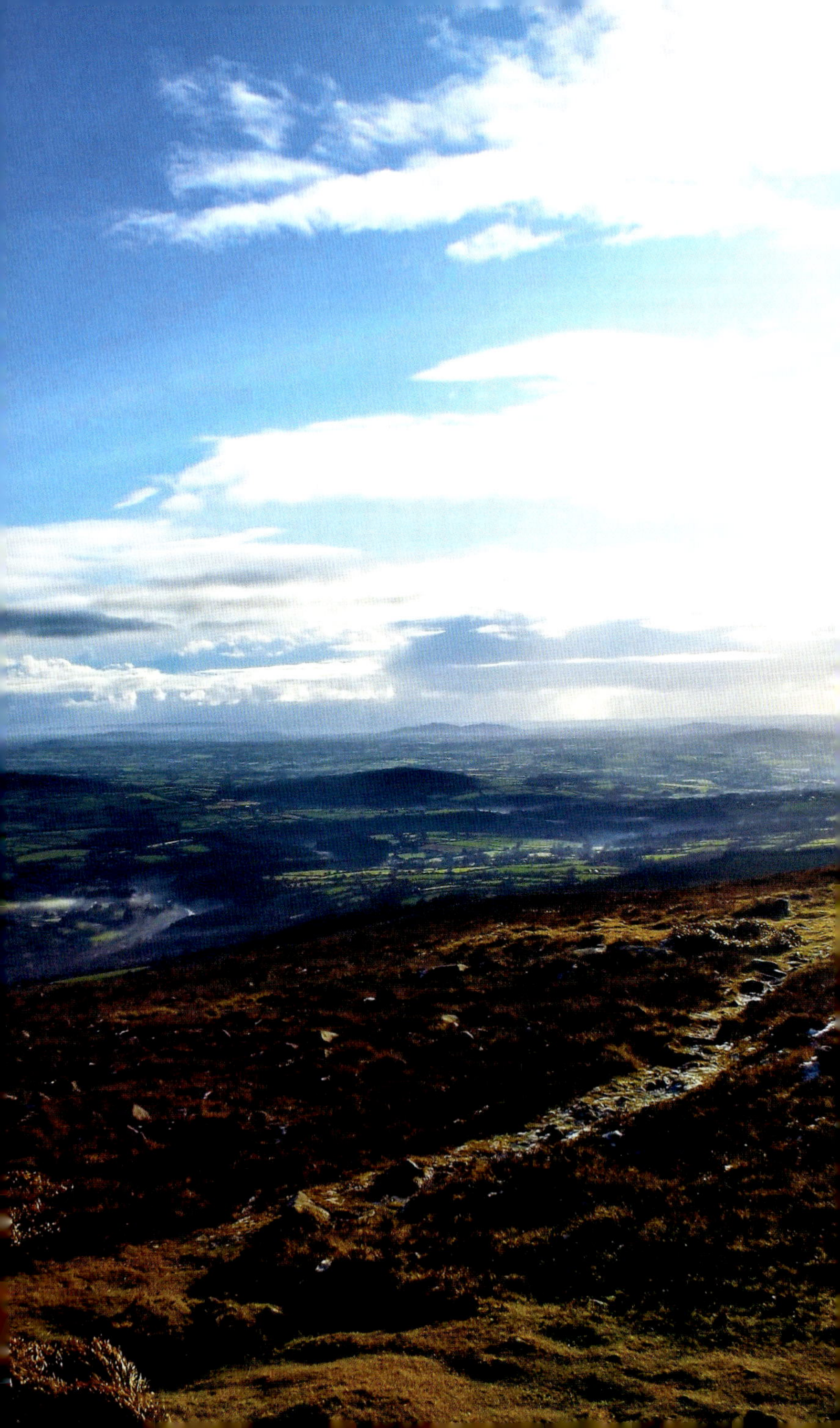

39

Brandon Hill
Co. Kilkenny

A wonderful hike to Kilkenny's high point

Brandon Hill is Kilkenny's highest point (515m) and is situated near the picturesque villages of Graiguenamanagh and Inistioge. This walk takes a little time to reveal its views, but once you enter the forest and reach the open mountainside, it really gets going! There is a large cross and Neolithic cairn at the summit. From here, enjoy spectacular views of the nearby Blackstairs Mountains (including Mount Leinster), as well as the Comeraghs, Galtee and Knockmealdown Mountains. Trace the ribbon of the River Barrow as it meanders through Carlow and Wexford down to Waterford Harbour. Good paths and signs throughout. Hiking boots recommended.

LENGTH:	TIME:	DIFFICULTY:	OSI MAP NO:
7.5km	2–3 hours	Medium	68

EASTWEST MAPPING: Blackstairs, Mount Leinster & The Barrow Valley

⊙ NEED TO KNOW

From Graiguenamanagh, take the R705 south. After 600m, turn right onto L4209. Follow this road for 3km and then turn left. After 1km, arrive at Raheendonore Car Park B on your right. This is a free car park with a picnic table and information board.

Coordinates: 52.5208 -6.9957

◄ A view from Brandon Hill towards the Atlantic

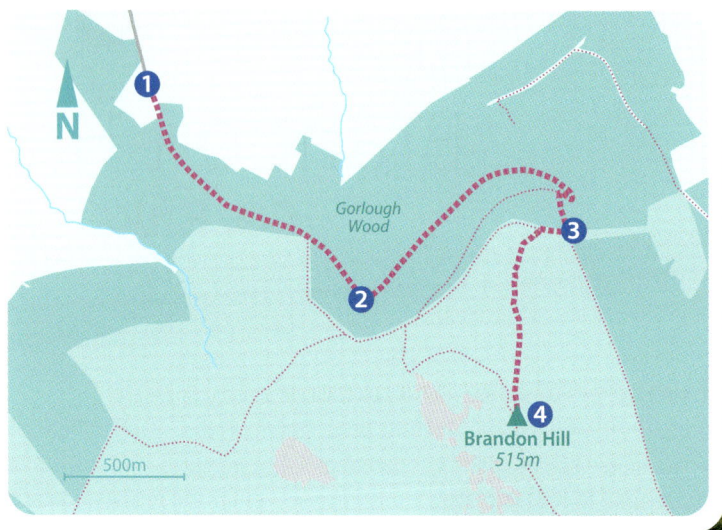

Gorlough
Wood

Brandon Hill
515m

500m

N

The Hike

1   Exit the car park, turn right and pass by a yellow and black barrier. After 500m, keep straight ahead and see a sign for Brandon Hill Summit Walk. Follow these signs throughout the hike.

2   After 1.5km, meet a junction of paths. Keep to your right and continue uphill, following the signs. At 2.3km, arrive at a clearance and enter the forest in front of you.

3   At 2.5km, cross over a metal gate and turn immediately right, following the signs. You are now on a stony path. One hundred metres later, you have an option to continue straight up the path for a gentler climb or turn left for a shorter, steeper path to the summit. We recommend taking the steeper, left path to the summit as it brings you through turf and heather.

Enjoying Brandon Hill summit ▲

4 At 3.7km, reach the summit, which has a large cross, cairn and circular information point. It also has a useful audio point that you can scan with your phone and listen as it tells you about Brandon Hill. From the summit, you can see the River Barrow as it meanders down to Waterford Harbour and the Atlantic Ocean. There are super vistas across the midlands and of the Comeragh, Galty, Knockmealdown and Blackstairs mountain ranges. When ready, retrace your steps to the car park.

Myths and legends

Brandon Hill is believed to have been inhabited for more than 4,000 years, with evidence of Neolithic tombs, huts, field systems and ritualistic sites for animal and perhaps even human sacrifice. There are rumours of a headless horseman passing by at night on the Inistioge side of the hill. There is also the legend of Freney the Robber, who at the end of the 1800s stole from local rich people and is believed to have taken refuge and buried his treasure on Brandon Hill. Locals say that fifty years later the treasure was found by men out digging turf. However, their employer, the turf farmer, told them it was only buttons, sent them to get their dinner and then kept the money for himself. No good could ever come from an act like that.

▲ A winter's day climb to Brandon Hill

A view of Mount Leinster from Brandon Hill ▲

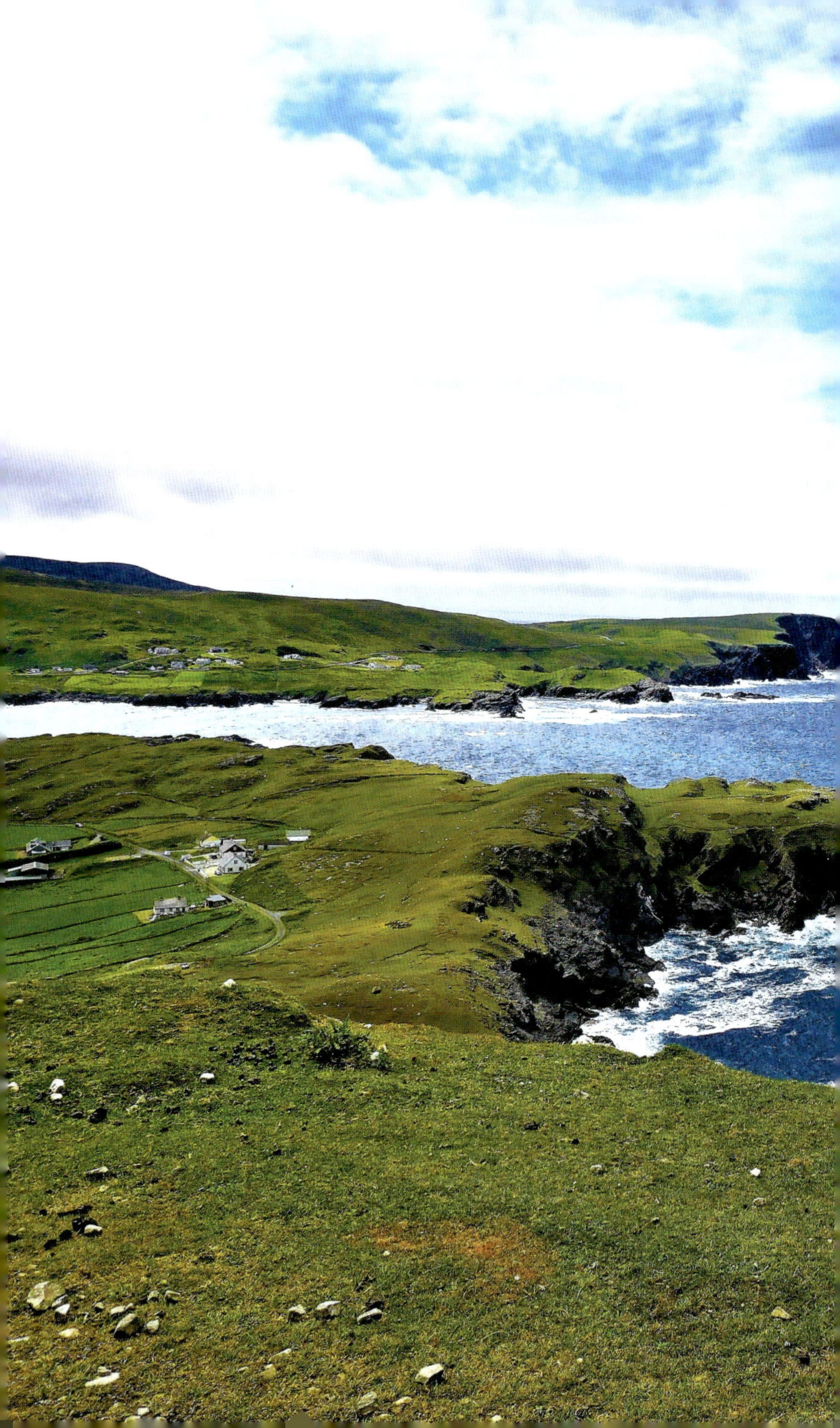

The North

40

Slieve League
Co. Donegal

A thrilling hike along the Slieve League sea cliffs

Rising 601m from the Atlantic Ocean, Slieve League has the second highest sea cliffs in Ireland (after Croaghaun on Achill Island) and the eighth highest in Europe. This thrilling hike offers one of the most magnificent vistas in Ireland, including the Giant's Desk and Chair at the base of the cliffs and views of the Atlantic Ocean as far as the eye can see. There are good paths throughout. This walk should only be undertaken in calm weather with clear visibility. Hiking boots recommended.

LENGTH:	TIME:	DIFFICULTY:	OSI MAP NO:
5–9km	2–4 hours	Easy–Medium	10

⊙ NEED TO KNOW

From Killybegs, take the R263 to Carrick. Turn left in Carrick at the sign for the cliffs. Follow the road until the Rusty Mackerel pub and turn right. Continue up the road until you come to the lower car park. There are two charges at this car park – €5 for two hours or €15 for the day. The visitor centres outside Carrick provide car parking and shuttle buses to the cliffs. Check online for prices.

Coordinates: 54.6265 -8.6644

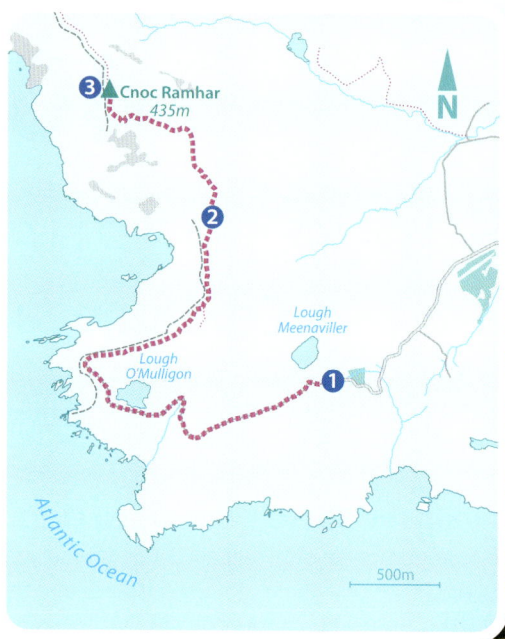

The Hike

1 From the car park, head up the paved road and through the pedestrian gate. Continue up the road, which is very steep at the start but soon eases off. Children can explore some of the rocks and hillocks that run alongside the road. Be mindful of service traffic. After 1.8km, arrive at the viewing platforms for the Slieve League cliffs and see the Giant's Desk and Chair. After enjoying the views, continue up the stone path. As you climb, you get different views of the cliffs.

2 At 2.7km, keep to your left and continue to climb. The path remains excellent throughout. For the easy 5km option, retrace your steps at this point back to the car park. Otherwise, continue on the path.

Descending Slieve League ▲

3 At 4.3km, reach a fork in the path. At the fork, you could extend the hike by taking the right-hand path to the summit of Slieve League. However, this path can become very difficult in places and there are two dangerous airy ridges that need to be negotiated. Only very experienced hikers should consider attempting this. For this hike, take the left path and climb to the top of Crockrawer. After enjoying the views simply retrace your steps, keeping right at any junctions you meet.

Myths and legends

Slieve League means 'Mountain of the Flagstones', a title that captures the towering cliffs that stand as silent witnesses to centuries of stories and traditions and the enduring spirit of the land. There is a trig point on One Man's Path that is set on top of an ancient structure of unknown origin. At the top of Slieve League is an early Christian monastic site where the remains of Ade McBric's chapel can still be seen. Alongside the chapel, there are also remains of the monks' stone beehive dwellings. The two sea stacks in front of the cliffs are called the Giant's Desk and Chair because of their shape and dimensions but also because Fionn Mac Cumhaill liked to rest there!

Giant's Desk and Chair, Slieve League ▲

41

Glencolmcille to the Sturrall
Co. Donegal

An exhilarating hike along the Donegal cliffs

This hike along the Glencolmcille sea cliffs is a truly exhilarating experience. Visit the Napoleonic lookout tower that looms high over the abyss of the Atlantic Ocean. See the incredible Sturrall Ridge and the amazing sea stacks of Port. You are unlikely to meet many people on this route. Paths include stone tracks and informal grass trails. Hiking boots essential.

LENGTH:	TIME:	DIFFICULTY:	OSI MAP NO:
4–6km	1.5–3 hours	Easy–Medium	10

⊚ NEED TO KNOW

From Glencolmcille, turn right onto the L5055. After 130m, turn left and stay on the L5055. After 350m, turn left, and after 850m, turn left onto Garveross. Keep going for just over a kilometre and park at the end of the road. There is room for a couple of cars. Be careful not to block the road.

Coordinates: 54.7189 -8.7394

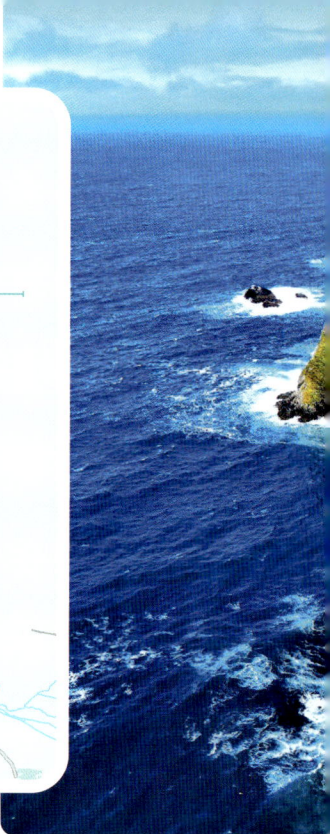

The Hike

1 From your car, head up the stony path beside you that leads to a gate. Pass through the gate and close it after you. Follow the red (Tower) and purple (Drum) arrows uphill. As you climb, beautiful views start to emerge of Glen Head and the coastline.

2 After 950m, take the grass path to the left where the signs indicate. You are now climbing uphill on a grassy and peaty path.

3 At 1.7km, reach the Napoleonic signal tower. There are stunning views of the Donegal coastline here. Head right along the cliff tops. There is a fence along the way, but be careful close to the cliff edge. As you hike, the incredible Sturrall Ridge headland emerges, and in the distance the amazing sea stacks of the deserted village of Port come into view. For the easy 4km option,

The Sturrall Ridge ▲

stop at any point along here and simply retrace your steps to your car. Otherwise, continue along the cliff edge.

4 At 2.2km, the fence posts run out. Slow down before this point and STOP! When the posts run out, there is a sheer drop beyond that is not easy to see from on top. Do not let children run ahead of you here. At this point, turn inland and follow the grass path steeply downhill and continue along the informal path heading towards the Sturrall.

5 At 2.8km, reach the Sturrall. At this point, you can choose to extend your hike by following the cliff path north towards Port. When ready, retrace your steps to your car. Stunning views of Glencolmcille emerge as you near the village.

Myths and legends

Glencolmcille is a beautiful, remote village most strongly associated with St Columcille but it also has a rich pre-Christian tradition dating back 5,000 years. St Columcille (or Columba) is one of the three patron saints of Ireland, along with St Patrick and St Brigid. He was born in 521 CE to King Fedlimid mac Fergus and Eithne, Princess of Leinster. He was also a great-great grandson of Niall of the Nine Hostages, who kidnapped St Patrick as a youth and brought him to Ireland. Of course, Patrick went on to convert Ireland to Christianity. Columcille is not only an important figure in Ireland; as the founder of monasteries in Iona and mainland Scotland, he was a key catalyst for the spread of Christianity in northern Britain. Columcille established one of the earliest Christian pilgrimage sites at Glencolmcille. Pilgrims would visit each of the fifteen penitential stations that are set out along the valley. To this day, the penitential stations include beautifully carved cross-inscribed slabs, simple cairns and a holy well. The first station is a modified megalithic tomb, its appropriation into a Christian pilgrimage providing a fascinating blend of ancient sacred spaces with Christianity. An example of an early high cross can be seen on an engraved standing stone close to Columcille's Chapel. Columcille is reputed to have battled with demons at Glencolmcille. These were the very same evil spirits that St Patrick had driven out of Croagh Patrick in Mayo but now appeared across the sea in Donegal. He is also said to have encountered the Loch Ness monster, battled with Pictish druids and performed miracles as he preached Christianity in Scotland.

The Sturrall with the sea stacks of Port in the distance ▲

42

Mount Errigal
Co. Donegal

Welcome to the roof of the north

At 751m, the conical quartzite peak of Errigal is both the highest and most recognisable mountain in Donegal. From below, Errigal can look unclimbable, but fear not! In recent years a new rock path has made the hike much easier. The views are beautiful from the beginning and only grow in stature as you progress. Enjoy breathtaking views of the Derryveagh Mountains, myriad loughs, the Atlantic Ocean, Tory Island, the Aranmore Islands and down to Benbulbin in Sligo. The twin summits only add to the drama of this amazing hike. Paths are well defined throughout. Hiking boots recommended.

LENGTH:	TIME:	DIFFICULTY:	OSI MAP NO:
6km	2–3 hours	Medium	1

⊙ NEED TO KNOW

From Letterkenny, take the N56 north for 10km. Turn left onto the R255, and after 22km arrive at the parking area for Mount Errigal on your right. If there are no spaces, just park carefully along the side of the road.

Coordinates: 55.0251 -8.09

Mackoght
555m

Mount
Errigal
751m

N

R251

Dunlewey
Lough

500m

Magical Mount Errigal ▶

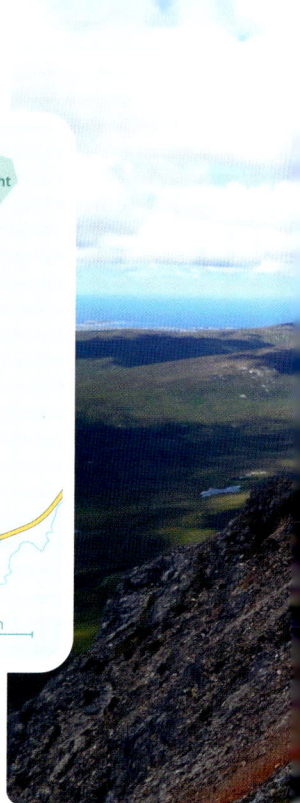

The Hike

1 From your car, head up the path on the left. Pass through a gate and continue uphill on the path alongside a lovely stream.

2 The path continues steadily uphill. After 1.5km, stay to the left when you reach a path that stretches off to the right to Mackoght. The path stretches higher and the twin summits will come into view.

3 At 3km, arrive at the top of Mount Errigal, which has twin summits that can be accessed by crossing a narrow but safe pathway. After enjoying the wonderful scenery, retrace your steps to your car. Enjoy your picnic in the shadow of Mount Errigal amidst the views of the Poison Glen.

Bright and windy on Mount Errigal ▲

Myths and legends

Errigal was named by the mythical race of the Fir Bolg or 'Bag Men' who travelled to Ireland from Greece. They were the fourth group of people to settle in Ireland. They were so awed by Errigal that they worshipped it as they had worshipped Mount Olympus. Errigal is also where Lugh, the great 'Light' king of the mythical Tuatha Dé Danann, fought his terrifying grandfather, Balor of the Evil Eye, who was from the monstrous Fomorian race. Lugh won the day by using a sling to defeat Balor. The Fomorians were said to come from under the sea and were enemies of Ireland's first settlers and opponents of the Tuatha Dé Danann, although some members of the two races had offspring. The epic battle between the two races at Moytura has been likened to other Indo-European myths of a war between gods, such as Olympians and Titans in Greek mythology. The Fomorian giants represented the wild or destructive powers of nature, while the Tuatha Dé Danann were associated with light, sun and wisdom and were often depicted as kings, queens, druids, bards, warriors, heroes, healers and craftspeople.

Moving between Errigal's twin summits ▲

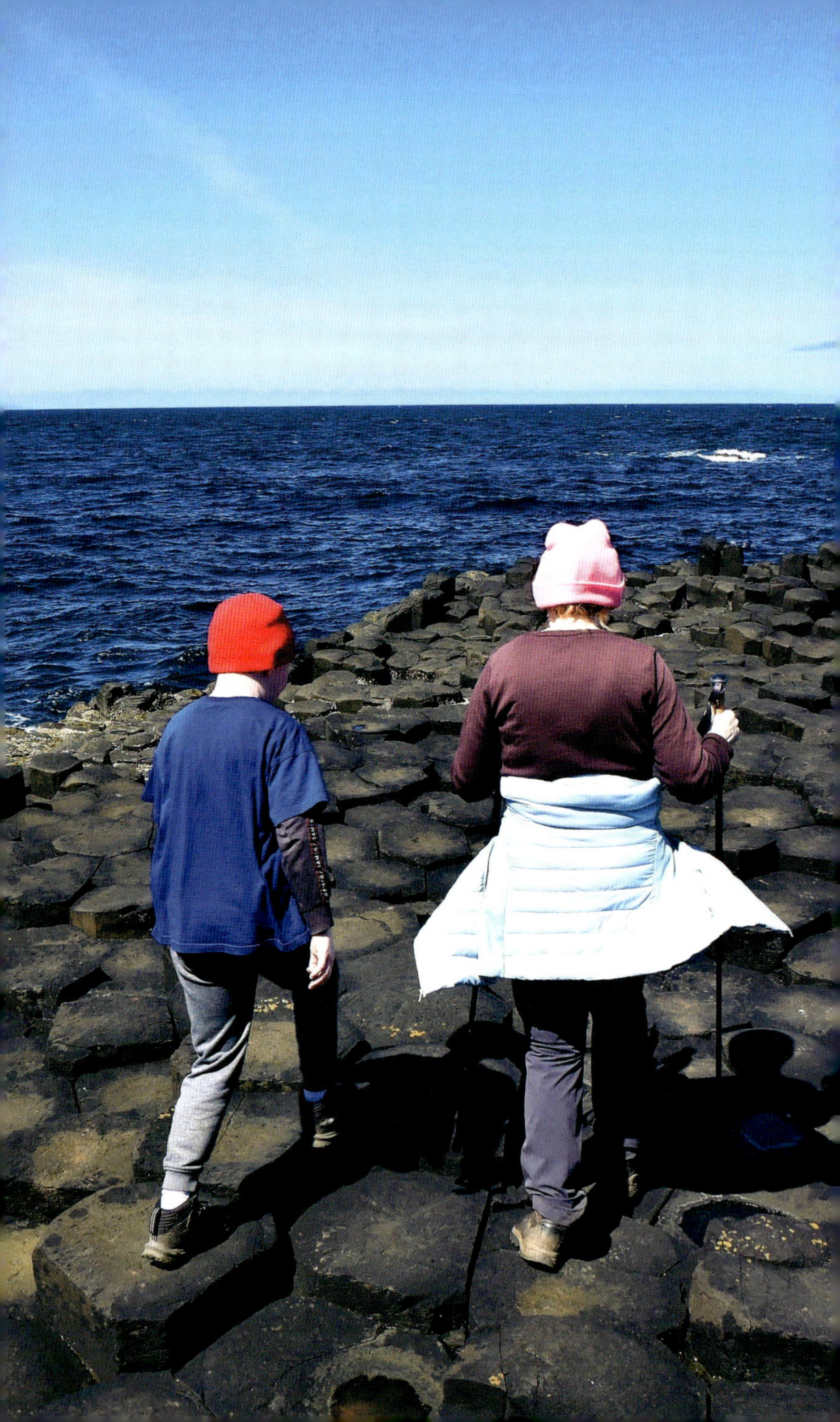

43

Dunseverick Castle to the Giant's Causeway
Co. Antrim

An incredible cliff-top hike to the iconic Giant's Causeway

There is something truly thrilling about entering the world-renowned Giant's Causeway from this cliff route. The drama builds as you round one beautiful headland after another, the scenery becoming ever more spectacular as you approach the Causeway. See amazing rock formations such as the Organ and the Amphitheatre and descend to the Causeway via the Shepherd's Steps. Explore the iconic hexagonal basalt rocks that formed the Causeway about 60 million years ago. Access to the Causeway is free via the cliff route. The visitor centre and onsite eating and shopping facilities only add to the experience. On your return, you can retrace your steps along the cliff path. Alternatively, you can take a local bus back to Dunseverick. There are clear paths throughout. This hike is best enjoyed in clear visibility. Hiking boots recommended.

LENGTH:	TIME:	DIFFICULTY:	OSNI MAP NO:
7–14km	4–6 hours	Medium–Experienced	5

◀ Walking on the hexagonal basalt rocks

From Ballycastle, go west along the A2 for 16km. Arrive into Dunseverick and see the castle remains. The free car park is a little further on your right. It has a picnic area.

Coordinates: 55.2376 -6.4492

The Hike

1 From the car park, follow the path through the picnic area and turn left. Follow the path along the coast following the sign for Castle Viewpoint Giant's Causeway. The views take a little time to properly reveal themselves, so be patient on this first section. After 1km, there is a viewing point for the beautiful Port Moon. Continue along the path from one headland to the next, with stunning seaviews throughout. As you approach the Giant's Causeway, the scenery becomes ever more dramatic. Amazing rock formations such as the Organ and the Amphitheatre can be viewed from high above.

2 At 6km, arrive at the Shepherd's Steps high above the Causeway. Head down the steps on your right. These steps will likely be busy. When you meet another path, turn left and head for the Causeway.

3 At 7km, reach the Giant's Causeway. Sit on Fionn Mac Cumhaill's boot and the Wishing Chair and explore the black hexagonal basalt rocks that extend as a causeway out into the sea. There are also other fascinating geological features to be seen. This is a truly amazing place to have a break. Once ready to leave, you have two options. The first is to retrace your steps on the cliff top back to Dunseverick. Alternatively, you can walk towards the visitor centre and out onto the main road. From there, it is possible to get a local bus (e.g. Causeway Rambler Bus) back to Dunseverick, which costs about £3 per person. Check prices and times online.

High above the Giant's Causeway ▲

Myths and legends

The Giant's Causeway is home to one of Ireland's best-loved myths. The mythological giant Fionn Mac Cumhaill created the causeway to Scotland by throwing rocks in the sea so that he could fight his fearsome Scottish rival, the giant Benandonner. However, on arriving in Scotland, Fionn saw that Benandonner was way bigger than himself and fled home. Benandonner chased him back on the causeway. Fionn ran home to his wife Oonagh, not knowing what to do, but she came up with a plan. When Benandonner arrived looking for Fionn, Oonagh told him that he had gone hunting down in Co. Kerry. She showed Benandonner around and asked him if he would like to see her baby. Benandonner was terrified to see the size of the baby. If the baby was that big at six months, how large was his father? Of course the baby was Fionn wrapped up in sheets! Benandonner fled in a panic back to Scotland, tearing up most of the causeway behind him as he went. In order to press home his advantage, Fionn tore out a piece of ground and threw it after Benandonner. The ground landed in the Irish Sea and is now known as the Isle of Man. The ground that Fionn tore up was filled up by water and became known as Lough Derg.

Relaxing in Fionn Mac Cumhaill's boot ▲

44
Carrick-a-Rede Rope Bridge
Co. Antrim

Cross a swaying rope bridge high above the North Sea

This short but memorable walk involves crossing a rope bridge high above the North Sea to Carrick-a-Rede Island. The rope bridge was first erected by salmon fishermen over 250 years ago. There are amazing views across the Antrim coastline from the Giant's Causeway to Fair Head, including Rathlin Island and Sheep Island. On a clear day you can see across to Scotland. A good head for heights is required. Clear paths throughout. Hiking boots not required.

LENGTH:	TIME:	DIFFICULTY:	OSNI MAP NO:
3km	1–2 hours	Easy	5

⊙ NEED TO KNOW

From Ballycastle, take the B15 west for 8km to the sign for the rope bridge. Turn left and park in the car park. The site is busy, so we recommend booking your tickets online beforehand. Children need to be able to cross by themselves so should be five years or older.

Coordinates: 55.2392 -6.348

◀ Crossing the Carrick-a-Rede Rope Bridge

The Hike

1 Leave the car park by the path for the bridge. After a kilometre, arrive at the rope bridge.

2 Present your ticket, take a deep breath and cross the swaying bridge. Spend some time on the island with its stunning views and abundant sea birds.

3 When ready, take another deep breath and cross back over. Take the left path as it offers lovely views across the island. All too soon this path rejoins the main path and you retrace your steps to the car park.

Carrick-a-Rede Island ▶

Atlantic Ocean
(North Channel)

N

Whitepark Road

B15

500m

Carrick-a-Rede Rope Bridge ▲

Myths and legends

Carrick-a-Rede ('rock in the road') rope bridge was erected in 1755 to allow fishermen better access to salmon and to reduce reliance on a boat to reach the island. The rope bridge actually connects two parts of an extinct volcano. Catches of up to 300 salmon a day were common until the 1960s but over-fishing and pollution led to a severe decline in stock and the last fish was caught in 2002.

Many tales of bloody massacres, both mythological and historical, are related to Rathlin Island, which is clearly visible from Carrick-a-Rede. Cú Chulainn prevented the titanic Fomorians from kidnapping Eimhear, the daughter of the King of Rathlin, by slaying them on the shore. In a later bloody battle, Conghal, a great warrior and later High King of Ireland, massacred the army of the King of Uardha (probably from Norway) in order to prevent them invading Rathlin and kidnapping Taise, the daughter of the King of Rathlin. Conghal married Taise, and Dún Taise fort was built in her honour in Co. Antrim. In 1575, Sir Francis Drake and the Earl of Essex led a massacre in Antrim that killed up to 600 of the MacDonnell clan. Sorley Boy MacDonnell sent his family members to Rathlin Island for sanctuary as he led a resistance against an Elizabethan plantation in mainland Ulster. The Earl of Essex boastfully reported that MacDonnell helplessly watched the massacre from the mainland and was 'like to run mad from sorrow'.

North Sea waters around Carrick-a-Rede ▲

45

Fair Head
Co. Antrim

A breathtaking hike along the sublime Fair Head

This wild, remote and incredibly beautiful cliff route offers stunning views of Rathlin Island, Scotland, Murlough Bay and the Atlantic Ocean. There are also a number of unusual rock formations. Waymarker posts and informal grass and rock paths help with navigation. Care should be exercised near the cliff edges. The walk should not be attempted in foggy or cloudy conditions. Hiking boots recommended.

LENGTH:	TIME:	DIFFICULTY:	OSNI MAP NO:
5–7km	1.5–3 hours	Easy–Medium	5

⊙ NEED TO KNOW

From Ballycastle, take the A2 east. After 500m, take a left onto Cushendall Road and after 4km turn left onto Torr Road. Stay on this road for another 4km. Turn left onto Murlough Road. Travel down this narrow road until you reach the free parking spaces on your left. You will see Scotland in front of you.

Coordinates: 55.2086 -6.13

◀ The beautiful Fair Head coastline

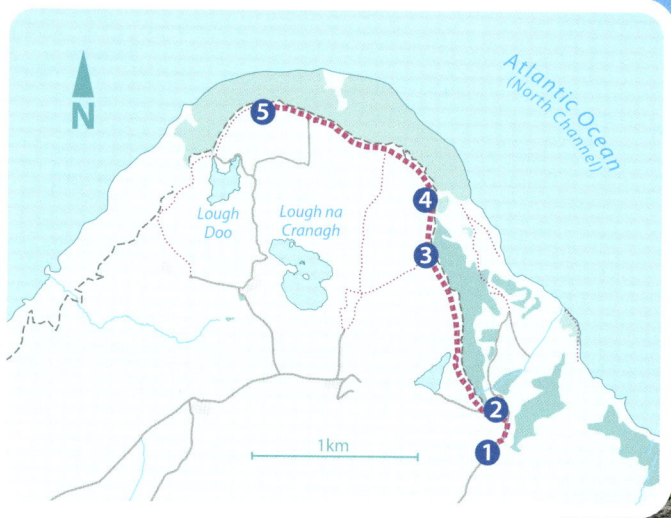

The Hike

1 From the car park, walk down the road towards Murlough Bay. The views towards Scotland are stunning.

2 After 200m, turn left onto a track until you meet a gate. You have missed the left track if you go past the large cross on the road. Pass the gate on the right and follow the informal track as it leads right, meandering through bracken and furze across the cliff top. After 600m, cross a stile and pick up the waymarkers. Then cross another stile, still following the waymarkers.

3 At 1.2km, arrive at a grassy junction. Continue straight and aim for the cliffs in front of you. Cross the next stile and continue.

Relaxing on stunning Fair Head ▲

4 At 1.8km, the path becomes rockier. You are very close to the edge of the cliffs, so take due care. You are now on the Grey Man's Path, an incredibly exhilarating section of the hike. Inland, you can see the beautiful Lough na Cranagh, Lough Doo and Knocklayd. For the easier 5km option, stop at any point along the cliff edge and retrace your steps to the car park.

5 At around 3.5km, there is an inviting rocky outcrop where you can stop and have a break. There are stunning views of Rathlin Island and all along the Antrim coast towards Ballycastle and the Giant's Causeway. When ready, retrace your steps to the car park. This hike can be shortened or lengthened as desired as the cliff line keeps going!

Myths and legends

The great Irish heroes Fionn Mac Cumhaill and Cú Chulainn had many adventures in Antrim. A lesser known but more enigmatic figure is the Grey Man. One of the dramatic features of the Fair Head cliff walk is the Grey Man's Path, which descends steeply down the cliff face to the shore below. The Grey Man appears in many guises, sometimes as an evil spirit, sometimes as a devil horseman and some-times as a holy man. He is also spoken of as a sea creature or an ancient sea god. In all manifestations, he seems linked to the grey mists and fogs that roll in off the north Antrim coast. The Children of Lir are also linked to this area. The Sea of Moyle lies between Fair Head and Kintyre in Scotland and it is here that the Children of Lir spent 300 years after they had been turned into swans by their wicked stepmother. They had previously spent 300 years on Lough Derravaragh in Co. Westmeath and after the Sea of Moyle spent a further 300 years on Inishglora Island off the north Mayo coast. The swans often had to seek refuge from the raging storms of the Sea of Moyle. One tradition is that Fiachra and Conn sheltered at the mouth of the Cushendall River in Antrim, from which the village and river take their name (Cois Abhainn dá Eala – river mouth of the two swans). Another place of shelter may have been at a small rock (Carraig na n-Éalaí – Swans' Rock) near the shore of Murlough at Fair Head.

Taking a break on Fair Head, looking out on Rathlin Island ▲

46

Cave Hill
Belfast, Co. Antrim

An extraordinary hike in the heart of Belfast city

This wonderful looped hike starts right in the heart of Belfast city and brings you up to the imposing Cave Hill that overlooks Belfast. Cave Hill is so named for the five caves located on the side of the cliffs. The summit offers tremendous views of the city and Belfast Lough. It is great fun to spend some time picking out well-known landmarks, such as the Titanic Belfast visitor attraction on the former Harland and Wolff shipyard site. Refreshments are available in beautiful Belfast Castle. There are good paths and signs throughout. This site can be busy, especially in summer, so get there early to ensure parking. Hiking boots recommended.

LENGTH:	TIME:	DIFFICULTY:	OSNI MAP NO:
7km	3 hours	Medium	15

⊙ NEED TO KNOW

Belfast Castle and Cave Hill Country Park are in the north of Belfast city. Parking is free and there are several car parks throughout the grounds.

Coordinates: 54.6427 -5.9428

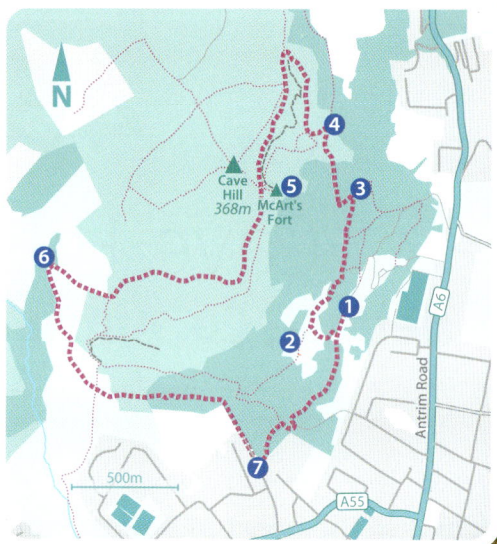

The Hike

1 Park opposite the impressive Belfast Castle and make your way back down the road you drove in on. After 50m, at another car park, turn right up the hill and follow the signs for Cave Hill Trail. These are the signs you will follow throughout the hike.

2 After 300m, follow the narrow path to the right as it continues to climb steadily uphill.

3 After 900m, take a sharp turn left. Keep following the arrows and climb uphill. Take rest breaks if necessary.

4 At 1.4km, turn left again and follow the arrows. Along this section, you will see one of the hill caves above you. This cave is best admired from the path as it is difficult and dangerous to access. Instead stay on the path and terrific views across Belfast start to emerge. Follow the path as it climbs uphill.

A view towards McArt's Fort and Belfast City from Cave Hill ▲

5 At 2.5km, pass an information board and turn left to access McArt's Fort on top of a very impressive cliff. Take a break and enjoy stunning views across Belfast city and Belfast Lough and down to the Mourne Mountains. When you rejoin the main path, there is an option to go straight across onto a grassy path, climb a stile and head up to the summit of Cave Hill itself. Alternatively, if the views from McArt's Fort are enough for you, rejoin the main path and continue left downhill.

6 After 4.2km, arrive at a junction of paths. Take a sharp left. There is a sign here but it is faint and difficult to see. Continue downhill. At just over 6km, emerge out onto a tarmac road.

7 About 200m later, turn left back into the Cave Hill Country Park. At 6.4km, follow the path to your right down the hill. Swing left at the bottom of the hill and follow the tarmac road back to your car. Belfast Castle and gardens are well worth a visit and there is a café there as well.

Myths and legends

Cave Hill, originally known in Irish as Beann Mheadagáin (Hill of Madigan), was named after an ancient king. However, the name changed over the years to Cave Hill from the many caves in the hillside. These are thought to have been created from early iron mines that were dug into the cliffs. The McArt Fort is named after the sixteenth-century Ulster chieftain Brian Mac Art O'Neill. However, the site itself dates back to the late Bronze Age or Iron Age, when a promontory fort existed here. When you arrive back at Belfast Castle, secure a bit of luck for yourself by visiting the Cat Garden and finding all the cats!

▲ The impressive Belfast Castle and gardens

Dramatic Cave Hill ▲

47

Slieve Donard
Mourne Mountains, Co. Down

A stunning climb to the highest peak in Ulster

At 850m, Slieve Donard is the highest peak in the Mourne Mountains and in the province of Ulster. This hike offers a great mix of woodlands, waterfalls and open mountainside views. While the incline may be steep in places, the scenery is worth the effort. The views from the summit include the many distinctive peaks of the Mourne Mountains and on a clear day it is possible to see the Isle of Man, Wicklow, Donegal, Wales and Scotland. There are good paths throughout. Depending on the time of year and day, this route will be more or less busy. Hiking boots recommended.

LENGTH:	TIME:	DIFFICULTY:	OSNI MAP NO:
9.5km	4–5 hours	Experienced	29

ACTIVITY MAP: The Mournes
HARVEY SUPERWALKER XT25: Mourne Mountains

⊙ NEED TO KNOW

From Newry, take the B8 to Hilltown. Go through Hilltown and after half a kilometre turn right onto the B27. After 1.5km, turn left onto the B180 and follow the road to Newcastle. Continue onto the quays and turn right and then left into Donard Park. The car park is free and has a large overflow car park at the back. From here, you will see Slieve Donard towering above you.

Coordinates: 54.2062 -5.8943

◄ The Irish Sea from the summit of Slieve Donard

The Hike

1 From the car park, make your way through a large grass picnic area, keeping to the left. Pick up a path on your left beside some trees. You can also use the waymarker posts signed with a mountain. The path rises steeply through the forest. At 560m, go left across a bridge. Then turn right and follow the path.

2 At just over 1km, reach another bridge. Turn right here and then immediately left. At 1.5km, turn left as you emerge onto a broad path. Soon after, continue up the path to your right. As you climb this path, the river valley between Slieve Donard on your left and Slieve Commedagh on your right opens out in front of you. Behind you, there are stunning views of Newcastle and the Irish Sea.

3 At 4km, arrive at the top of the col with the Mourne Wall straight in front of you. It is well worth having a look over the wall as there are tremendous views across the rest of the Mourne Mountains from here. When ready, turn left along the wall and climb steadily to the top of Slieve Donard.

4 After 800m, arrive at the summit cairn. The views are truly amazing, especially with the Irish Sea so close below you. We call this the Land of Nod as people generally seem to go quiet and lie down here for while! When ready, retrace your steps back to the car park, enjoying wonderful views all the way.

The agility of youth on Slieve Donard ▶

Newcastle

Slievenabrock
438m

Slievenamaddy

Shan Slieve

Slieve
Commedagh
767m

Slieve Beg
596m

Slieve
Donard
849m

Thomas's
Mtn

Milestone Mtn
460m

*Donard
Forest*

Irish Sea

N

1km

Myths and legends

There are two ancient burial cairns on the summit, one of which is the remains of the highest known passage tomb in Britain or Ireland. In the past, the cairns had a more well-defined shape and it is thought the Great Cairn had an east-facing entrance leading to an inner chamber and was seen as an entrance to the Otherworld. In earlier times, the mountain was named after the mythical figures of Boirche and Slángha, the former being a cowherd and king with supernatural powers and the latter said to be the first physician in Ireland. In the Annals of the Four Masters, it is said that Slángha was buried in the Great Cairn. In the fifth century, the mountain was named after St Donard, who allegedly made the Great Cairn his hermit's cell and used the Lesser Cairn as an oratory. Up until the 1830s, people climbed the mountaintop in late July each year, a Christian pilgrimage that mapped onto the pre-Christian Lughnasa (harvest) ritual. Other places in Ireland still retain this Christian/harvest pilgrimage in late July, such as Croagh Patrick.

Descending Slieve Donard towards Slieve Commedagh ▲

48

Slieve Binnian
Mourne Mountains, Co. Down

Catch sight of the ghostly Blue Lady

Slieve Binnian is one of the more distinctive and jagged peaks in the Mourne Mountains. This incredible looped hike takes you into the heart of the Mourne Mountains. You will pass by the beautiful Blue Lake, Ben Crom reservoir and Annalong Valley and encounter incredible, scramble-friendly rock formations. At all times, the views are simply stunning. Paths are well defined throughout. Hiking boots essential.

LENGTH:	TIME:	DIFFICULTY:	OSNI MAP NO:
9.5 km	4–5 hours	Experienced	29

ACTIVITY MAP: XT25

HARVEY SUPERWALKER XT30: Mourne Mountains

⊙ NEED TO KNOW

From Newry, take the B8 to Hilltown. Go through Hilltown and after half a kilometre turn right on to the B27. Continue on this road past the Spelga Dam for 14km. Then turn left onto Head Road and continue for 2.5km before taking a sharp left onto Oldtown Road. Continue for 4km; the free public car park is on the left. If this is full, drive up the stony lane beside it, where there are two more car parks, which have a daily charge of £5.

Coordinates: 54.1288 -5.9433

◀ Slieve Binnian summit

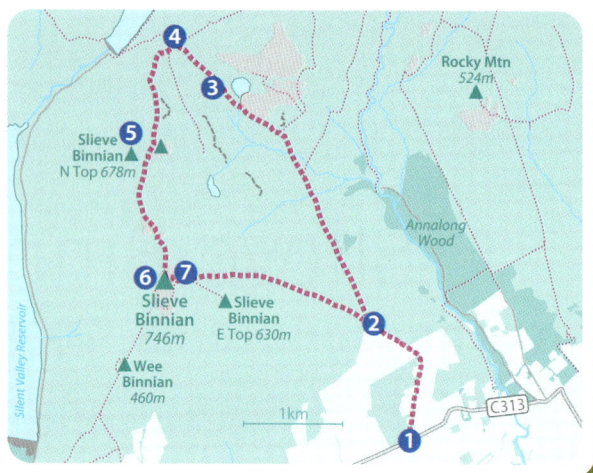

The Hike

1 From the car park, head up the stony path beside you. After 800m, pass through a gate, closing it behind you.

2 At 1km, proceed along the path as it veers to the right. Cross several delightful streams, while all around several of the Mourne peaks progressively reveal themselves.

3 The path continues uphill, and after 3.5 kilometres, arrive at the Blue Lake lying serenely at the foot of Slievelamagan. This is a great place for a rest and on the left, you can see along the spine of Slieve Binnian – your next destination!

4 Continue past the Blue Lake and at 4.5km crest the top of the path at the junction between Slieve Binnian and Slievelamagan. A small diversion here is worthwhile. Instead of turning directly left for Slieve Binnian, go straight ahead to see the incredible Ben Crom reservoir below you, as well as several other Mourne peaks. When ready, return to the junction and head up the path towards Slieve Binnian. This is quite a steep path at this point and can be windy, especially at the start of the incline. However, as you proceed higher, the wind usually dies down and incredible views across the Mournes reveal themselves.

5 At 5.8km, arrive at Slieve Binnian's North Tor. It is well worth spending some time here to explore some of the incredible rock formations. When ready, continue along the path towards the summit. The path is a little confusing near a large stone outcrop but keep to the left and you will soon see what appears to be a gap in the wall. Make your way up and through this gap and enter the plateau at the top of Slieve Binnian.

6 At 7.5km, reach the summit. Enjoy transcendent views of the Silent Valley, the Irish Sea and Mourne peaks all around you.

7 For your descent, make your way down left through the gap just before the large stone tors. Take care descending here as it is quite steep and prone to scree. Continue downhill, keeping the Mourne Wall beside you to your right. On your left, enjoy amazing panoramas across the Annalong valley. After descending for 2.5km, arrive at point 2 on the map. Follow the path back to the car park. Don't be surprised if you find yourself repeatedly turning around to take one more last look. This landscape soaks deep into the soul. The Mourne Mountains offer a whole range of amazing hikes that are well worth exploring.

Myths and legends

According to local legend, the 'Blue Light of Binnian', which appears as a ball of blue phosphorescent light that crosses the ground, is the restless spirit of a young woman who was murdered by her husband and is believed to have been buried somewhere on the slopes of Binnian. Others say that the blue light blocks the path to haunted trees where an ancient chieftain lies buried.

Enjoying one of the many unusual rock formations on Slieve Binnian ▲

49

Slieve Gullion
Co. Armagh

Explore the enchanting Ring of Gullion

Slieve Gullion is the highest point in Co. Armagh and boasts one of the highest passage tombs in Ireland. The longer hike option starts in an enchanting forest park and leads to open mountainside with views of the Ring of Gullion and the Irish Sea. The Ring forms a rampart of low, rugged hills around Slieve Gullion. At the summit, there are beautiful vistas of the Cooley and Mourne Mountains and the midlands plain. The easy 3km option starts at the Slieve Gullion Viewing Platform. Paths are generally well defined, although parts can become boggy in wet weather. Hiking boots essential.

LENGTH:	TIME:	DIFFICULTY:	OSNI MAP NO:
3–15km	1–5 hours	Easy–Experienced	29

⊙ NEED TO KNOW

From Dublin, take the M1 north towards Newry. Exit at junction 20 on the B113 on the Lower Foughill Road. Just after 3km, take a left, and after a further 2km the entrance is on your right and leads to the car park. There is a daily parking charge of £5. There are toilets, a playground and a children's forest park. Be aware that closing times vary according to the season. Parking at the Slieve Gullion Viewing Platform is free, with no closing times.

Coordinates for 15km experienced route: 54.1163 -6.4084
Coordinates for 3km easy route: 54.1193 -6.4438

◀ Approaching the Cailleach's lake

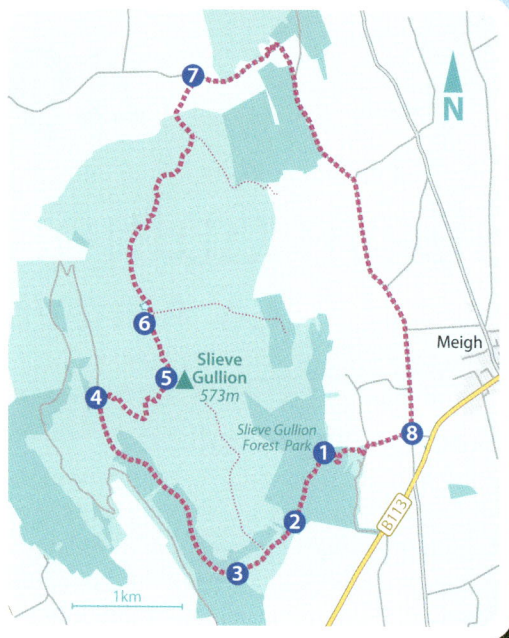

The Hike

1   From your car, make your way to the left across the car park to where you enter the Giant's Lair. Follow the black and blue arrow signs. There are many wonderful areas for children to enjoy along this path. Keep to the left at any junctions of paths.

2   After 700m, follow the arrows first to the left and then take the right up the hill. This is a lovely path with signs providing information about trees.

3   At 1.2km, turn right up the hill on a hairpin bend towards a barrier across the road. At the top of this little road, meet a wider road and turn left up the hill. There can be traffic on this road. Continue uphill. This can be a tough stretch of climbing and children may need to be distracted. Beautiful views of the Slieve Gullion Ring Dyke emerge as you climb.

Exploring Slieve Gullion summit ▲

4 At 4.2km, pass a car park on your left and find the mountain path up to Slieve Gullion summit on your right. There is a little yellow sign to mark where the path begins. This is an exciting path with incredible views all around.

5 At 5.7km, reach the summit of Slieve Gullion. Similar to Newgrange, the inner chamber of the Neolithic passage tomb here is aligned to light up at the winter solstice. Enjoy an amazing panorama towards the Cooley and Mourne Mountains and the midlands plain. When ready, take the path north towards the Cailleach Béara lake.

6 At 7km, arrive at the Cailleach Béara lake. After another couple of hundred metres, reach Slieve Gullion North top. Follow the path as it continues north and starts to descend. The path turns into a grass trail; follow this downhill. In the distance, you will see a white cottage and this is the line you will take downhill. At 8.5km, go through a farm gate, remembering to close it after you.

7 After another kilometre, pass through another farm gate and turn right onto the road. At 10.8km, continue on the road and ignore the road to your left. After another kilometre, continue straight ahead and ignore the road to your left. While the views are lovely, children may become bored, so it might be time to introduce sweets and/or games. The road is quiet, so kicking a stone down the road works well!

8 Continue along this road and at 14.5km turn right up to the road towards the Slieve Gullion car park. After 300m, turn left and follow the road around to the car park. There are plenty of picnic tables in the playground and it is a lovely place to rest after your hike. Although everyone will be tired, it is likely that the sight of the slides and zip lines may well prove irresistible to your children and you may need to allow more time for fun!

Easy 3km option: Park at the car park on point 4 of the map, i.e. the Slieve Gullion Viewing Platform. Climb to the summit indicated on point 5 and then retrace your steps to the car park.

Cailleach's lake ▲

Myths and legends

There are many myths in this region and the helpful information boards at Slieve Gullion will introduce you to many of them. One of the most famous involves the famed Cailleach Béara. The Neolithic tomb on the top of Slieve Gullion is known as the Cailleach Béara's House. In one tale, the legendary Fionn Mac Cumhaill was tricked by the Cailleach who pretended she was an old woman who had lost her ring in the lake at the top of Slieve Gullion. Fionn felt sorry for her and dived into the lake to retrieve the ring. When he resurfaced, he was bewitched and the Cailleach had turned him into an old man with hair as white as snow. Eventually the Cailleach relented and returned his youth, but his golden hair was forever turned white. As a word of warning, the spell was so powerful that it still lingers by the lake today. Anyone brave or foolish enough to swim here will emerge with a shock of white hair.

50

Cuilcagh
Co. Cavan/Co. Fermanagh

At 666m, Cuilcagh Mountain is the highest point in counties Cavan and Fermanagh. We outline two hikes here: the well-known 'Stairway to Heaven' and a wilder route to the summit.

50A Cuilcagh: Stairway to Heaven

An incredible boardwalk that rises to a precarious viewing platform

The Stairway to Heaven route provides well-defined tracks and boardwalks across beautiful rolling bogland that rise to a viewing platform offering breathtaking views of the surrounding lowlands. This route does not bring you to the summit of Cuilcagh. Hiking boots are recommended but not essential.

LENGTH:	TIME:	DIFFICULTY:	OSI MAP NO:
14km	3.5–4 hours	Experienced	26

◄ Descending the Stairway through the clouds

From Swanlibar, Co. Cavan, take the N87 and enter Northern Ireland. The road changes to the A32 and after 9km turn left onto Marble Arch Road and continue for 4.5km. Then turn left onto Marlbank Road, and after a further 3.5km the car park is on the left. It is advised to prebook parking online (£6), although payment on the day is usually accepted. If full, there is a free car park nearby on Marlbank Road, but it will add another couple of kilometres to the walk.

Coordinates: 54.2504 -7.8160

The Hike

1 From the car park, head up the wide path towards the mountain. There is beautiful rolling countryside, and a lovely gushing river accompanies you along the way.

2 After 1.5km, you have the option of detouring to your left onto a charming boardwalk that brings you through the bog. This path ends all too soon and you will shortly arrive back onto the main path.

3 Continue walking on the path. At 3.5km, the stony track gives way to a boardwalk, which is a welcome change.

4 The boardwalk continues for another 3.5km until it reaches the steps up to the viewing platform. It is steep but doesn't last too long. Take a well-earned rest and enjoy the stunning views all round. When ready, retrace your steps to your car. When you leave the car park, we recommend turning left; after 1km you arrive at the Killykeeghan National Nature Reserve on your right. This free spot has picnic tables, toilets and lovely views. And more walks if you want them! The nearby Marble Arch Caves are also well worth a visit.

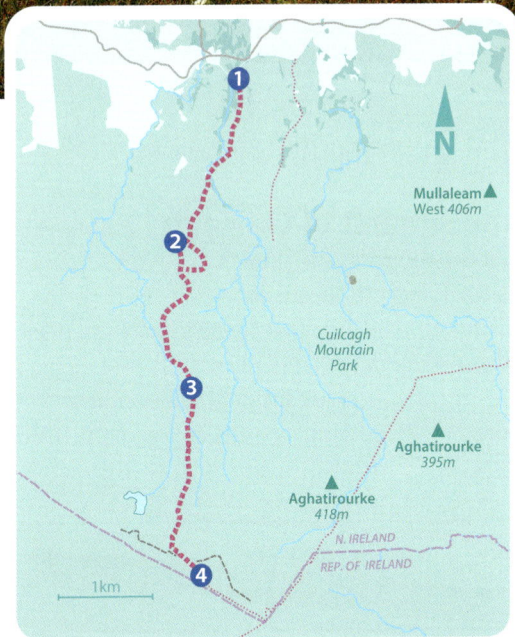

▲ Bog cotton on Cuilcagh

50B Cuilcagh Summit

A wild hike to the summit of Cuilcagh

This wild and remote hike approaches the summit of Cuilcagh from the other side of the mountain and provides a contrasting experience to the Stairway, if an equally stunning one. This connoisseur's route uses informal bog paths that skirt the rim of a broad escarpment that leads to the summit, on which there is a large cairn. You will encounter very few people on this route. Some navigational skills are required. Hiking boots essential.

LENGTH:	TIME:	DIFFICULTY:	OSI MAP NO:
10.5km	4–5 hours	Experienced	26

▲ A view of Cuilcagh around the escarpment

The Hike

1 From the car park, head up the path beside the picnic tables. Keep on the stony track as it winds its way uphill, ignoring any offshoots. At just over 1km, the track swings sharply to the left, but just keep following it uphill.

2 After 1.5km, arrive at a small power station. Your route lies directly up the hill you see in front of you. At the gate of the power station there is a large rock. Directly across from this rock on your right is a path through the rushes on a bank. Take this path and follow it to the fence, where you cross a stile. Pick up an informal path that runs parallel to a fence on your right. Follow this path uphill. The path improves nearer the top of the hill. As you near the summit of Benbeg, keep following the path as it bends slightly to your left.

3 At Benbeg, you will come across a lone standing post. Nearby is a beautiful boghole surrounded by peat hags. Off in the distance on your right is the summit of Cuilcagh. Your route follows the rim of the escarpment as it curves its way from Benbeg to Cuilcagh. The bog path is narrow but clear.

4 At 4.6km, the path bends slightly away from the rim as it moves inland and starts to climb more steeply.

5 After climbing for over 200m, emerge onto the summit plateau of Cuilcagh. Note this point as it has a small cairn that you will need to earmark for your return journey. Turn right and make your way across the stones to the summit cairn of Cuilcagh.

6 At 5.4km, arrive at the summit cairn of Cuilcagh. There are stunning views here and plenty to explore. After a break, retrace your steps to your car.

Hiking across the escarpment to Cuilcagh Mountain ▲

Approaching the summit of Cuilcagh Mountain ▲

Myths and legends

The Cuilcagh region is steeped in geology and mythology. The hills around Cuilcagh are named after Fionn Mac Cumhaill's wolfhounds, Bran and Sceolan. Legend has it that they were chasing a cailleach (witch) across the mountains but she got the better of them and turned them to stone. In addition, Cuilcagh is not far from the source of Ireland's longest river, the River Shannon. One legend reveals how the Shannon manifested at the end of the last glacial period. The goddess Sionann, granddaughter of the great Celtic god of the sea, Manannán Mac Lir, went to the Shannon Pot (the pool where the Shannon rises) in search of the great Salmon of Wisdom. She had been warned not to approach the salmon. The salmon was angered at seeing her and caused the pool to overflow and drown her. Such was the overflow that the river was formed and poor Sionann was pushed deep to the bottom, never to be seen again. Her name was given to the river as a reminder of her fate. The drowning of a goddess in a river was common in Irish mythology and may represent the dissolving of her divine power into the water, which then gives life to the land.

To our fearless, fun-loving and inspiring son, Levi, without whom this book could not have happened. To the team at Gill who believed in our book, thank you for your professionalism and beautiful design.

We hope you and your family have plenty of adventures in Ireland's incredible landscape.

Happy hiking,

Mairéad and Fergal